Understanding
Human Sexuality

Understanding
Human Sexuality

Frederick Cohn, M. D.

Clinical Associate Professor
Department of Obstetrics & Gynecology
University of New Mexico School of Medicine

Adjunct Assistant Professor
Department of Health Education
University of New Mexico

with the editorial assistance of

Charles E. Moritz, Ph.D.

Prentice-Hall, Inc.

Englewood Cliffs, New Jersey

Library of Congress Cataloging in Publication Data

COHN, FREDERICK (date)
  Understanding human sexuality.

  Includes bibliographies.
  1. Sex (Psychology)   2. Sex (Biology)   I. Title.
  [DNLM: 1. Sex education.   2. Sex manuals.   1. HQ31
  C679u 1974]
  BF692.C63   612.6   73–20476
  ISBN 0–13–937425–6
  ISBN 0–13–937417–5 (pbk.)

© 1974 by Prentice-Hall, Inc.
Englewood Cliffs, New Jersey

10   9   8   7   6   5   4   3   2   1

Printed in the United States of America

PRENTICE-HALL INTERNATIONAL, INC., *London*
PRENTICE-HALL OF AUSTRALIA, PTY. LTD., *Sydney*
PRENTICE-HALL OF CANADA, LTD., *Toronto*
PRENTICE-HALL OF INDIA PRIVATE LIMITED, *New Delhi*
PRENTICE-HALL OF JAPAN, INC., *Tokyo*

To Bob, Larry, Janice, and Sandy

contents

preface   xv

acknowledgements   xvii

part one   **A Background**   1

1   where are we? what is it all about?   3

Sexuality Is Learned, 3
Where Is Sexuality Taught? 5

2   validity   9

Determination Of The Truth, 10
Truth In Sexual Matters, 10
Bases Of Information In This Book, 11
Truths Versus Attitudes, 12
Summary, 13

3 semantics **15**

The Use Of General Terminology, 16
The Use of Scientific Terminology, 16
The Vernacular, 17
Scrambled Words, 18
Epilogue, 18

**4 an historical sketch of western man's
sexual attitudes and customs** **19**

Ancient Jews, 20
The Classical World, 23
Early Christianity, 25
Early Medieval Ages, 27
Increasing Permissiveness And Reactions To It, 31
The Rise Of Romance, 29
"The Enlightenment" And The Eighteenth
   Century, 35
Victorianism, 36
Conclusion Of The Sketch, 39

part two **Sexual Biology** **43**

5 sexual anatomy and physiology of the male **45**

Testes, 46
Genital Ducts And Associated Glands, 48
Penis, 51
Erection, 52
Impotence, 54
Ejaculation, 54
Male Hormonal Physiology, 55
Male Menopause, 57

6 sexual anatomy and physiology of the female **60**

Mammary Glands, 60
Hormonal Activity And The Mammary Glands, 63

Ovaries, 66
Uterine Tubes, 69
Uterus, 69
Vagina, 71
Mons Pubis, 73
Labia Majora, 73
Labia Minora, 73
Clitoris, 74
Vestibule, 74
Hymen, 74
Bartholin's Glands, 75
Skene's Glands, 75
Hormonal Activity In The Sexually Immature Female;
    Anovulatory Menstruation, 75
Hormonal Activity In The Sexually Mature
    Nonpregnant Female; Ovulatory
    Menstruation, 77
Hormonal Activity In The Sexually Mature
    Pregnant Female, 78
Relationship Of Sex Hormones To
    Female Sexuality, 79
Menopause, 80

7 human sexual physiology   **81**

Historical Background, 82
The Work Of Masters And Johnson, 83
Human Sexual Response, 83
Total Female Response, 84
Individual Organ Response In The Female, 86
Female Orgasm, 92
Total Male Response, 92
Individual Organ Response In The Male, 93
Male Orgasm, 95

**8 the relation of fertilization and
    implantation to genetic engineering**   **97**

Fertilization And Implantation, 97
New Techniques In Genetics, 100
Implications Of Genetic Techniques, 102

9 pregnancy   **105**

Fetology, 105
Tests For Pregnancy, 110
Physiological Changes In The Female
      During Pregnancy, 111
Parturition, 113
Placenta, 119
Analgesia And Anesthesia, 120
Routine Prenatal Care, 121
General Attitudes Regarding Pregnancy, 122

10 psychosexual development   **126**

The Biological Interpretation Of Psychosexual
      Development, 127
The Psychoanalytical Interpretation Of
      Psychosexual Development, 128
The Sociocultural Interpretation Of
      Psychosexual Development, 134
Conclusion, 135

11 sexual intercourse   **137**

Two Types Of Sexuality, 137
Two Important Addenda To Sexual Love, 139
Some Parameters of Sexuality, 139
Motivational Aspects Of Sexual Intercourse, 140
Sexual Motivations For Intercourse, 142
Nonsexual Motivations For Intercourse, 142
The Need For Determining Why Sexual
      Intercourse Is Undertaken, 144
Common Problems Which Patients Bring To
      Physicians Regarding Sexual Relations, 144

**12 counseling young people about
      sexual relations**   **152**

The Pros and Cons Of Adolescent Intercourse, 153
Truisms About Sexual Intercourse, 154
Counseling Young People About Sexual
      Intercourse, 156

13   gender roles   **158**

New Truisms, 159
Female Gender Role, 160
Male Gender Role, 163

14   masturbation   **165**

Definition, 166
Number Of Masturbators, 166
Frequency Of Masturbation, 166
Mechanism Of Masturbation, 167
Sexual Motivation, 167
Nonsexual Motivation, 168
Summary, 169

15   homosexuality   **170**

Definition, 172
Sexual Methods, 173
Incidence, 173
Etiology, 174
General Discussion, 177
Facets Of Homosexuality, 179

part three   **Sex And Society**   **183**

16   the problems of overpopulation   **185**

Underdeveloped Nations, 186
Developed Nations, 187
Epilogue, 189

17   contraception   **190**

History Of Contraception, 191
Criteria For The Perfect Contraceptive, 191
Nonappliance Methods Of Contraception, 192
Appliance Methods Of Contraception, 193

18 contraception (continued): sterilization   **204**

The Operative Technique In The Male:
  Vasectomy, 204
Operative Techniques In The Female, 206
Indications For Sterilization, 209
Motivational Aspects Of Contraception, 210
Epilogue, 212

19 abortion   **213**

Incidence, 214
Who Seeks Abortion? 214
Methods Of Abortion, 217
Complications, 220
Religious Attitudes Toward Abortion, 221
Legal Aspects Of Abortion, 222
Morality Of Abortion, 224

20 venereal disease   **226**

Syphilis, 227
Gonorrhea, 234
Public Health Measures For Control And
  Eradication Of Venereal Disease, 236

21 an anthropological approach to sexuality   **239**

Anthropological Techniques, 240
Conclusions Derived From Anthropological
  Studies, 240
Basic Concepts Common To Human Societies, 242
Conclusion, 243

22 sex and the family   **244**

The Traditional American Family, 245
The Family Of Today, 246
Solving The Problems, 249
The Family Of The Future, 251
Conclusion, 253

23 religious attitudes toward sexuality **254**

The Stand Of Religion On Five Major
    Sexual Topics, 255
Conclusion, 257

24 sex and the civil law **258**

Restrictions On Marriage, 258
Laws Regarding The Role Of Sex In Marriage, 259

25 sex and the criminal law **261**

Legal Requirements Concerning Sexual
    Intercourse, 261
Crimes Involving Sexual Intercourse, 264
Other Aspects Of Sex And Criminal Law, 265
Conclusion, 266

index **269**

preface

My professional background and academic position have allowed me the opportunity of approaching human sexuality from two distinct points of view. As a physician specializing in obstetrics and gynecology, I daily encounter sexual problems of patients; and as a sex educator, I have the opportunity of imparting information to students in such a way that they may avoid these self-same problems in their future.

Extensive literature already exists about human sexuality. Yet for the most part, I have found that it has been compartmentalized by various academic and scientific disciplines with little communication among them. To compound the difficulties, it seems that each discipline has somehow adopted a unique vocabulary of its own, which makes the reading difficult and in many cases incomprehensible, for those outside any specific discipline. I am impressed that although much of the material has extensive practical significance, little has been done to present it in an integrated way which would have practical value for the usual reader.

With consultative help, I therefore have tried to write this book as an integrated unit, assimilating and consolidating as much material from the various related disciplines as possible, yet keeping the book reasonably compact. This purpose negates writing a sexual encyclopedia. Other books of that type are readily available. Furthermore, this purpose prevents extensive coverage of sexual deviations, which, to be sure, make interesting reading, but are of little practical significance for the average reader.

At times the material will be embellished by some philosophical touches and opinions of my own. In particular, while I acknowledge the existence of mechanistic sexuality, namely sexual encounter in which orgasm is orgasm regardless of with whom or how attained and in which the act seemingly is more important than the participants, I emphasize that there is still another type of sexuality which allows for deeper interpersonal relationship.

I therefore address this book to the average reader who is interested in a better comprehension of current sexual practices and a better understanding of his own sexual motivations and needs. At the same time I hope the text may broaden the horizon of the sex educator, be he professional or parent, by presenting the subject matter in a meaningful, integrated, and simplified way.

FREDERICK COHN
Albuquerque, New Mexico

acknowledgements

As this book is an outgrowth of a course in human sexuality given at the University of New Mexico, I wish to acknowledge those individuals who made the course possible, specifically Doctors Ella Mae Small and Dale Hanson of the Department of Health Education at the university. I wish also to acknowledge those who collaborated with me in teaching the course and contributing to its success, namely Doctors E. G. Belzer, Jr., and Paul Dearth. It is also appropriate to thank Dr. Robert Munsick of the Department of Obstetrics and Gynecology at the Medical School for his support.

I am particularly grateful to Dr. C. J. Eaton for his assistance with clinical photography and to Mrs. Marge Thornton for secretarial help. Dr. Alan Frank gave me special assistance on the topics of psychosexual development and homosexuality, and Dr. Helmuth Vorherr edited the section on lactation. To both of them I owe special commendation.

As writing a book is a new experience for me, I wish to thank Charles E. Moritz for his assistance in preparing the manuscript and the editors of Prentice-Hall, particularly Edward E. Lugenbeel, for their interest and encouragement.

Lastly, I would like to thank my family and my partners for allowing me to take the time from a busy professional career to accomplish this project.

Understanding
Human Sexuality

part one

A Background

where are we? what is it all about?

Why Study Sexuality? *It has long been assumed that sexuality is an instinctual process. To say this another way, even if no teaching were done, one would be able by virtue of one's human qualities to perform sexually with satisfaction. There is a basic drive of a sexual nature in all humans. However, the application of that drive—the way by which that drive finally reaches its fulfillment—is, I believe, a learned experience. To direct that learning satisfactorily seems to me a sufficient reason for studying sexuality.*

Sexuality Is Learned

There are two strong arguments that sexuality is learned. The first involves the oddity of having a child born with ambiguous sexual differentiation. Such a child, although it is hormonally and physically a female, may, because of enlargement of the clitoris, be raised initially as a male child. In like manner, a male child, because of defects in the penile area, may be raised as a female child. If this sexual identification is not corrected before the age of two, it has been learned that the child is best raised as the gender initially designated. This means that if a child is thought to be a female, raised for two years as a female, but is later found to be a male, the child is best raised for the remainder of her life as a female. Reconstructive surgery can be undertaken to establish female genitalia. Despite the fact that this child has male hormones, the physiological makeup of a male, and should have the "sex drive" of a male, still in the initial two-year period the child has learned on its own to be a female. The learning in that brief time is of far greater import than any instinctual or hormonal function. In like manner, a female child initially identified as a male should subsequently be physically and surgically assigned as a male if she is past her second birthday. The rationale behind these procedures is well founded in pediatric and psychiatric literature. Those individuals whose sexual identity has been changed after the age of two frequently have suffered severe emotional reactions.

The second argument that sexuality is largely learned is based on the outstanding work of Harry Harlow with monkeys. He demonstrated that early observational experiences of monkeys have a profound effect on their adult sexual behavior. He noted that monkeys raised in total isolation from birth and thus deprived of any contact with their mothers or peers, were totally incapable of performing with a mate when placed in a sexual situation. This phenomenon is most obvious if the mate also had reached sexual maturity in isolation. In these experiments a female monkey in heat (a state of sexual excitation that can be observed and scientifically determined) was placed with a male monkey, also sexually mature and also reared in isolation. To the observer it appeared that the pair were aware that they were supposed to do something but were at a loss as to what it was. The animals often became agitated, restless, and frustrated. Other monkeys, who had previously been involved in sexual activity or had previously observed other monkeys in sexual activity, were then introduced into the scene. These experienced monkeys knew exactly what to do and soon taught the others. Interestingly, the few inexperienced female monkeys who did become pregnant in this experimental study subsequently gave birth to offspring but were unable to take care of the young satisfactorily and, in fact, cruelly rejected them. A similar type of learning of sexual activity has been observed and reported by individuals who raise domesticated cats and dogs.

It is certainly unscientific to draw absolute conclusions regarding human sexual behavior on the basis of experiments performed on lower forms. However, we do know that in man the young are more helpless than in other primate species. We also know that among primates, the human infant requires the longest period of time to reach maturity. It therefore seems logical to suppose that a similar type of sexual teaching must exist for the young of man as exists for the young of higher apes and domestic animals. To the best of my knowledge, no one has done a study on humans parallel to the study on monkeys just described, and it would be folly to suggest such be done. On the basis of the preceding information, however, I believe we can assume that human sexual activity is learned and in some way taught.

Where Is Sexuality Taught?

With the basic assumption that sexuality is learned, the question arises: Where and how is sexuality taught and learned? There are four areas: the home, the peer group, the sexual milieu, and the school.

THE HOME.   It is obvious that sexuality is initially learned from parents. These are the first people the child encounters. He encounters them at a time during which he is rapidly maturing and easily influenced. He is also highly curious and receptive. I wish to say as an aside here that a great deal of the sexuality learned from birth to possibly age 8 to 10 is not erotic in nature, that is, it does not cause arousal or sexual desire. As an example, seeing breast-feeding at an early age is a part of sexual learning but causes no eroticism in a young child, although it may well do so at a later date. Certainly a child will be exposed to other sexual learning in the home. He will see his parents, or his brothers and sisters, in various stages of undress. He may even see them in some phase of sexual activity. The child will, however, not respond erotically to these observations.

The child will be taught certain attitudes in the home. Attitudes toward such factors as undress, handling the genitalia, and cleanliness will be established at an early age.

However, one of the problems involved with formal sex education in the home is that it can rarely be taught in an impartial fashion. The average parent will give very specific instructions about sexual behavior in living. The parent generally will give the child only one way, the parent's, of handling sexual situations, and it is assumed to be the correct way. It is a rare parent who will proceed to instruct his child in that attitude which the parent espouses, yet allow the child to know that there are alternatives or variant attitudes of sexual behavior.

Now the question arises as to whether the child should receive further instruction on sexuality in a more formalized way from that derived in the home. The obvious variable in the situation is the qualification of the parents to handle the teaching of sexuality. Some parents are well qualified, emotionally and factually, whereas others are deficient on both counts. I personally do not feel it is entirely fair for parents, just because they are parents, to be totally responsible for the sexual education of their child. Other lines of education are needed to assure a greater breadth of sexual knowledge, which is important to the child's future.

THE PEER GROUP. A second major source from which a child learns sexuality is the peer group. Among leading sociologists, John Gagnon believes that this is the group from which the child should learn about sex. The child relates immediately with his peer group, and it is with members of this group that he will have sexual activity, if he has it at all during his younger days.

However, there are serious problems associated with peer group teaching. First, the peer group frequently deals with wrong information. Peer group knowledge is at best second-hand in the young adolescent stages. It consists of what other members of the group have heard or thought they heard, frequently gathered from older boys or girls, parents, or teachers. If some parents are ill-prepared to discuss sexuality, we are then obliged to conclude that peer groups, as a whole, are often less prepared to handle sexual education. Teaching by peer groups is fraught with misinformation.

The second problem of peer group teaching is that a set of values is engendered with sexuality. There is nothing aseptic or clinical about the sexual procedures discussed by the younger adolescents. Each peer group has its "do's" and "don'ts," depending on the specific group, and accordingly they will or they won't. Thus those who are learning may not only glean second-hand information, they are also directed about what to do with the information, whether this be petting, intercourse, venereal disease, or other related directives.

THE SEXUAL MILIEU. By sexual milieu I refer to the sexual environment to which a child is exposed. This includes movies with their various ratings, television with heavy emphasis on dramatic entertainment, advertising, billboards, sex-oriented books and magazines, and, more recently, love comics. All these contribute dramatically to a child's attitude toward sexuality and what is right, wrong, good, and bad. As time goes on, it may be that this third area will be the single most influential area of sexual training. Certainly, if there is a continuing decrease in our society toward interpersonal communication, then a noninterpersonal type of communication may prevail.

This area, it seems to me, is an unmanageable one, and I hope we can rely on the prevalence of the other three programs to keep it in proper perspective.

THE SCHOOL. The fourth potential area for sexual training lies in the formalized school system. Teaching sex in school is currently a very controversial subject. It has been tried and has been successful in some areas; it has failed in others. The Scandinavian countries took a lead in sex education and continue to maintain the forefront in educating their young in sexual matters. However, the concepts toward which they have striven and the values they have created are not necessarily those which are currently espoused by middle-class America. I cannot categorically answer the question, "Should the school teach sex education?" I can only give my opinion as to why I think they should. Schools do have the obligation at least to introduce the subject of sexuality if for no other reason than to provide a source of accurate information for those students who wish to correct misconceptions or who believe themselves to be inadequately informed and have questions to be answered.

However, there are two rather obvious inherent dangers in a formalized sex education program. The first involves what should be taught, at what age level, how, and whether adult concepts are being introduced into a childlike situation. Answers to this set of questions I leave to those educators who regularly instruct below the college and university level. I call the reader's attention to the SIECUS program, on which information can be obtained by writing to the Sex Information and Education Council of the United States, 1855 Broadway, New York, New York 10023.

The second danger concerns me more. It embodies those factors which more than any others motivate me to write this book. This danger is that sex education all too often is taught in a factual, inhumanized, cold, and probably indifferent manner. Total sexual satisfaction remains a potent weapon toward individual fulfillment and happiness. To present sexuality without presenting the milieu of human feelings that accompany it is to denude it. I believe humanization of sexual behavior should be an integral part of any presentation.

References

HARLOW, HARRY F. 1971. *Learning to Love*. San Francisco: Albion. Also in paperback, 1973, New York: Valentine Books.

SIMON, WILLIAM, AND JOHN H. GAGNON. 1967. "The Pedagogy of Sex," *Saturday Review*, 18 Nov.: 74.

2

validity

The Need To Avoid Error.   In the area of human sexuality and its relation to human feelings, it is of major importance that we be as close to 100% accurate as possible in the information presented, for what is presented may well serve as some basis for the way in which the students or reader will act, react, and feel in sexual situations. If we err, we may cause confusion, some degree of unhappiness, or both. Since I am writing this book in an attempt to dispel emotional misery, not cause it, I feel strongly that we should not err.

As an example, let us consider masturbation. Not too long ago, it was believed that masturbation caused psychological regression and in some instances would cause the masturbator to go insane. Masturbation was also believed to be harmful to one's growth and development. Scientifically we are now sure that these previous "valid" statements were in error. In actuality masturbation does not cause the reputed consequences. Studies by Kinsey revealed that 95% of all males masturbate to orgasm at some time during their sexual lives. We certainly do not see a similar percentage of insane or growth-stunted males in the population. What we do see, however, is a generation that has developed and retained strong guilt feelings about masturbation. We find feelings of uncertainty. We find that masturbation is a delicate subject to discuss with our students and our children. We may have reached the point of being able to talk glibly about masturbation in generalities, but we are reluctant to answer such questions as: Should I masturbate? If the answer is yes, then: How often? Where? When?

Thus, historically once a concept has gained the status of being valid, it exerts tremendous influence on the way people act. Possibly more important, it also influences how they feel about these actions. Even if the statement is later proved invalid, it may alter people's actions but does not necessarily alter the feelings that previously had accompanied those actions.

Determination Of The Truth

Realizing, then, the importance of truth and validity in sexual matters, how do we determine what is true and valid? Let us analyze first the way we find truth in nonsexual matters. Two methods have been widely employed.

THE SCIENTIFIC METHOD. The first is the well-known scientific method. By it one hypothesizes what one believes to be true, gathers data from experimentation, and if the observations confirm the hypothesis beyond all reasonable doubt, a fact has been obtained and a new validity is assured.

LOGIC. The second method, possibly more philosophical, is that of logical reasoning. "If there is creation, there has to be a creator." If one can prove by analysis, similar to that employed in geometry, a conclusion based on previously known facts, then again a fact has been obtained and a new validity assured.

Truth In Sexual Matters

However, in the realm of human sexuality, these two standard methods, particularly the latter, have not proven successful. In the unique area of sexuality, "truth" seems to come from two different sources: authoritarian statements and statistical surveys.

AUTHORITARIAN STATEMENTS. Certain authors have gained a degree of respect in their specific fields. These authors make statements and claims that take on the aura of "truth." Thus a statement is true because Freud said it is true. Or a statement is true because it appears in an authoritarian book, such as the *Enclopedia of Sexual Behavior* or possibly in David Reuben's book, *Everything You Always Wanted to Know about Sex but Were Afraid to Ask.* Despite the credibility of the authors, however, if one closely examines the evidence, one cannot help but feel that one is exposed to the opinion of the author rather than what one would call definite facts.

The shortcomings of these individual experts is dramatically exposed by Patrick M. McGrady, Jr. in his book, *The Love Doctors,* in which he analyzes the background of "the curious breed of professionals who are masterminding our love lives."

STATISTICAL SURVEYS. Statistical surveys involve the gathering of information by questioning individuals about their sexual habits. The difficulties inherent in this method are several. The individual interviewed may not tell the truth, either on purpose or because he simply cannot recall the actuality. Questions of the interrogator may be slanted or may not adequately cover the topic being considered. Sampling of the population may be slanted or inadequate. Interpretations of the replies are fraught with potential error.

Bases Of Information In This Book

After considerable reflection and extensive reading, I present the information in this book on the following bases:

1. The anatomical and physiological material is as accurate as can be obtained today. However, the reader should realize that the information is subject to change as scientific investigations proceed. He should be prepared accordingly to alter his thinking from time to time as necessity may require. An excellent example of this refinement and change occurred recently in our knowledge of chromosomal count in the human. At one time we were certain that the human cell contained 46 autosomes plus two sex chromosomes (either two X's or an X and a Y). With more sophisticated methods of observation we now believe that there are but 44 autosomes plus two sex chromosomes.

2. Information, such as that of the Kinsey reports, based on in-

terviews and statistical analysis is presented as just that: statistics. The defects of interviewing techniques and the hazards of drawing absolute conclusions therefrom should be emphasized to the reader. Material presented in this light then has some significance and value.

3. The work of Masters and Johnson is very well done and seems to be basically valid. They have approached their studies by the scientific method and have followed uniform scientific techniques. Their findings have yet to be duplicated by other investigators and corroborated. Moreover, ramifications and refinements are to be expected as research progresses in this vanguard of scientific investigation.

4. Other information in the book I would pose as attitudinal—that is, it reflects an opinion, and more frequently than not the majority opinion. To be more explicit about this attitudinal information, let us take an example. Take the simple statement, "It is wrong to have sexual intercourse with your neighbor's wife." On the surface this appears to be a true statement, and there are certain subtruths about it that can be regarded as valid. Legally the statement is true, so that to make it a valid statement, one can say, "It is legally wrong to have sexual intercourse with your neighbor's wife." One can also make a valid statement by saying, "By most religious standards it is sinful to have sexual relations with your neighbor's wife." However, you cannot have the audacity to say that it is absolutely valid that it is wrong to have intercourse with your neighbor's wife. This is an attitude.

Let us go one step further, because attitudes may be of prime importance in life. The attitude of your behavior with your neighbor's wife is one which society would prefer to maintain under present circumstances. It is probably a necessary attitude if we are to preserve the family structure as a fundamental way of life. Well and good, but one cannot say this attitude is a truth, for it is not. One cannot say it is an absolute, because it is not.

Truths Versus Attitudes

The reader might contend at this point that I belabor the issue of differentiating between truth and attitude. I think not. The difficulty is that when truths or valid statements are taught, particularly in childhood, they generate a tremendous amount of feeling. They are most often taught by a parent, teacher, or other highly regarded adult figure. When these truths are then disregarded, they cause a feeling of guilt, anxiety, or fear in that person who has disobeyed, as it were, these fundamental truths. As described later (p. 133), these feelings of guilt, anxiety, or fear are incompatible with a healthy sexual existence and are probably the causes of most of the sexual pathology we see today. Anything that would engender unhealthy emotions should be removed, if possible, from our teaching.

Let us take the example of a young lady who has been brought up to believe that she should be a virgin at the time of marriage. If she is not, the emotional trauma will likely be far greater if she has been taught that such virginity is a basic truth than if she has been taught it is an attitude about which there is a somewhat ambivalent view at the present time.

Fortunately, several students of sexuality, among them Kirkendall, Maslow, and Reiss (see references), have attempted to formalize the various attitudes regarding sexuality that currently exist. Although each reader undoubtedly has his own set of attitudes, namely those with which he feels most comfortable, he can, after studying the works of these authors, possibly formulate new attitudes or better understand his own.

Summary

An individual in his lifetime is faced with a series of so-called truths, which as time progresses may be proven to be untruthful. Yet, despite the lack of authority for these statements, they still possess some real value to a society that is made up of people. They are significant in individual development and in interpersonal relationships. The individual must then evaluate each sexual attitude, try to determine why it evolved in the first place and what were its prior reasons for validity. He must then fit these findings into today's pattern of living as attitudes, but no longer as truths.

References

Kirkendall, L. A. 1961. *Premarital Intercourse and Interpersonal Relationships*. New York: Julian Press.

McGRADY, PATRICK M., JR., 1972. *The Love Doctors.* New York: Macmillan.

MASLOW, A. H. 1968. *Toward a Psychological Being,* 2nd ed. New York: Van Nostrand.

REISS, I. L. (ed.). 1966. "The Sexual Renaissance in America," *Journal of Sexual Issues,* 22: 1–140.

3

semantics

In any discipline one must deal with words that are pertinent to the material being presented. One certainly could not use or teach arithmetic without using numbers, nor could one teach chemistry without the proper symbols related to the substance involved. Sexuality also has its pertinent nomenclature. Sexuality, however, also has a unique problem. Sexual words in addition to describing a phenomenon are likely to arouse the emotions of both addresser and addressee. The number 7 does not cause anxiety in an algebra class, nor does H_2O cause any degree of consternation in the chemistry class. Quite in contrast, sexual words in a class on human sexuality do generally cause the arousal of emotions. The word intercourse may or may not cause some emotional reaction, but the term fucking certainly does. To further complicate the situation, sexual words for some readers may well cause embarrassment, revulsion, feelings of guilt, or *even defiance. Readers may run the gamut of emotions from appreciation to hostility.*

The reaction evoked within the teacher is also quite variable. There may be embarrassment or a general feeling of discomfort. The difficulty seems to be that teachers, physicians, clergymen, and many parents have accepted certain rules regarding speech and have been taught that certain words are taboo in either mixed company or in the classroom. Upon reflection one can see these restrictions make little or no sense. Certainly everyone in an adult audience today knows the usual four-letter words and with rare exceptions has used them at some time or other. Even among younger people, those past the ages of 7 or 8, such words are familiar.

The problem then centers on the relationship of a teacher with his student and getting over the hurdle of intercommunication devoid of awkwardness and embarrassment. In the following, I am suggesting methods by which the problem can be overcome. I am sure others have mastered their own techniques for handling the situation, but either they have not written about them or I have not become familiar with their techniques. I am presenting only those methods which I have used or with which I am familiar. One must learn to handle sexual semantics on a one-to-one relationship or in teaching a group.

The Use Of General Terminology

Certain words and expressions can be found in the daily newspapers or in general parlance. Among these are sexual satisfaction, sexual outlet, making love, and climax. There is also sexual union, a phrase that has a rather austere ring and is perhaps best reserved for use by the clergy. Toward the legalistic side are the terms cohabitation, sexual relations, and adultery. All these terms are useful, but when one attempts to teach by using such language, one soon finds the vocabulary inadequate. One shortly finds oneself using euphemisms that really do not hit the nail on the head.

The Use Of Scientific Terminology

This method is seemingly favored by those who are biologically or medically oriented. Here we find such terms as penis, vagina, coitus, orgasm—in general, terms with Latin or Greek origin. The main problem with this type of terminology is that it frequently takes sex out of everyday experience and puts it into an area that is not commonplace or common knowledge. It furthers the concept of a mechanistic sexuality rather than a human sexuality. Possibly among people in lower economic levels it is somewhat ridiculous to use such words because they lack meaning. These people have their own vocabulary for sexual entities. It is therefore essential in communicating with such people that the scientific words, when introduced, be carefully explained and accurately defined so that their meaning is not lost or confused.

One value of this method is that it saves the teacher from embarrassment and probably places him above emotional involvement. Another is that if the student wishes to read investigative literature, scientific nomenclature will constitute the method of presentation.

The Vernacular

Here are the common four-letter words and their adjunct terms of longer spelling. That is, if one wants to say fuck, one says fuck, disregarding whatever effect this might have on the audience. The course in sex education at one major university requires that the students use these words openly in unison. They say them. They sing them. They shout them in an attempt to remove the feelings that have developed over the years around using this type of vocabulary.

There is a certain advantage in using these words, as one can completely level with one's students. One is calling a spade a spade and thus can establish a rapport that otherwise might not be obtainable. However, using this vocabulary requires a rather mature person, one who is self-composed, and one who is willing to defend himself calmly against whatever hostility might develop from the student or the parents. It also involves thumbing one's nose at conformity. In general, the younger teacher seems more capable than the older teacher in using these terms comfortably and in a way which the audience does not resent. The educator is doing himself and his students an injustice, however, if he is forcing himself to use these terms. If this vocabulary does not come naturally, then I think it is better to ignore and forget this method.

Scrambled Words

Eric Berne, M.D., in his book, *Sex in Human Loving*, advocates the use of vernacular words wherein the spelling is slightly altered. Thus for example, tunc represents cunt, kirp represents prik (prick), swerk represents skrew (screw), and cuff represents fuck (fuck). This method, oddly enough, has been used by some quite successfully. One can say, for example, "I like cuffing, but I don't want a boy who will swerk me just for the glory of it."

In introducing this method to students, the initial reaction is one of a bit of laughter and a sort of "so what" attitude. However, as communication progresses, it is interesting to note that an individual, who earlier was embarrassed by using sexual terms, will discuss sexual entities and phenomena quite comfortably and easily with the use of scrambled words, almost not realizing what he or she has said.

Epilogue

I appreciate that many forms of communication of a sexual nature are nonverbal. An extensive literature is developing suggesting that "body language" is of possibly greater significance than the spoken word. The interested reader is referred to the book, *Body Language*, by Julius Fast.

References

BERNE, ERIC. 1971. *Sex in Human Loving*. New York: Pocket Books.

FAST, JULIUS. 1972. *Body Language*. New York: Pocket Books.

MORRIS, DESMOND. 1972. *Intimate Behavior*. New York: Random House. Also in paperback, 1973, New York: Bantam Books.

4

an historical sketch of western man's sexual attitudes and customs

This chapter has been written by E. G. Belzer, Jr. Ph.D. of Dalhousie University, New Brunswick, Canada.

Because of technology, civilization is moving at an extremely fast pace. In one generation, for example, we have gone from Kitty Hawk to the moon. Sociological changes tend to parallel this acceleration. Thus in one generation social changes occur which earlier would have spanned several generations. It therefore behooves us to understand historical changes in perspective, because what we describe as characteristic at any given moment in history may neither be appreciated nor accepted a short time later. The generation gap per se is an excellent example of this phenomenon. The younger generation moves so rapidly that the older generation has difficulty keeping up.

So it is with sex. The scientific advance in sexual studies in the last fifty years has exceeded all the advances of prior generations. It thus may be difficult for some members of the older generation to appreciate the views of the younger generation on sexual matters. The older generation, however, can take solace in the probability that the present up-and-coming generation will likewise be just as exasperated by the sexual views and activities of their offspring.

A person who has some knowledge of sexual history stands a better chance of giving more rational consideration to current sexual issues. When he appreciates the ebb and flow of restrictive and permissive erotic tides, the reader is not likely to assume that his own mores represent the zenith of cultural evolution.

It should be pointed out, however, that despite advances in sexual technology, there are only a certain number of sexual feats which can be accomplished. Our ancestors apparently were quite aware of all the diversifications of sex, as illustrated by the accounts of the Biblical cities of Sodom and Gomorrah.

The current trend of thinking is that any sexual activity between consenting adults is legal and acceptable, providing there is no offense to the sense of public decency. We are currently living in an era of sexual freedom, which, however, at any time can veer and return us to a type of sexual puritanism.

Because of its brevity, the historical account presented here is simplified. It is presented with the expectation that it will offer a rationale for the generation gap, broaden the reader's tolerance for sexual mores which are not his own, and encourage him to read more extensively among the excellent references given at the end of the chapter.

Ancient Jews

Prior to about 400 B.C., the separation of man into a carnal and spiritual dichotomy was not characteristic of Jewish culture. The early Jews' conception of the universe did not pit natural against supernatural worlds. The Jewish patriarchs did not expect their very human desire for immortality to be satisfied by a ghostly afterlife. Rather, immortality was obtained by a biological continuation of their "seed" or family lineage. These people seem to have had the attitude that sexual pleasure is a good and natural part of life, but that there are rules within which it should be obtained. Thus, the ancient Jews are said to have had an essentially naturalistic tradition.

Realizing their notions about the importance of family lineage, one might predict quite correctly that the Jews' rules discouraged non-reproductive sex. A Jewish prayer says, "And so our Creator and Maker ordered us to be fruitful and multiply, and whoever does not engage in reproducing the race is likened unto one who is shedding blood."

This requirement to reproduce pertained only to men. Why? The Jews, as did pre-Aristotelian people in general, saw the female's role in reproduction as providing a seed-bed in which the male's seed was sown. The female did not have "seed," so if she did not marry or reproduce or both, it would not be a failure to propagate the lineage. Paradoxically, if a Jewish man sowed his seed in a gentile woman, the child was not considered a Jew. Thus could nomads move on without feeling they were leaving some of their people behind.

The purpose of marriage was essentially reproduction. If a union was not fertile, the man was expected to dissolve the marriage or use concubines as fields in which to sow his seed. It was especially grievous if a man died without having produced children unless his widow could be inseminated by one of his close relatives. The child of such a union ("levirate marriage" from the Latin "levis" for "husband's brother") was regarded as the dead man's offspring, thus preserving his lineage.

You can thus see that separate standards were applied to men and women. The double standard also applied to adultery. The commandment forbidding adultery was not intended to limit a married man's erotic activity to his own wife. It forbade only coitus between a married Jewess and any man other than her husband. Thus, the Jewish man, who had probably married as a teenager, could seek erotic pleasure with single Jewesses, or with non-Jewish women regardless of their marital status. The important thing was for a Jew to know that his wife's children were truly his own, for purposes of reckoning property inheritance as well as to assure biological immortality.

The ancient Jews also differed from the mainstream of contemporary Western outlook in their attitude toward fornication and illegitimacy. Noncommercial fornication, excepting rape, was not taboo in general. Unless her father specifically ordered her not to, a girl twelve and one-half years of age might legally begin erotic activity. Hebraic fathers had almost unlimited authority over their wives and children. A father could receive more money for his daughter when he contracted for her marriage if she was a virgin. Thus, a father could claim cash compensation from a man who took his unbetrothed daughter's virginity. Betrothed people were regarded as married from the standpoint of sex relations, including adultery. Children were considered bastards only if they were the result of an illegal sexual union, such as adultery or incest.

Both the Jewish taboo on nonreproductive eroticism and the double standard were evident in their attitudes about homosexual activity. Male homosexual activity was taboo not only because it was nonreproductive but also because it was associated with the ceremonies of neighboring tribes who worshiped rival gods. Breaking this taboo was punishable by stoning to death. Female homoeroticism was not as severely condemned, presumably because neither the wasting of seed nor rival gods was involved. A woman known to have had homosexual experience was not permitted to marry a man who held an important religious position, but she was not killed. On the other hand, the double standard demanded death by stoning for a Jewess who prostituted herself, whereas the male Jew's liaisons with gentile prostitutes were accepted.

In summary, some of the sexual attitudes and customs transmitted to us through the ancient Jews are as follows. Erotic pleasure is good, but there are behavioral rules within which it should be sought. Men and women are to be governed by separate standards of sexual morality. Women should be more closely controlled to protect the family structure and the clarity of inheritance rights. The man is the ruler of the family, and his wife is his sexual property. He has "absolute" say over the sexual life of his daughter, whose virginity he should try to preserve until after marriage. Nonreproductive eroticism is taboo, particularly if a wastage of seed is involved.

Other attitudes still in circulation that are shared with the Jews of long ago include the following. A menstruating woman is unclean and sexual relations with her are taboo. It is very bad to expose your genitals or to look at those of another person; a Biblical lesson tells of a son, Ham, being cursed for accidentally seeing his father's genitals. The woman is to be honored as a mother and homemaker, but is not usually expected to venture into public life. All male babies should be circumcised.

The Classical World

The "Classical World" refers to three distinct ancient civilizations. The Greek civilization, prior to approximately 400 B.C., and the Roman civilization were basically naturalistic. The Greek civilization after approximately 400 B.C. was characterized by dualism, the doctrine that man has two natures, physical and spiritual.

Classical cultures shared with the Jewish culture the assumption that men were generally more important than women. It was through the males that culture was supposed to be transmitted and society's problems solved. There are other similarities, as well as important differences, between the sexual mores of the Classical and Jewish cultures.

Among the early Greeks there was only a vague relationship between religion and morality. For example, the monogamous form of marriage was demanded not for what we would ordinarily call religious reasons, but for secular reasons. Their system of inheritance of property required that a certain number of each generation be of known parentage. A lasting monogamous marriage was also valued as a means whereby the husband could obtain needed domestic help.

Extramarital sexual activity was evidently common enough for Classical men so that usually they did not relate to their wives as lovers. On the other hand, wives were the sexual property of the husbands. Adulteresses were severely punished, and the husband was apt to kill the interloper. As with most generalities, there are exceptions to the rule. Extramarital coitus for Spartan women, for example, was sometimes encouraged as a means of providing more warriors. Also, in pre-Augustinian Rome, a cuckolded husband more likely than not merely turned his adulterous wife over to her man of the moment and found himself another woman.

The inequality between a husband and wife appears to have been still less favorable for the Classical woman than it was for her Jewish counterpart. For example, the Greek wife did not usually appear in public with her husband, nor was she encouraged to be socially or intellectually active outside the home. Apparently the concept of virginity in the Classical World was different from that of today. A woman lost her virginity by marrying and thus yielding her freedom to a man. This virginal status was different from the condition of never having had coital experience, which was known as *"virgo intactus."* The latter condition did increase marriageability, but was not considered a moral virtue per se.

If a Greek woman did not become a wife, she might become an *hetaera* (Greek feminine for "companion") or a prostitute. Both were legitimate social roles, but the former was preferable. Hetaerae, unlike wives, were often well educated and accompanied men in social as well as sexual activities. Sexually active women had no need for a sense of shame, whether or not they accepted money from their partners. Male prostitutes rounded out the scene, making homosexual as well as heterosexual gratification available to the population.

In general, the human potential for developing an appetite for homosexual as well as heterosexual relations was much more widely recognized and accepted in the Classical World than it is today. The Imperial Romans never viewed male homoeroticism as favorably as did the early Greeks. On the other hand, female homosexual activity, Lesbianism, seems to have been more widely enjoyed in Rome than it was in Greece.

The female's potential for eroticism was given great respect in the Classical World. Hippocrates taught that if a woman's *hystera* (Greek for uterus) was not regularly excited by semen, the womb wandered about the body and the blood moved upward, clouding the mind and sometimes affecting the breathing. This condition was known as hysteria, and for 2000 years the Hippocratic school of medicine prescribed the obvious remedy for nervous, restless women. As recently as Freud's time physicians were taught that a man, having no womb, could not be afflicted with hysteria.

The generally positive attitude of the Classical World's naturalists, i.e., the early Greeks and Romans, toward sexual pleasure can be illustrated in other ways. The Romans insisted that sexual pleasure was a human birthright, and only in cases of dire necessity could the state interfere with it. The Greeks accepted masturbation as a healthy safety valve for human eroticism. The only situation in which it was generally frowned upon was in the case of adult men. The men were supposed to be able to obtain gratification with one of the various, readily available, potential partners. That the naturalistic Greeks and Romans took pleasure in viewing the human body is obviously reflected in their art.

A major point of contrast between the naturalistic Romans and the early Greeks was that the Hellenic sexual appetite seems to have been almost entirely free of brutality. The sexual appetites cultivated in Rome demanded activities that today are considered to be unspeakably cruel. Children, even babies in cradles, could be obtained to satisfy desires for pederasty, fellatio, or vaginal coitus. The Romans left detailed accounts not only of private bestiality where at least the human partner was willing, but also of sexual assaults upon captive humans in arenas by trained animals. There are reports of bulls, stallions, asses, zebras, giraffes, leopards, cheetahs, wild boars, large dogs, and various species of apes which were trained to copulate with women and to perform pederasty with men. Great suffering and even death resulted from these attempts to satisfy the voyeurism of the spectators. From the examples of the Hellenic and Roman cultures, one can see that very permissive sexual customs may develop in either the presence or absence of much cruelty and exploitation of other people.

Military ventures brought the Greeks into contact with Oriental peoples. Books from India first appeared in Greece around 500 B.C. By 400 B. C., the influence of the traditionally Oriental world outlook known as dualism had resulted in such a change that historians consider a new Greek civilization, the Hellenistic, to have emerged. Dualistic mentality dichotomized man into an inferior physical self and a superior spiritual self. The goal of a man's life ought to be the securing of a spiritual reward for the soul after the flesh has disappeared. Immortality was no longer biological, but was now spiritual. This new force was to influence not only the Greeks, but also some sects of Judaism, Christianity, and many of the religions with which Christianity had to compete for supremacy in the Western world.

Early Christianity

Christianity originated at a time and place of rapid transition and upheaval. The Greco-Roman civilizations were waning. Hellenistic dualism had strongly influenced the areas with asceticism. This resulted in friction with the more worldly naturalism, which was still much in evidence.

Jesus of Nazareth was a Jew from Palestine, a region that had been relatively uninfluenced by Hellenism. As might be expected, Jesus was basically naturalistic. Apparently he was not shocked by, but was concerned for, the welfare of sexually permissive people, including prostitutes. Some of his more dualistic detractors considered him a "winebibber of questionable morals." Judging from Biblical statements, Jesus favored a single standard forbidding adultery, rather than the double standard of his ancestors. His teaching on divorce was much stricter than that of traditional Judaism. However, no comprehensive set of rules by which to judge external behavior can be based on Jesus's ethic. Society must judge people against observable criteria, such as whether a couple was married when they had coitus. Jesus's teaching would have them judged on the basis of inner motive. For example, a person who had suppressed desires for adultery was no different from one who acted out such desires.

Paul spoke much more specifically about sexual matters than did Jesus. Consequently, the early Church's sexual mores were strongly Paulian. Concerning marriage, Biblical records of Paul's statements indicate he stood roughly midway between traditional Jewish insistence on procreation and factions, such as the Essenes, who had been so thoroughly influenced by Hellenistic dualism that they opposed sexual relations and marriage. During his earlier years, Paul had been rejected by a prospective bride. It was perhaps for this reason that he later urged others to emulate his celibacy if they could, but he sanctioned marriage.

Paul's position, not dualistic to the point of viewing sexual pleasure as an evil per se, but much more restrictive than that of the Greco-Roman naturalists and sensualists, characterized the Church in its earliest years. The original Christian dissuasions from sexual aspects of life were motivated primarily by an expectation that the world's end was near. The faithful were urged to prepare for the apocalypse rather than to concern themselves overmuch with earthly ephemerata. Activities such as homosexuality were condemned largely because they were so often associated with idolatry, the worship of false gods.

The early Church had to struggle for survival. Competing naturalistic religions of the Greco-Roman world included overt fertility symbols and erotic ceremonies in their stress upon the natural continuation of life. The Church reacted by gravitating closer to the opposite pole, dualism. It stressed the supernatural continuation of life and the evils of sexual pleasure.

By the third century, it was argued that any woman who had coitus for any reason other than procreation was a prostitute. Although for the first three centuries celibacy was not required of the lower ranks of clergy, it was considered "unseemly" for men to marry after they became priests. Around the fourth century, Augustine (354–430 A.D.) taught that marital coitus (*copula carnalis*) and nonmarital coitus (*copula fornicatoris*) were not significantly different; both were sinful. Pope Gregory (590–604 A.D.) later endorsed the doctrine that marital coitus was always sinful, stressing that pleasure "befouled" it. An early Christian prayer, which I understand is still used in certain versions of the faith, states, "Behold, I was conceived in iniquity and in sin hath my mother conceived me."

Early Medieval Ages

It is clear that by 385 A.D. the Church had succeeded in its struggle for survival and was in control of the Roman region. The death penalty for ecclesiastical offenses, including adherence to a rival dualistic religion, Mithraism, was introduced. As the faith spread northward, its ascetic teaching about sexuality ran into resistance. Among the sexually permissive traditions which the Christians found prevailing, and which continued to have many adherents for centuries thereafter, were as follows: virginity was not prized; marriage was usually on a trial or temporary basis; women as well as men actively sought lovers; polygamy was common; and having been born out of wedlock was not a disgrace. Of course, resistance to the Church's sexual asceticism was never entirely subdued, but efforts to enforce Church teaching resulted in much violence and martyrdom. The efforts were successful enough for the years 400 to 800 A.D. to be characterized by "morbid asceticism and contempt for this world" and to have gone down in history as the "Dark Ages."

During this period the Church elaborated its antisexual teachings and vigorously sought to impose them upon the populace. The prevailing attitude was definitely no longer "sexual pleasure is good, and here are the rules within which it may be sought." Rather, it was "sexual pleasure is damnable, and here are the rules to keep you from damnation." Some of the rules seem to have been justified by "white lies" based on the proposition that "pious frauds" might be praiseworthy in efforts to save souls. Thus, Paul's prohibition of remarriage for a man who "put away," i.e., divorced, his wife was applied to widowers who "put away," i.e., buried, their wives. The Old Testa-

ment story of Onan, who was killed when he evaded the duty of in-
seminating his brother's widow by withdrawing his penis and spilling
"seed" on the ground, was interpreted to the people as referring to
masturbation.

The Biblical story of the original sin of Adam and Eve was explained as being sexual intercourse, bolstering the attitude that sexual
activity was sinful. Whereas pre-Christian Saxon men treated women
as property, their converted brothers tended to treat them as property
who were the source of sin. If a woman was to be thought of highly,
she had to emulate Mary, the mother of Jesus, who in 451 A.D. was
declared by the Council of Chalcedon to be a perpetual virgin and the
mother of God. In 1854, it was further declared that Mary herself
was not conceived in the ordinary way.

If the women of the Classical World do not seem to have been
as free as women of the ancient Jewish world, women of the Dark
Ages were still less free. A married woman had no legal existence, so
a lawsuit against her actually made a defendant of the husband. Thus,
the civil law permitted a man to keep his wife in line by beating her.
Church law, however, required him to treat her mercifully. By this
time the Church had stripped women of the right to perform min-
isterial duties such as preaching, baptizing, and healing, which the
early Church had granted them.

Around the eighth century, the Church produced a series of
penitentials in which rules concerning sexual behavior were codified.
Among the punishable offences were thinking of fornication, which
drew forty days' penance, and nocturnal emissions, called "nocturnal
pollutions," which obligated the offender to rise at once and sing
seven penitential psalms. If the erotic dreamer was in church at the
time, he had to sing the entire Psalter. Married couples were permitted
only one coital posture. Penalties for using forbidden positions varied
from one position to the other. The most taboo, a rear entry, called
for seven years' penance. Marital coitus was illegal on Sundays,
Wednesdays, and Fridays, which account for slightly more than five
months of the year. The marriage act was taboo for forty days prior
to Easter and for three days prior to attending communion, at which
frequent attendance was required. The penitentials also kept husbands
and wives from coupling during the time between conception and
forty days after childbirth.

Many people have difficulty believing that people could be made
to obey such rules. There is no way of knowing how effective the en-

forcement was. It was based on the people's belief that their clergy could tell them what God considered damnable, that is, who was the sinner. The fourth Lateran Council of 1215 ruled that every person must make an oral confession on his sins to a priest at least once a year and then pay the penalty. Their soul, conceived of as their conscious self or ego, would suffer eternal torture if they did not confess and then carry out the penance. People today often relate to physicians with similar faith. They submit to such procedures as radical surgery and electroshock treatments in a way that must seem incredible to someone outside our culture.

The Rise Of Romance

When a person's desire for an idealized lover is frustrated, the feeling which today we often call "being in love" is likely to arise. Throughout history, this emotion has been viewed in various ways. Although at some points it has been thought of as a minor affliction— "don't worry about it; it will go away"—toward the end of the eleventh century courtiers in southern France began to esteem and cultivate this feeling. The idea that "love and marriage go together like a horse and carriage, you can't have one without the other" seems not to have enjoyed wide circulation until the Romantic Era of the late eighteenth century.

From as early as the fifth century to as late as the fifteenth, the Church did not consider "love" a justification for marriage. Jerome insisted that "the man who loves, i.e. lusts after, his wife too ardently is an adulterer." Thus, the soil in which courtly love germinated included a marriage system that did not satisfy the human desire for love and affection. The milieu also included a familiarity with Maryworship, a chaste relationship with an idealized woman in which the man was a humble supplicant. Troubadours commonly referred to their ladies as "Madonna." In the thirteenth century, French troubadours who "worshiped" the wrong sort of madonna were persecuted by the Church and fled to Italy. There they bolstered a spreading community of romantics.

Courtly lovers typically were married to someone other than the object of their passion. Often they would increase their ardor with protracted petting sessions, which were carried out while unclothed in bed, but which were not allowed to culminate in coitus or orgasm.

Indeed, it was believed that "true love" could be distinguished from "false love" in that the former limited itself to kissing and naked fondling, whereas the latter included coitus. Men who played these chivalrous games did not completely deny themselves orgastic gratification. For this they might turn to their own wives or to women of lower social status. The troubadours recognized that their passionate love, which was based upon unfulfilled desire for possession of the idealized beloved, would not survive marriage's daily contacts and easy accessability.

From the tradition of chivalry, Western man today has inclinations toward such ideas as (1) there should be fidelity between lovers who are not necessarily marriage partners, (2) love must be mutual and involve admiration and respect, and (3) if a man truly loves a woman, he will not engage her in "complete" sexual activity. Perhaps most important was the influence toward redefining the role of women. Generally, "romantic love" has not been compatible with viewing women primarily as sources of labor, children, and sexual gratification. Where men have chosen to cultivate this sort of emotion, they have usually had to elevate women's status to a more idealized plane, which sometimes included the opportunity for idiosyncratic development, as opposed to defining the female role in a stereotyped manner.

With the rise of the middle class in post-Reformation Europe, we find a new dimension added to the field of sexual ideals. The bourgeoisie were interested in values such as honesty, property rights, avoidance of illegitimacy (which confounds inheritance of property), and family stability—a set of values that was satisfactorily met neither by the ideals of courtly love nor by the dualistic asceticism of Church teaching. The Romantics came up with the revolutionary idea that one woman ought to perform all three functions which earthly women might serve: providing sexual pleasure, companionship, and children and domestic labor. The woman should be one's wife! One might here recall the Greek arrangement whereby the three functions were separately performed by different women: prostitutes, hetaerae, and wives. The Romanticists agreed with the Church's insistence upon monogamy, but abandoned its prohibition of fornication. They felt that sexual pleasure was important in marriage and that a bit of experience was needed in order to choose a mate wisely. Some Romanticists, however, believed that it was nature's rule for a monogamous union to last only until a more attractive mate came along, and it would be foolish to fight nature. This offended both the bourgeoisie and the Church. The Romantic notion is still popular that the intense emotional kind of love resulting from unfulfilled desire for the beloved ought to be the basis of, and is the justification for, marriage.

Increasing Permissiveness And Reactions To It

After the eighth century, Western civilization began to emerge from the four-century-long "Dark Ages" discussed earlier. The main theme was no longer one of extreme ascetic dualism, but of humanism and concern with the affairs of this world. There was a general weakening of the feeling that pleasure was evil. We have already discussed one of the important developments of this period—romantic love.

The pluralism in attitudes regarding sexual matters that is evident in contemporary Western societies was already well developed during these periods, making generalizations hazardous. At the same time we find evidence of increasing secularization, we also find signs of extreme sexual suppression and asceticism. Early in the twelfth century, shortly after the Church obliged all clergy, rather than just monks, to remain celibate, there appears to have been an increased concern over homosexuality. A council in 1102 ruled that priests should be degraded for homosexual acts and excommunicated if the behavior persisted. There were mass outbreaks of flagellation mania. Female demons known as succubi were widely reported to initiate sexual relations with sleeping men. Women, especially widows, virgins, and nuns, were similarly assaulted by incubi or male demons.

Evidence from Renaissance art indicates that some men began to heal the dualistic dichotomy of "sexual" versus "good" women, which had been epitomized by Eve and the Blessed Virgin. Sexual activity and goodness were no longer seen as incompatible. A mural of Pope Alexander's mistress surrounded by angels was painted on a Vatican chamber. A prostitute modeled for a portrait of Saint Barbara, and the painter Filippo Lippi fashioned a picture of Mary after his mistress.

Illegitimacy was not a great social handicap during the Renaissance. Great painters and poets of the period were frequently, if not usually, illegitimate. Married men of high social standing, including supposedly celibate clergy, were very commonly and openly fathers of illegitimate children. Pope Paul III had a son whose proposed marriage to an illegitimate daughter of Charles V was called off at the altar when the bride-to-be discovered that her thirteen-year-old fiance was a cretin idiot. Pope Alexander VI recognized five offspring, and worked toward making princes and princesses of them. He once issued a papal decree that Lucrecia Borgia, his unwed daughter, bore him a child. He later indicated, however, that the baby was the result of an incestuous relation between Lucrecia and Cesare, one of his sons. In German the word *pfaffenkind*, parson's child, was synonymous with "bastard." The men of many parishes in Spain and Switzerland insisted that their priests keep a concubine so as to protect their own wives from clerical attentions.

In December of 1494, not two years after Columbus and his crew returned from the New World, syphilis appeared in Naples. Its rapid spread throughout Europe was a good indication of the widespread permissiveness of the times. Syphilis not only illuminated but also influenced the history of sexual matters. Sixty-five years after the disease appeared, Fallopius had invented a type of condom for prophylactic purposes. Only centuries later were condoms widely used as contraceptives.

After the Crusades, armies of camp-following prostitutes returned to European cities. Civil and clerical authorities set up and supervised brothels where business could be regulated and taxed. Pope Julius II, a patron of the arts, founded a brothel in Rome. Prostitutes who did not confine their activities to brothels, thus making taxation difficult, were in danger of being arrested and charged by the Inquisitors with witchcraft. After syphilis appeared in Europe, the popularity of brothels declined.

Various faiths and life styles considered heretical by the Church were common enough during the Renaissance to cause Church leaders to feel threatened. In the thirteenth century the use of torture was authorized to combat heretics. Shortly thereafter the Inquisition began. During the fourteenth century a characteristic Renaissance attitude circulated in increasingly wider circles. People began to consider themselves as possessors of free will. Not only did individualism of a romantic nature appear, but so did evident rejection of all authority. Unbridled sexual license, selfishness at the expense of others, was widespread.

Prior to the Inquisition, the Church regarded belief in witches as a heathenish superstition. It ordered the death penalty for anyone who burned a woman in the belief that she was a witch. But by the time of Thomas Aquinas in the thirteenth century, those who denied that witches existed were the ones who were in danger of being imprisoned or killed as heretics.

Inquisition judges not only protected the faithful from witches, but themselves from poverty as well. Often part of the confiscated property of men and women who had been convicted of witchcraft was turned over to the judges. Charges of witchcraft increasingly focused on sexual matters. By 1400 the civil courts recognized a duty to execute persons whom ecclesiastical courts found guilty of copulation with the Devil. In 1450 the Church recognized the nightflying abilities of witches, making it difficult for a person to establish his innocence by having been seen a good distance from the scene of the sorcery. In 1484 Pope Innocent VIII ordered his inquisitors to use torture to extract confessions. The belief was held that a witch who died without confessing would suffer eternal torture in Hell. Therefore, it was merciful to gain confessions by inserting needles under fingernails, burning feet, and crushing legs with heavy stones. The relatively brief suffering imposed upon convicted witches to obtain confessions was seen as a mercy which would actually spare the poor souls a much worse fate in the world to come. Confessors of sexual misconduct with the Devil generally agreed that his semen was ice-cold and that his penis was painfully large and covered with iron or fish scales. One woman at an early witch trial confessed to copulating with the Devil and bearing his child. The monster child had a wolf's head, a serpent's tail, and an appetite for children's flesh, with which she provided it.

Confessions were extracted after the person's guilt had been legally established. Among the kinds of evidence upon which guilt of copulation with the Devil was legally established were the presence of freckles, warts or sties; places that had been insensitized to Inquisitors' pin pricks by earlier contact with the Devil; both the sinking and the floating of bound women who had been cast into water; and answers of "yes" to the question, "Do you believe in witches?" Answers of "no" were punishable as heresy. Respected theologians of the time agreed that the presence of an intact hymen was not evidence that a girl was innocent of copulating with the Devil.

Witch-hunting did not reach its peak until the end of the sixteenth century, when Protestant reformers began to participate. It is estimated that at the very least a total of 30,000 people were executed for being witches. One post-Reformation Saxon magistrate claimed that he alone had condemned 20,000 witches.

Three sexual issues have been identified as among the causes of the Protestant Reformation. Two have already been discussed: the rule obliging clergy to celibacy, the observance of which seemed to be less likely as a clergyman's rank increased; and the Church's practice in Rome of profiting from prostitution. The third was the Church's forbidding of divorce and its system whereby annulments might be obtained.

On the continent, the Reformation seems largely to have been a reaction to the extreme permissiveness and the resistance to authority, which was so widespread during the late Renaissance. However, in England the Reformation occurred just as the Renaissance was getting a belated start. Rather than a religious reaction, it was more of an historical accident in England. To marry Anne Boleyn, King Henry VIII wanted his marriage to Catherine of Aragon annulled by the Pope, inasmuch as divorce was not permitted by the Church. Among the reasons suggested for his wanting the annullment were: syphilis had affected his brain, resulting in satyriasis, an insatiable urge for coitus (he later changed wives five times in ten years and, according to rumor, kept a room in his palace for his prostitutes); the marriage with Catherine had resulted in no male heir to the throne; and he was intensely and romantically in love with Anne, so much so that he refused to court a French princess in her stead, even though the Pope was believed likely to grant an annulment to make possible Henry's marriage to the princess. When the annulment was not granted, Henry withdrew England from the Church of Rome and set himself up as head of the Anglican Church. For the first time since Christianity became the dominant religion of Western man, one person officially headed both the church and the civil government of a nation. Gradually, Church law and secular law became mingled, with the ultimate result that the civil courts acquired the job of trying punishable sexual acts. Many of the civil and criminal laws regulating contemporary Western man's sexual behavior have thus evolved from Church laws.

The Reformers created an environment in Europe that was a partial return to the antipleasure, antisexual atmosphere of the Dark Ages. There were important differences, however. For example, virginity was not seen as good in itself. Also, the asceticism was more broadly based than that of the Dark Ages, which had focused mainly on sexual restrictions. Another noticeable difference was that the Reformers used public punishment to control people more than did the clergy of the Dark Ages, who stressed guilt and fear of damnation more heavily.

By now the historic tendency for erotic customs to vacillate between extremes of permissiveness and restrictiveness must be evident. After the restrictiveness of the Reformation and Counter-Reformation periods, a relaxation of sexual restraint occurred.

"The Enlightenment" And The Eighteenth Century

During the seventeenth and eighteenth centuries, Western culture was profoundly influenced by the intellectual revolution known as "The Enlightenment." Sexual attitudes and customs reflected the faith that there were "natural" ways of behaving, and that religious, governmental, and economic organizations should not force people into "artificial" lives. The notion that man was tainted by original sin was rejected by members of the "return to nature" movement. A large measure of romanticism was included in the flavor of the times.

Rousseau, believing that love was a private affair, argued that social authorities should not be involved with marriages. Reflecting the effect of Calvin's "Doctrine of Predestination," Rousseau taught that it was the will of God and Nature that couples who were meant for each other should someday meet, never to part. To the contrary, Maurice of Saxony, one of the period's most famous generals, wrote that marriage for life was a betrayal of nature. The rally back to nature could not result in a homogenization of sexual attitudes and beliefs as long as there was no agreement on what was "natural." The same difficulty exists today.

Since it seemed unnatural to confine sexual activity to a bedroom, the out-of-door rendezvous became fashionable. Homosexual activities were classified as "unnatural," and they fell into disrepute after having enjoyed widespread popularity among the upper classes. Only in England, which differed from the continent in other important respects as well, was male homosexuality in vogue.

During this period in England, appetites for flagellation became so widespread that brothels specializing in this form of eroticism appeared. One enterprising inventor even created a machine capable of whipping forty patrons simultaneously. An appetite for rupturing

hymens became so popular among wealthy eighteenth-century British-
ers that a technique of stitching ruptured hymens was developed.
Thus, a girl might command the high fees paid to a virgin prostitute
several times.

Reactions to the free-wheeling eroticism, which arose in England
during the Restoration of the monarchy after the Puritanical rule of
Cromwell, and the gallant sex life of the pre-Revolution French
aristocracy led to suppressive measures especially aimed at women.
Puritan Englishmen demanded obedience from their wives. Women
were required to stay at home, devoting their lives to housework.
Rather than becoming active in social and romantic pursuits, daughters were expected to remain at home until their father had "married
them off." After their Revolution, Frenchmen also were wont to deny
women roles outside the home. The pre-Revolution gallants had
thought so highly of women that feminism and sexual equalitarianism
were associated with the hated aristocracy.

From the start of the Industrial Revolution until the end of the
eighteenth century, the leaders of Western man generally agreed that
the more people a country had, the wealthier and better off it was.
In the face of high year-in-year-out death rates, which were augmented
sporadically by unusually high mortality during epidemics, famines,
and wars, mankind was accustomed to thinking in terms of under-
population rather than overpopulation problems. In 1798, Thomas
Malthus published his *Essay on Population*, a work which flew in the
face of prevailing opinion about the implications of human reproduction. He argued that the means of sustenance can be increased only
arithmetically, whereas biological populations tend to increase geo-
metrically. This basic principle, still accepted by some as valid today,
underlies much of the current concern over the "population explosion."

Victorianism

The Victorian era was one of accelerating social change, the
thrust of which appears to continue into the present. During this
period, much of the Western world passed from a predominantly
agrarian to an industrial economy, from aristocratic to middle-class
and workers' societies, from a static, mechanistic view to an evolutionary orientation toward science and the world, and from dogmatism
to empiricism and relativism.

However, the term "Victorianism" has come to refer to a particular sort of orientation. Influenced by the Enlightenment, the Victorian mentality saw man as an essentially rational being. Eroticism was viewed in a negative light, not because it was thought especially sinful, as it was during the Dark Ages, but because it awakened such strong feelings. Primarily on this account sexual activity was seen as "animalistic" and disgusting. This sort of attitude seems to have been most prevalent in England between 1760 and 1860. It was declining during much of the actual reign of Queen Victoria (1837–1901).

Realizing they could not eliminate the disgusting sexual side of life, which fit in so badly with their self-concept of superior-to-the-animals rationality, Victorians occupied themselves with hiding it. Shakespeare's writing appeared with sexual material expurgated. It was even argued that the Bible was dangerous to people with unchaste minds. Due to the suppression of erotic literature, prices paid for the limited-edition copies that were widely circulated in underground markets were inflated.

Ultraprudish Victorian ladies, often informed their physician of disease signs and symptoms by pointing at manikins rather than pointing to or exposing themselves. When a physician had to make a tactile examination, it was commonly made through an intervening cloth in the presence of the woman's husband or mother. This shamefulness about the body carried over into sexual activities as well. Not only "proper couples" but also prostitutes and their clients usually did not disrobe completely.

Prudery and a fear of inciting "dirty thoughts" which might even lead to female masturbation probably account in large measure for the absence of bidets in English bathrooms even after they were common on the continent and English homes were generally equipped with plumbing. Worry over masturbation by boys was evidently more widespread. Indeed, some Victorian fathers had their sons wear "cages" to bed which somehow fit about the genital area. For greater protection some of the devices were equipped with spikes. In order to balance the picture, it ought to be realized that just when prudishness was at an extreme, there were also vociferous critics who rebelled against it.

Victorian gentlemen, preferring to think of their wives, mothers, and other female relatives as "pure," refused to acknowledge publicly a lady's abilities for receiving sexual pleasure. A standard gynecological text insisted that the notion that women had sexual appetites was a "vile aspersion" on femininity. Sexual desire in young women was labeled "pathological" by a leading gynecologist. In addition to being labeled "sick," sexually responsive women were sometimes simply considered "bad," "impure," or "unladylike."

During these times, England was regarded as the world's leading power and as such tended to be considered a model. Thus, Victorian concern for suppressing open eroticism influenced much of the world, including the United States. A Surgeon General of the United States Public Health Service wrote that ninety percent of the time, "decent" women did not experience anything pleasant in coitus. Precoital play was thought to be both unnecessary and "beastly." Coitus was usually limited to the position in which the couple lies face to face with the male on top. The widespread insistence on this position has been explained as a reflection of an authoritarian culture in which men needed to assert their dominance. The submerged sexuality of American life was associated with so great a fascination for sexual matters that piano legs frequently were covered with crinoline "pants" for the sake of modesty.

While Victorian notions of propriety were flourishing, so was prostitution. As always, strong social pressures and harsh legal penalties failed to annihilate homosexual activities. Flagellation hit another of its peaks in popularity during Victorian days.

Queen Victoria herself was instrumental in settling one of the sexual issues which was then being contended. The newly developed technique of administering anesthesia during childbirth was being opposed by fundamentalists, who cited the decree in Genesis that women shall bring forth children in sorrow. When Victoria took chloroform during the birth of one of her babies, the controversy was ended.

Another sexual issue that was important during this period was not resolved as easily. Indeed, the issue of what the socially approved roles of the sexes ought to be is still simmering, if not raging. The bourgeoisie insisted that a man should be the ruler of his wife and children, for which there was certainly historical precedent. The success or failure of his life revolved around his ability to "get on" in his particular vocation and to provide material goods for his family. "Ladies," who were distinguished from "working-class women," were judged on how well they conformed to the traditional roles of homemaker and mother. Respectable society considered it virtuous for a woman to be exposed to as few of the realities of life as possible. Part of the resistance against a lady's occupying a job outside the home must have been due to the prevailing sexual mores and the accompanying repute of working-class women. Many of them supplemented their meager earnings by engaging in prostitution with double-standard men from higher socioeconomic strata.

In summary, the Victorian era has left us with influences such as having sexual matters made so hush-hush that people build up highly erotic charges, which in turn eroticize their perception of the world about them. There is a great concern for proper appearance, with a relatively great disparity between approved and actual sexual behaviors. There is a tendency to disapprove of activities for women which do not revolve around their reproductive role. Many people feel that sex is dirty or animalistic. Behavior should be rational, and it is appropriate for a person to rebel against customs which no longer seem to make sense to him.

Conclusion Of The Sketch

Sexual attitude and customs have always been undergoing revolution. Periods of relative permissiveness have alternated with times of greater restrictiveness. Negative attitudes toward erotic matters have given way to positive ways of looking at them, only to become dominant with a later reversal of the tide. However, the alternations have not been like those of a pendulum, which returns to the same place periodically. Many differences as well as similarities exist among all periods.

World War I accelerated the withdrawal from Victorian ways. The German Empire, Austro-Hungarian Monarchy, Czarist Russia, and the Ottoman Empire fell. The Western World drew up new codes for living, and among them new rules concerning sexuality. During the war, industrialization accelerated and women successfully filled jobs ordinarily considered man's work. The possibility for economic independence for masses of women gave added impetus to their demand for equality brought about by industrialization and freedom. By the 1920's, women's rights as free and equal citizens were recognized in the constitutions of most Western World nations. However, economic, religious, and ethnic barriers have been much more resistant.

Sigmund Freud's work was also of historic import. He strongly disagreed with the Enlightenment philosophers and the Victorians, who saw man as an essentially rational creature. Scientific research into human sexuality and reproduction has lagged behind most other important areas of inquiry. However, the work of such modern pioneers as Kinsey, Martin, Pomeroy, and Gebhard, all members of Indiana University's Institute for Sex Research; Pincus, Chang, and Rock, developers of the "pill"; and Masters and Johnson, scientists who have studied human sexual responses, have effectively opened the door to research in these areas. Much of the material in the rest of this book will deal with recent and current developments and trends in Western man's sexual knowledge, beliefs, issues and behaviors.

References

BIRD, JOSEPH W., AND LOIS F. BIRD. 1967. *The Freedom of Sexual Love.* Garden City, N.Y.: Doubleday.

BRUSENDORFF, OVE, AND PAUL HENNINGSEN. 1965. *A History of Eroticism: Antiquity.* New York: Lyle Stuart Press.

CLEUGH, JAMES. 1964. *Love Locked Out: An Examination of the Irrepressible Sexuality of the Middle Ages.* New York: Crown.

COLE, WILLIAM GRAHAM. 1959. *Sex and Love in the Bible.* New York: Association Press.

COLE, WILLIAM GRAHAM. 1966. *Sex in Christianity and Psychoanalysis.* New York: Oxford.

ELLIS, ALBERT, AND ALBERT ABARBANEL (eds.). 1967. *The Encyclopedia of Sexual Behavior.* New York: Hawthorn.

GOLDBERG, BEN ZION. 1962. *The Sacred Fire: The Story of Sex in Religion.* New York: Grove Press.

HUNT, MORTON M. 1959. *The Natural History of Love.* New York: Alfred A. Knopf.

JOHNSON, WARREN R. 1968. *Human Sexual Behavior and Sexual Education,* 2nd ed. Philadelphia: Lea & Febiger.

KARLEN, ARNO. 1971. *Sexuality and Homosexuality.* New York: W. W. Norton.

LEWINSOHN, RICHARD. 1958. *A History of Sexual Customs.* New York: Harper & Brothers.

MASTERS, ROBERT E. L. 1962. *Forbidden Sexual Behavior and Morality.* New York: Julian Press.

TAYLOR, G. RATTRAY. 1970. *Sex in History.* New York: Vanguard Press.

part two

Sexual Biology

5

sexual anatomy and physiology of the male

Human sexuality has a solid biological basis. One cannot ignore the anatomy and physiology involved. On the other hand, understanding sexual anatomy and physiology in great detail in no way guarantees satisfactory sexual activity. In sex education undue time and emphasis have often been placed on anatomy and physiology to the exclusion of other topics, more often than not those dealing with the psychological aspects of sexuality. Therefore the chapters presented here on anatomy and physiology will be confined to those aspects having practical or clinical significance. This will allow the remaining pages of the book to be devoted to a broader view of sexuality. For greater detail on sexual anatomy and physiology, the reader is directed to the references.

Testes

The testes, or testicles (Figs. 5–1, 5–3, 5–4), are twin glandular organs, responsible for the production of sperm and male hormones. Each testis is about 1 to 1.5 inches long and 0.75 to 1 inch in diameter. Each contains a complex of small tubules, (Fig. 5–2) lined with glandular epithelium composed of two types of cells (Fig. 5–2). The first type is spermatogenic, giving rise to sperm; the second type is sustentacular, giving nourishment to the developing sperm cells. The tubules

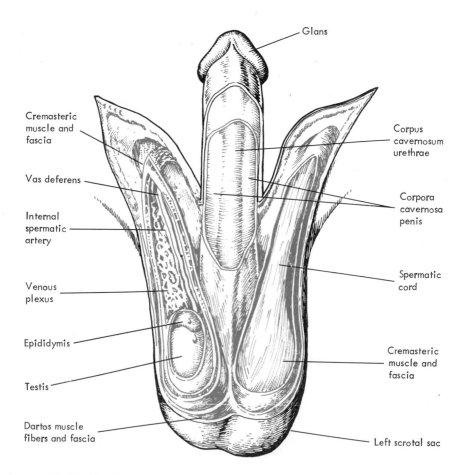

FIGURE 5-1. Penis and testes.

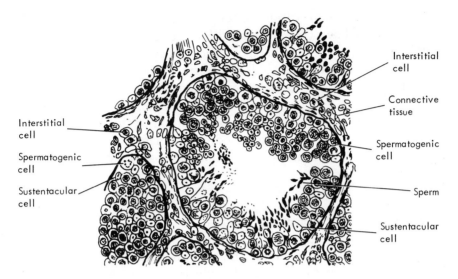

FIGURE 5-2. Tubules of the testis. X170. (From Bloom and Fawcett. 1968. *A Textbook of Histology.* Philadelphia: W. B. Saunders.)

are surrounded by connective tissue in which lie specialized cells, known as interstitial cells or cells of Leydig (Fig. 5–2), which are responsible for the production of the male hormone, testosterone.

The testes are housed in a pouch of skin termed the scrotum, the two halves of which are marked on the external surface by a ridge extending from the base of the penis to the anus. The left sac is characteristically lower than the right. The scrotum is actually a continuation of the skin covering the body. The testes develop embryologically on the posterior wall of the abdominal cavity. During the seventh month of development, the testes descend, pushing the skin outward to form the scrotum. The cause of descent is unknown. If the testes do not migrate downward, the condition is termed cryptorchism. The cryptorchid testis can produce male hormone but cannot produce viable sperm, presumably because the temperature within the abdomen is too high. Descent into the scrotum allows the testis to lie in a cooler environment.

Either of two sets of muscles can elevate the individual testis, and it is probable that at times the two sets act in unison. The cremasteric muscle (Fig. 5–1), which lies adjacent to the spermatic cord, is under both voluntary and involuntary control. A gentle stroke of the scrotol skin or inner aspect of the male thigh will result in contractions of the cremasteric muscle and ascent of the testicle on that side. The dartos muscle fibers (Fig. 5–1) lie within the scrotal wall and are under involuntary control. In cold environment, they contract, elevating the testes closer to the body wall. In warm environment, such as hot weather or water, the testes are more pendulant. Immediately prior to ejaculation, the testes are elevated involuntarily.

A small plexus of veins (Fig. 5–1) surrounds the vas deferens on either side of the body. These blood vessels may become varicose and for reasons unknown may play an important part in male infertility if this varicosity occurs.

Genital Ducts And Associated Glands

In each testis, the tubules that produce the sperm empty their products into a network of ducts, which, in turn, lead to a highly convoluted tubular structure, the epididymis (Figs. 5–1, 5–3, 5–4). The epididymis caps the testis and extends downward the full length of the posterior surface of the testis. It serves as a site for temporary storage of sperm produced by the testis. At its lowest point, the epididymis becomes continuous with the vas deferens, also termed the ductus deferens (Figs. 5–1, 5–3, 5–4). The causative organisms for both gonorrhea and genital tuberculosis have a predilection for the epididymis, where they may cause scarring and eventual male infertility.

The vas deferens on either side of the scrotum may be felt near the junction of the scrotum with the body wall as a firm, rubberlike tube about one-eighth of an inch in diameter. It is at this site that each vas is cut in vasectomy to sterilize the male (Fig. 18–1). A vas deferens, bound by connective tissue to adjacent blood vessels and nerves, constitutes a spermatic cord (Fig. 5–1). Within the cord, each vas courses upward, penetrates the body wall, and loops behind the bladder (Figs. 5–3, 5–4). At this site, each vas enlarges into an ampulla (Fig. 5–3), which serves as a reservoir for sperm.

Adjacent to each ampulla is a seminal vesicle (Figs. 5–3, 5–4). Each of this pair of vesicles is a saclike gland, which secretes a portion of the seminal fluid. This fluid is sticky and yellow in appearance. It contains the sugar, fructose, which is considered important in sperm nutrition. The fluid also contains pigments that are of medicolegal significance in cases of rape. Seminal fluid, when exposed to ultraviolet

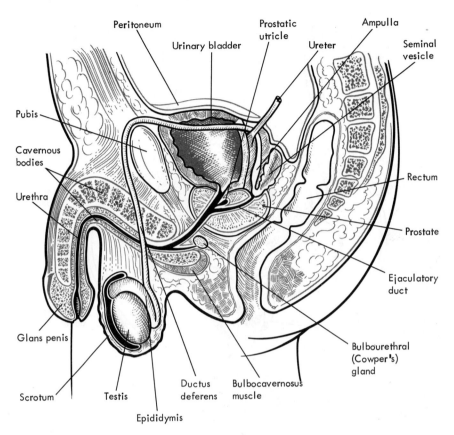

FIGURE 5-3. Sagittal section of the male genital system. (After Turner and Bagnara. 1971. *General Endocrinology*. Philadelphia: W. B. Saunders.)

light, becomes fluorescent because of these pigments. The presence of seminal fluid in the vaginal canal indicates that coitus has occurred, whether or not sperm are also present.

Each ampulla of the vasa deferentia narrows and receives the duct of the adajcent seminal vesicle, forming a new structure termed the ejaculatory duct (Fig. 5–3). The pair of ejaculatory ducts empty their mixture of sperm and seminal fluid into the urethra.

The ejaculatory ducts, as well as the adjacent section of the urethra, are embedded in the prostate gland, which lies at the base of the bladder (Figs. 5–3, 5–4). Several ducts from the prostate open into the urethra near the site of the openings of the ejaculatory ducts (Fig. 5–4). The prostate secretes a thin, milky, highly alkaline fluid, which

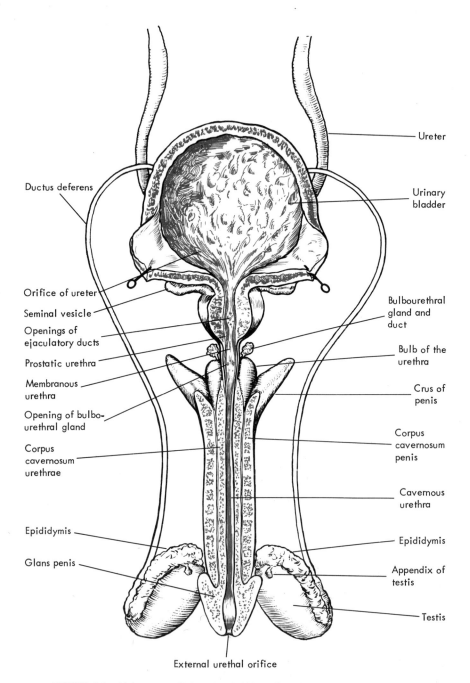

Ureter

Ductus deferens

Urinary
bladder

Orifice of ureter

Seminal vesicle

Openings of
ejaculatory ducts

Prostatic urethra

Membranous
urethra

Opening of bulbo-
urethral gland

Corpus
cavernosum
urethrae

Bulbourethral
gland and
duct

Bulb of the
urethra

Crus of
penis

Corpus
cavernosum
penis

Cavernous
urethra

Epididymis

Glans penis

Epididymis

Appendix of
testis

Testis

External urethal orifice

FIGURE 5-4. Male urogenital system. (After Crouch, J. E. 1972. *Functional Human Anatomy*. Philadelphia: Lèa & Febiger.)

contains a complex of substances, among which are proteins, calcium, citric acid, cholesterol, enzymes, and acids. This secretion is nutritive to the sperm and provides a medium for sperm transfer. The prostate may be palpated by a finger inserted within the rectum.

Clinically, the prostate is one of the more important pelvic organs of the male. It is subject to infections, among them being gonorrhea. Prostatitis, or inflammation of the gland from whatever cause, is accompanied by the usual symptoms of any infection, such as pain, fever, or chills. In the case of the prostate, blood may tinge either the semen or urine under pathological conditions. As either aging or disease occurs, the prostate may enlarge and impede or completely block the flow of urine. Several surgical procedures are available to remedy this enlargement (hypertrophy). An incision can be made through the abdominal wall and a portion of the gland removed; or a transurethral resection can be performed, whereby surgical instruments are introduced by way of the penile urethra to the region of the enlarged prostate.

The urethra (Figs. 5–3, 5–4, 5–5) in the male serves the dual function at separate times of conveying urine from the bladder and the ejaculate from the ejaculatory ducts and prostate gland to the exterior. Its total length is approximately 8 inches. There are three divisions of the urethra (Fig. 5–4): the prostatic urethra, which is about 1 inch long; the membranous urethra, which is about 0.5 inch long; and the cavernous or penile urethra, constituting the remaining length of the tube.

Two small bulbourethral (Cowper's) glands (Figs. 5–3, 5–4), each about the size of a pea, lie adjacent to the membranous section of the urethra, into which their respective ducts enter.

Numerous minute glands, the urethral glands, are present in the wall of the urethra and are especially abundant along the penile urethra. They are responsible for continuous lubrication of the tube.

Penis

Basically, the penis consists of three cylindrical masses of erectile tissue (Figs. 5–1, 5–5), capped by the glans or head. Two of these cylinders, the corpora cavernosa penis, lie dorsal and lateral. The third, which surrounds the urethra, is called the corpus spongiosum or corpus cavernosum urethrae. Its position is ventral and median. Erectile

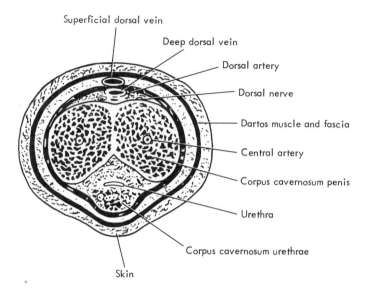

Superficial dorsal vein

Deep dorsal vein

Dorsal artery

Dorsal nerve

Dartos muscle and fascia

Central artery

Corpus cavernosum penis

Urethra

Corpus cavernosum urethrae

Skin

FIGURE 5-5. Cross-section of the penis.

tissue with qualities similar to a sponge can be engorged with blood which changes the tissue from a flaccid state to a firm erect state. Dense connective tissue binds these cylinders and a meshwork of nerves and blood vessels together. The entire complex is covered by skin which folds back on itself over the glans to form the foreskin or prepuce. The inner surface of the prepural skin bears small glands which secrete an oily substance called smegma. It is the prepuce which is surgically removed by circumcision. The glans of the penis is richly endowed with nerve endings and hence is the most sensitive part of the organ to sexual stimulation.

The base of the penis is wrapped by the bulbocavernosus muscle (Fig. 5–3). This muscle by contraction squeezes out the last drops of urine following urination. Rhythmic contraction of this muscle during ejaculation forces semen to spurt from the urethra.

Erection

The physiology of erection is being increasingly studied as the problems of impotence come to the fore. Despite the statement by some authorities that the mechanism of erection is well understood, there is increasing evidence that the process is more complicated than previously supposed.

Nerves originating in the sacral section of the spinal column—that is, from the small of the back—supply the penis, including its blood vessels. These nerves can be stimulated by electric shock. When such is done, the blood vessels of the penis increase markedly in diameter with consequent increased blood flow into the penis. This blood fills the spongy tissue of the cavernous bodies, resulting in erection. Previously it was thought that at this time the veins draining the penis were constricted, causing more blood to remain in the erect organ. However, more sophisticated studies show that five or six times more blood flows out of the penis during erection than during non-erection. Were the veins constricted, one would expect less circulation.

Stimulation of the nerves is mediated through the parasympathetic nervous system, which must be intact for erection to occur. Stimulus can occur in one of two basic ways. First, the penis itself may be stimulated, and reflex action through the sacral area of the spinal cord will act on the blood vessels to bring about erection. Or second, stimulus for erection may come from higher centers of the brain. Sight, smell, or touch of a female may cause the brain to send impulses by way of the sacral area to the penis causing erection. Tactile stimulation of other parts of the body may likewise cause erection by more complicated nerve pathways. Stimulation of the male breast, for example, may send impulses to the brain, thence to the sacral area of the cord and the penis. However, if the reflex arc between the penis and sacral area is disturbed or destroyed, no amount of stimulation, either through the brain or by direct stimulation of the penis, will result in erection. On the other hand, if the spinal column is severed above the sacral area, the possibility of erection still exists. This phenomenon has been noted in paraplegic men. By stimulation of the penis itself, they can be induced to have an erection and ejaculate, but these activities cannot occur from fantasizing or other methods of mental stimulation.

Loss of erection is also under nervous control. The sympathetic nervous system is believed to be involved. If the sympathetic nerves to the penis are stimulated during an erection, loss of erection will occur. There is also evidence that the brain has some inhibitory influence on erection of the penis. Evidence is scanty, but it is known that when a man is hung and the neck acutely broken, erection frequently occurs. It is assumed that this is due to some release of inhibition which the brain exercised.

Priapism is persistent erection despite repeated or multiple orgasms. This condition is rare but extremely painful when it does occur. With prolonged erection, blood clots may form within the penis. Appropriate surgery is now available to relieve this unpleasant state.

Impotence

With rare exceptions failure to obtain an erection is the cause of impotence. There is primary impotence and secondary impotence. Primary impotence exists in a male who has never been able to have an erection. Secondary impotence exists in a male who has had erections but is unable to do so at some later date and time.

Causes of impotence may be either organic or nonorganic. Such disease states as diabetes, spinal cord tumors, or prostatitis may injure nerves in the penile area or affect the sacral area of the spinal column, resulting in impotence. Drugs or chemicals which an individual may be taking may result in similar failure. However, nonorganic causes, generally psychological in nature, are much more frequent. Some of these cases are fascinating, such as the man who is impotent with his wife but not with his mistress, or the man who is impotent with both his wife and his mistress but who is able to have a nocturnal emission. In such cases, inhibition of one sort or another is the probable cause.

Ejaculation

Ejaculation is the forcible emission of semen from the male reproductive tract. It can occur with or without erection, although the two usually are combined.

There is a pre-ejaculatory emission of a clear, mucoid fluid which at our present state of knowledge is thought to be principally a product of the bulbourethral glands, although the urethral glands may contribute in small degree. This flow may consist of a few drops, or may be emitted to the point of copiousness. Sperm may or may not be present in the fluid. The fluid, however, is not part of the ejaculate per se, and the process of its emission is not an integral part of ejaculation.

Ejaculation can be divided into two separate phases. The first phase is designated as seminal emission. By this is meant the delivery of sperm from the epididymides and fluid from the seminal vesicles and prostate into the prostatic urethra. This process is brought about by the rhythmic contractions of these ducts and glands, activated by the sympathetic nervous system.

The second phase is designated as true ejaculation, or the forcible expulsion of semen from the penile urethra. This action is brought about by contractions of the bulbocavernosus and ischiocavernosus muscles and simultaneous constriction of the sphincter urethra at the base of the bladder.

The stimulus for production of additional sperm seems to be the lack of sperm in the various tubular structures. As yet we do not know the physiological feedback mechanism that activates production of additional sperm. This is equally true of the fluid secretions composing the seminal fluid. Although younger males may be able within short intervals of minutes to ejaculate fluid several times in succession, older males require a period of replenishment varying up to several hours before ejaculation is again possible. However, because of the feedback mechanism, the more ejaculate used, the more stimulus there is to produce more.

The male is consciously aware of ejaculation and impending ejaculation. This awareness seems to reach the conscious level in two distinct stages. In the first stage, the male has the feeling that an ejaculate is coming, and in no way can he constrain, control, or delay this process. The physiological mechanism behind this feeling seems to be collective pooling of the semen in the prostatic urethra before the second stage occurs. The second stage of the ejaculatory process is the expulsion of the semen from the penile urethra.

There seems to be a relationship between the volume of the ejaculate and the male's pleasurable sensation of the act of ejaculation. Males who have not ejaculated for an extended period of time describe a subsequent initial ejaculation as extremely intense, whereas a subsequent ejaculation after a shorter duration of abstinence is described as less intense. This is in direct contrast to females, who seem to enjoy a subsequent orgasm more than an initial orgasmic experience.

Male Hormonal Physiology

The anterior pituitary gland (Fig. 5–6), by means of its gonadotrophic hormones, controls the growth and reproductive functions of

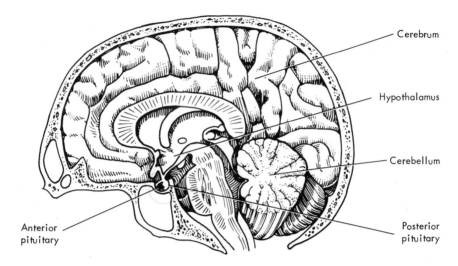

FIGURE 5-6. A mid-section of the brain, showing the relationship of the hypothalamus to the pituitary body. (From Krieger, D. T. 1971. "The Hypothalamus and Neuroendocrinology." *Hospital Practice*.)

the testes. The anterior pituitary, in turn, is controlled by the hypothalamus, a part of the brain lying immediately above the pituitary.

The anterior pituitary produces a hormone called the interstitial-cell-stimulating hormone (ICSH). This hormone is chemically identical with the luteinizing hormone (LH) of the female (cf. p. 77). ICSH initiates and sustains the hormonal activity of the interstitial cells of the testes (Fig. 5–2). These cells secrete testosterone, which enhances primary male characteristics. That is, it is involved with growth and eventual size of the penis as well as growth and secretory activity of the accessory sex glands. It also influences the growth and development of secondary male characteristics, such as male hair distribution, a larger larynx than in the female, broader shoulder girdle and narrower pelvis, and typical male nipples.

It has been supposed that the anterior pituitary secretes a second hormone that directly controls spermatogenesis, which is similar to the follicle-stimulating hormone (FSH) in the female (cf. p. 76). The amount of sexual activity also plays a part in sperm production, as mentioned earlier, and it may be that such activity influences production of the postulated hormone. A reciprocal relationship exists between testosterone and ICSH.

Male Menopause

In the sense that menopause means a hormonal change and cessation of the menses in the female, this term is inapplicable for the male. But in the sense that menopause is accompanied by psychological changes, the term "male menopause" is a practical one to designate changes in attitude that some men undergo during their forties or fifties. This change is not nearly as universal as among women. It is psychological and not hormonal in nature, inasmuch as therapy with testosterone has proven ineffective.

The average man at this time of life has frequently reached the height of his career. Although he certainly may continue to be successful, it is unusual for him subsequently to reach a higher plateau in his life's work. Characteristically, from this point on, the movement is either sideways or downhill.

The menopausal male in his family situation often considers himself as the "forgotten man." He feels he is being taken for granted and reproached for any failures, actual or fancied, during his lifetime. Furthermore, he is usually involved with a menopausal woman, namely his wife, who is having problems of her own and may no longer devote the time needed to bolster his male ego.

In his work the man is also frequently reproached as being an "old fogy" by younger men eager for his position. They frequently give him little credit for the experiences he has had or the accomplishments he achieved during his lifetime.

He also has second thoughts regarding his sexual capabilities and attractiveness. Here, too, his wife's change of attitude frustrates him and possibly confuses him even more.

Dr. Thomas D. Hackett has suggested that male rebellion to these frustrations fall into three categories. The first of these he calls the Gauguin syndrome, named after the French banker, who at 40 walked out on his wife, family, and position in Paris and went to Tahiti to become a famous painter. Some men take this approach, actually leaving their positions and in some cases going so far as to desert their families, dropping completely out of the world to which they have been accustomed.

The second he describes as the scapegoat wife syndrome, in

which the male in a rather cruel fashion begins to blame all his short-comings on his wife. She becomes no longer attractive to him, and her faults, either real or fantasied, appear out of all proportion to actuality. He stresses frequently that he was seduced into the marriage, that she tricked him, and that all his troubles are secondary to her shortcomings.

The third he describes as the sacred amulet syndrome. This situation is most often found in men who have taken great pride in their sexual prowess. When their performance diminishes, they seek out a younger woman, "the sacred amulet," to restore their prowess. Often this woman is a decade or two younger than he. She frequently comes from a lower socioeconomic class so that she regards him with some awe and thinks he is a great "catch." At the beginning of this relationship, the male finds himself more virile with her and credits this newly found virility to her. She has somehow magically restored his youthful powers.

In his book, *The Revolt of the Middle-Aged Man*, Dr. Edmund Bergler states that such rebellion is doomed to failure, because the cards are truly stacked against the middle-aged man. Bergler's thesis is that with years of experience behind him, the middle-aged man believes that if he could relive his life, he would handle it differently and much more effectively. In taking a second chance, he forgets, however, that he himself is the same regardless of how he changes his external milieu. He forgets that the mistakes he thinks he made in the past, including his choice of mate, are really not accidental. They are the outcome of his psychological makeup, and this psychological makeup has not been changed in any way by middle age.

In fairness, not all men go through such a rebellion, male meno-pause, or whatever one wishes to call it. There is no question, however, that it is becoming a more frequent occurrence in our society. The increase in divorce rates and the association of middle-aged men with younger women have become facts of life in American society, much to the dismay of many a married woman (see also Chapter 22, Sex and the Family).

References

BERGLER, EDMUND. 1957. *The Revolt of the Middle-Aged Man*. New York: Grosset & Dunlap.

CIBA COLLECTION OF MEDICAL ILLUSTRATIONS. 1965. Vol. 2, *The Reproductive System.* Summit, N.J.: Ciba Pharmaceutical Products.

DICKINSON, ROBERT L. 1949. *Atlas of Human Sex Anatomy.* Baltimore: Williams & Wilkins.

GRAY, HENRY. 1973. *Anatomy of the Human Body.* 29th ed., ed. by C. M. Goss. Philadelphia: Lea & Febiger.

GUYTON, ARTHUR C. 1971. *Textbook of Medical Physiology,* 4th ed. Philadelphia: W. B. Saunders.

6

sexual anatomy and physiology of the female

The format of this chapter is to present the anatomy and physiology of the female reproductive organs and mammary glands with a minimum of unessential detail. Thereafter the sexual aspects of the female are considered in a sequential manner, beginning with birth, passing through adolescence and the reproductive years, and ending in menopause.

Mammary Glands

Although these glands are not components of the reproductive system, they are included in this book because they are significant in human sexuality.

Breast tissue is present in both sexes. In the male, as well as in the immature female, it is rudimentary. In the female, however, the breast reaches its typical exquisite development during her early reproductive life, closely associated with appropriate hormonal activity.

Externally, the female breast (Figs. 6–1, 6–2) extends outward from the chest wall as a conical or hemispherical protrusion. The left breast generally is larger than the right one. In some individuals, prominent hair follicles are found in the cleavage between the breasts or surrounding the area of the nipple. This is a normal phenomenon and does not indicate an hormonal problem. Immediately beneath the center of each breast is the areola, a circular area of markedly darker color than the surrounding skin and of different texture. The surface of the areola is roughened and wrinkled by the presence of the openings of various glands. Some of these secrete a viscid fluid, which protects the areola and nipple from the irritating effect of an infant's saliva at the time of suckling. The areola surrounds the nipple. The surface of the nipple has 15 to 20 pinpoint openings from which milk

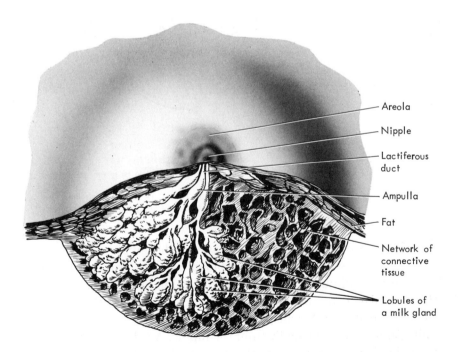

Areola

Nipple

Lactiferous duct

Ampulla

Fat

Network of connective tissue

Lobules of a milk gland

FIGURE 6-1. Human breast with the lower half dissected to show internal structures. (After Luschka in *Gray's Anatomy*, ed. by C. M. Goss. 1973. Philadelphia: Lèa & Febiger.)

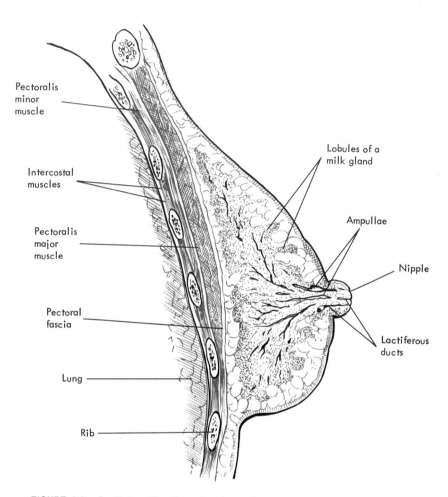

FIGURE 6-2. Sagittal section through a human breast. (After Eycleschymer and Jones in *Gray's Anatomy*, ed. by C. M. Goss. 1973. Philadelphia: Lèa & Febiger.)

exudes in drops at the time of lactation. The nipple itself contains erectile tissue, which by engorging blood becomes firm and extended under proper stimulus. At the time of suckling, the nipple assumes a shape similar to the prosthetic nipple seen on baby bottles.

Internally, the female breast consists of 15 to 20 multilobulated milk glands arranged radially from the nipple. A network of connective tissue holds them in place. Fatty tissue is also distributed among the lobes, the size of the breast being related mainly to the quantity of fatty tissue present. Each milk gland is composed of numerous lobules, each of which is drained by a small duct. These ducts coalesce to form a major lactiferous duct, leading to the surface of the nipple. Just before opening on the surface of the nipple, each major lactiferous duct has an expanded section, the ampulla, which serves as a reservoir for the milk. The milk itself is a combination of water, minerals. carbohydrates, and fats.

A great deal of fanfare has been made regarding the relationship between breast size and female libido; the concept is promulgated that the larger the breast, the more feminine the individual. In fact, surgical procedures have been devised to enlarge the breasts. The current method in vogue is to place a plastic balloon under the breast through a very small incision. The balloon is then expanded by the introduction of saline solution, thus pushing whatever breast tissue is available away from the chest wall. Silicone injection, one of the older procedures, has fallen into disrepute. Silicone wandered from the breast and had a tendency to become infected.

Historically one finds each culture has its own concept of what constitutes an ideal feminine physique. Disparity exists in our own culture, with *Playboy* having one standard and *Vogue* another.

Hormonal Activity And The Mammary Glands

The human body has two means of coordinating itself: by nerve impulses and by hormones. Nerve impulses are carried by nerve fibers, which within the central nervous system (brain and spinal cord) form tracts and outside the central nervous system constitute nerves. Hormones are chemical secretions produced by ductless glands, located at various places in the body. These ductless glands secrete their products directly into the blood stream, which then distributes the chemical messengers to the site or sites of action.

Sexual activity requires interplay of both methods of coordination. I have chosen to use the breast and milk production as a model of the complexity of this interplay. I have also chosen to present the material in greater detail than is used elsewhere in the text, not because the subject is of major importance, but rather to illustrate the physiological complexity that can exist in a normal biological phenomenon.

GLANDULAR DEVELOPMENT OF THE BREASTS. In a growing female, estrogens and progesterone, all of which are hormones derived mainly from the ovaries after puberty, induce the enlargement of the breasts and their glandular development. In addition, insulin, growth hormone, thyroxin, and cortisol are needed for the intricate development of the breast. If pregnancy occurs, the placenta becomes a source of even more plentiful amounts of sex hormones, which activate even greater development of the milk-producing structures of the breasts. At the same time, apparently, estrogens and progesterone inhibit the actual production and flow of milk.

PRODUCTION OF MILK.   After birth of a child has occurred, with accompanying loss of the placenta, there is a consequent and corresponding marked reduction, almost to zero, of estrogens and progesterone. Removal of these hormones permits the release of the hormone prolactin by the anterior pituitary gland at the base of the brain. Prolactin then acts on the secretory cells of the mammary glands, which, in turn, produce milk. However, the production of milk by the glandular cells and the flow of milk through the ductules are separate processes.

THE "LET-DOWN" OR FLOW OF MILK.   While prolactin induces the secretion of milk, the hormone oxytocin, produced in the hypothalamus and stored in the posterior pituitary gland, activates the flow of milk. Muscle cells surround the glandular cells of the mammary alveoli and the small milk ducts. These muscle cells contract in response to oxytocin, which is released by the stimulus of suckling. This contraction results in ejection of milk into the larger milk ducts and sinuses from which the milk can be removed by the suckling baby. This process is known as milk ejection or milk "let-down."

For a day or two following birth, if the baby is breast-fed, the stimulus to produce milk is present. About the third day after delivery, milk "comes in" and flows freely whenever suckling occurs.

Suckling by the infant causes production of new milk and the let-down of milk already produced. When a baby sucks on the nipple, no milk is immediately obtained, but within 45 to 60 seconds milk appears at both nipples, regardless of which one is used for suckling. Suckling causes sensory impulses to pass over the nerves from the breast to the spinal cord and upward to the hypothalamus of the brain (Fig. 5–6). The hypothalamus is centrally located within the brain and is noted for its intricate and multitudinous connections with surrounding areas of the central nervous system. It lies immediately above the pituitary gland with which it has two means of physiological interplay. One is by way of nerve cells present in the hypothalamus but with long processes extending into the body of the posterior pituitary (pars nervosa of the neurohypophysis). The other is by way of a portal system of blood vessels arising as capillaries in the hypothalamus and ending as capillaries in the anterior pituitary, thereby carrying high concentration of hypothalamic secretions directly to the anterior pituitary before being diluted by blood elsewhere in the body. By direction of the hypothalamus, activated by nervous impulses derived from the suckling process, the posterior pituitary releases oxytocin into the blood stream to bring about milk ejection (milk let-down). Also, prolactin is increasingly released from the anterior pituitary gland during suckling, with the result that the prolactin enhances milk secretion.

As long as the breast is emptied of milk, the circuit continues to operate. Failure to empty the breast arrests the activity in the hypothalamus and pituitary and stops the production of milk. If a baby is breast-fed, return of regular menses may not occur for several months, but if suckling does not occur, menses usually will begin within 12 weeks after delivery in 65% of the women.

RELATIONS OF HIGHER CENTERS OF THE BRAIN AND MILK FLOW. The hypothalamus (Fig. 5–6) is located adjacent to higher centers of the brain. Thus, impulses from such centers of the brain as those for sight, smell, and memory may play a part in the functioning of the hypothalamus. In this way, the entire past experience of an individual may enter into her reaction to breast-feeding. Thus the phenomenon of milk let-down may be complicated by past experiences of the mother. For example, a woman's first sight of breast-feeding occurred while she was riding a bus. The woman next to her rather abruptly unzipped her blouse, exposed her breast, and placed a baby on it, much to the revulsion of the observer. At a later time the observer, in attempting to breast-feed her own infant, was subconsciously again revulsed and unable to produce milk. The point is that if a postpartum woman is undergoing emotional trauma, she may be unable to produce milk, even if the nervous and endocrine systems are intact and the baby and the breast are normal. Somehow control from a higher center of the brain than the hypothalamus interferes with the reactive mechanism. Note, however, that there is no correlation between breast size and the ability to breast-feed an infant. Women with only slight breast development can breast-feed their babies with complete success.

Breast-feeding clearly shows for the first time in this book, and perhaps for the first time in the reader's thinking, the intricate relationships involved in the whole subject of sexuality. There are no "casual" experiences. Every experience and any experience leaves an imprint in the brain and on the nervous system of the body. If the experience is repeated, a predetermined pathway has been set up which more or less develops into a conditioned response. Hence in sexual activity, if you once develop a specific pattern of handling a sexual situation, it becomes increasingly difficult to turn and handle it in a new way. The inclination will be to follow the set route.

Ovaries

The paired ovaries (Figs. 6–3, 6–4) lie in the pelvic cavity to the right and left of the upper portion of the uterus and below the corresponding uterine tube. Each is about 2 inches long, 1 inch wide, and 0.5 inch thick. However, the size varies, diminishing with advancing age, so that in elderly women an ovary is often no larger than a good-

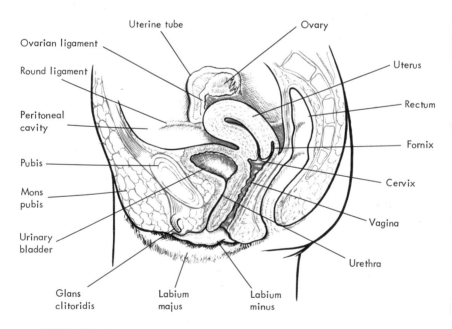

FIGURE 6-3. Sagittal section of the female pelvis. (After Turner and Bagnara, 1971. *General Endocrinology.* Philadelphia: W. B. Saunders.)

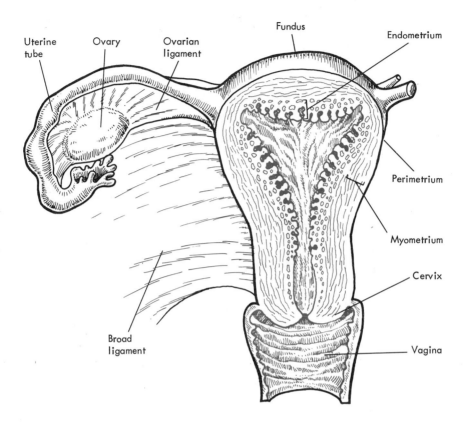

FIGURE 6-4. Uterus and related organs. (After Reith, Breidenbach, and Lorenc. 1964. *Textbook of Anatomy and Physiology.* New York: Blakiston of McGraw-Hill.)

sized pea. The surface of the ovary is wrinkled and pinkish-white in hue. Each ovary lies relatively free within the abdominal cavity but loosely attached to the uterus and side wall of the pelvis by ligaments (Fig. 6–3). A small yellowish spot on the surface of an ovary may be present; this is a corpus luteum from which an egg has recently been expelled. Smaller greyish areas may also be present, each representing the healed site of a prior egg expulsion.

Internally, the ovary (Fig. 6–5) is divided into two zones: an outer zone, the cortex; and an inner zone, the medulla. The medulla is primarily nutritional in function. It is composed of blood vessels and connective and nervous tissues. Significance of the nervous tissue is not yet completely clear. The cortex is responsible for the production of

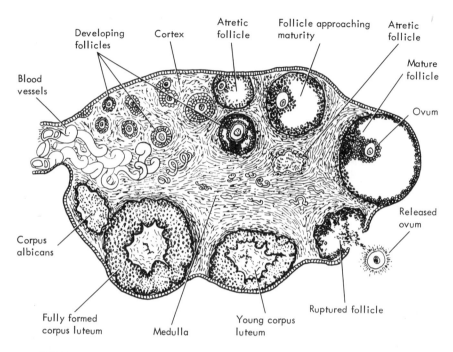

FIGURE 6–5. Cut surface of an ovary. (From Patten, B. M. 1968. *Human Embryology*. New York: Blakiston of McGraw-Hill.)

eggs and the hormones estrogen and progesterone. Usual illustrations of the cut surface of an ovary (Fig. 6–5) give a composite picture of events therein, representing what occurs over a sequential period of time, let us say a 28-day cycle. In an actual ovary one would never see all the phases of activity illustrated by these composite drawings.

The cortex contains between 200,000 and 400,000 immature eggs. It is believed that all these are present at birth and that following birth there is no increase in the number of potential ova. There is, however, controversy on this point. Several developing ova may be present in the ovary at any one time, but usually only one of them in the human reaches maturity each month. The potential ovum develops to maturity in a small, cystic structure, termed a follicle, which moves to the surface of the ovary. The follicular cells that surround the ovum and compose the wall of the follicle are responsible for the production of estrogens. At the surface of the ovary, the mature follicle ruptures, and the egg, surrounded by a layer of cells, is expelled into the peritoneal cavity.

The wall of the follicle, which remains within the ovary following explusion of the egg, then undergoes significant changes in form and function. It collapses, becomes glandular, attains a yellowish hue, and begins the production of estrogens and progesterone. At this stage it is termed a corpus luteum. If pregnancy occurs, it continues to produce progesterone. If pregnancy does not occur, the clump of cells contracts, scars, becomes a corpus albicans, and production of progesterone ceases.

Most of the developing ova never reach maturity. They degenerate within the substance of the ovary by a process called atresia. Follicles undergoing such degeneration are called atretic follicles. Eventually they are completely reabsorbed by the body.

Uterine Tubes

The uterine tubes (Figs. 6–3, 6–4), also called the Fallopian tubes, are paired muscular canals that extend outward from the upper corners of the uterus to a distance of 4 to 6 inches. Each tube courses the length of its respective ovary and terminates in a fimbriated opening. Since the end of the tube is not in direct contact with the ovary, eggs expelled from the ovary must travel in the open body cavity at least a few millimeters before entering the tube. Movement of the egg into the tube is believed due to three factors. First, there exists the possibility of chemical affinity, or chemotaxis, between the egg and the tubal entrance. Second, the fringed lip of the tube is mobile and may engulf the egg in tentacular fashion. And third, the tube is supplied with hairlike organelles called cilia, which beat in unison, creating a current that sweeps the egg into the tube and toward the uterus. Propulsion of the egg within the tube is further enhanced by peristaltic contractions of the tube in the direction of the uterus.

It is significant to note that movement of the egg into a uterine tube is indeed a dynamic process. Women who for medical reasons have had one tube and the opposite ovary surgically removed have in some instances still become pregnant. In these cases the expelled egg has migrated from one side of the body cavity to the other, a distance of 6 inches or more, before gaining entrance to the reproductive tract.

Uterus

The uterus (Figs. 6–3, 6–4) in the adult nulliparous female is an organ about the size and shape of a pear. It lies in the midline of the body above the pubic bone between the urinary bladder and the rectum, where it is held in place by ligaments attached to the pelvic wall. The uterus can be palpated by a finger inserted within the rectum or vagina. By proper stimulation during pregnancy it can increase to the size of a watermelon, a change not duplicated by any other organ. This change takes approximately nine months to complete. By comparison, return to normal size following pregnancy is accomplished in only six weeks. The uterus is not considered an endocrinologic organ, for women who have undergone hysterectomy, or removal of the uterus exhibit no alteration in their endocrine pattern. The organ is, however, influenced by the secretions of certain endocrine glands.

Arbitrarily, the uterus is divided into two regions, more on the basis of function than anatomy. The upper portion is the fundus or body of the uterus. It is here that the fertilized egg is implanted and housed through pregnancy. The lower portion is the cervix, the major function of which is to retain the contents of the uterus until delivery occurs.

FUNDUS. The wall of the fundus has three distinct layers: the perimetrium, the myometrium, and the endometrium.

The perimetrium is that section of the lining of the body cavity, or peritoneum, which covers the uterus. It is a thin glistening layer of cells.

The myometrium is the extensive muscular layer of the uterus. These muscles are arranged in circular and helical fashion in such a way that their contraction brings a downward movement to bear on any contents of the uterus. Thus, when labor commences, contraction occurs first at the upper end of the uterus and moves as a wave progressively downward toward the cervix, functioning to expel the fetus.

The endometrium is the innermost of the three major layers of the uterus. It, in turn, is composed of a thin glandular lining of the uterine cavity and a thicker layer of connective tissue lying between this lining and the myometrium. The endometrium is highly glandular and well supplied with blood vessels. It is mainly this endometrium that is sloughed off at the time of menses. The glandular components of the endometrium are capable of sustaining early stages of development of an embryo until such time as the placenta is developed (cf. p. 100). The endometrium is esquisitely sensitive to small amounts of female hormones.

CERVIX. The cervix projects as a thick ring into the upper

portion of the vaginal cavity (Figs. 6–3, 6–4). Its inner surface is a continuation of the endometrium of the uterus, and its outer surface a continuation of the lining of the vagina. The body of the cervix is a strong set of circular muscle fibers, supplied with nerves and blood vessels, and capable of extensive dilation. The primary function of the cervix is to retain the growing products of conception within the uterus. This is no mean task, considering the contents during pregnancy are a baby of seven pounds, a placenta of a pound and a half, plus the weight of additional fluid and membranes surrounding the infant. Contractions of the uterus force the cervix to dilate, resulting in eventual passage of the baby and afterbirth through the cervix to the vagina and out. The cervix, in fact, is the second strongest muscle of the female, the strongest being the muscle of the jaw.

There are medical conditions in which the muscles of the cervix are not sufficiently strong to retain the fetus and associated structures, and delivery occurs prematurely. Such a weakened cervix is called an incompetent cervix. Fortunately, a surgical procedure is available to correct this difficulty.

By means of suitable instruments a physician can easily observe the cervix and obtain a smear of its cellular coating. This is called a Papanicolau smear and is used to diagnose the presence or absence of cervical cancer, the second most common cancer found in women.

Vagina

The vagina (Figs. 6–3, 6–4, 6–6) is a musculomembranous tube, which extends from the external genitalia to the uterus. It, too, as does the uterus, lies in the midline of the pelvis, interposed between the bladder and the rectum. The upper end of the vagina ends as a blind pouch, the fornix, into which the cervix of the uterus projects at an angle. As a result of this projecting cervix, the anterior wall of the vagina is shorter (6 to 8 centimeters in length) than the posterior wall (7 to 10 centimeters in length).

Unless an object is introduced into the vagina, the walls remain in apposition and only a potential cavity exists. The vagina, however, is capable of marked distension and expansion, as may occur at the time of introduction of the penis and even more so at the time of childbirth.

The vagina serves three important functions. It serves as a chan-

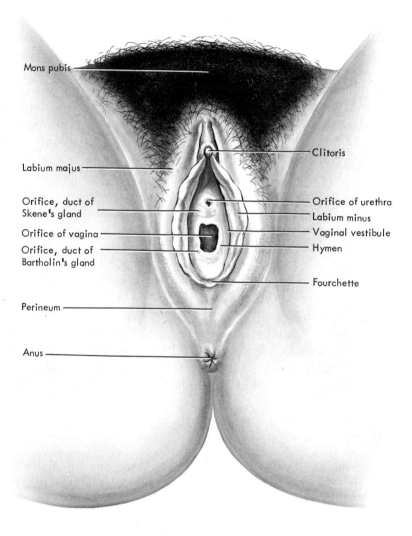

Mons pubis

Labium majus

Orifice, duct of
Skene's gland

Orifice of vagina

Orifice, duct of
Bartholin's gland

Perineum

Anus

Clitoris

Orifice of urethra
Labium minus
Vaginal vestibule
Hymen

Fourchette

FIGURE 6-6. External female genitalia.

nel for the escape of the menstrual flow; it is the female organ of
copulation; and it forms part of the birth canal during labor. The
vagina is kept moist by a small amount of secretion from the cervix.
During sexual excitement, according to the observations of Masters and
Johnson, the vagina is capable of self-lubrication, somewhat like a
sweating process, although the exact source and mechanism of this
lubricating material is not as yet known.

Mons Pubis

The mons pubis or mons Veneris (Fig. 6–6) is the fatty cushion that rests over the front surface of the pubic bone, just above and to the sides of the cleft which constitutes the entrance to the reproductive and urinary tracts of the female. After puberty, the skin covering the mons pubis is covered by kinky hair. Generally speaking, the distribution of the pubic hair differs in the two sexes. In the female it occupies a triangular area, the upper border of which marks the upper margin of the pubic bone; this patch of hair is termed the escutcheon. In the male, on the other hand, the pubic hair occupies a similar location but also extends upward as a peak toward the umbilicus and downward over the inner surface of the thighs.

Labia Majora

Extending downward and backward from the mons pubis are two rounded folds of fat tissue covered with skin which are termed the labia majora (Figs. 6–3, 6–6), also colloquially called the outer lips of the vagina. They vary in appearance according to the amount of fat present within them and are less prominent after childbearing. In children and virginal women they usually lie in apposition and completely conceal the underlying parts, whereas in women who have borne children, they often gape widely. Each labium majus presents two surfaces. The outer surface corresponds in structure to the adjacent skin and after puberty is covered with hair. The inner surface is a moist, smooth, and glistening mucous membrane, resembling the inner lining of the oral cavity.

Labia Minora

If the labia majora are parted, two elongated, flat, reddish folds are seen lying parallel to, and within, the labia majora. These are the labia minora (Figs. 6–3, 6–6), colloquially called the inner lips of the vagina. They vary greatly in size and shape from female to female. Each labium minus is a thin fold of tissue, covered on each side by mucous membrane. The labia minora converge anteriorily and divide into two folds which surround the clitoris. The upper or forward fold constitutes the prepuce clitoris. The lower fold constitutes the frenulum clitoris. Strain placed on the labia minora results in stimulation of the clitoris by tightening the folds which surround it.

Posteriorly the labia minora fuse to form the fourchette.

Clitoris

The clitoris (Figs. 6–3, 6–6) is a small cylindrical body situated between the anterior ends of the labia minora. It rarely exceeds 2 centimeters in length, even during erection. It is encased by a prepuce and bears a frenulum at its base. It is the counterpart in the female of the penis in the male. It has a glans about the size of a small pea and two tracts of erectile tissue, which are the equivalents of the corpora cavernosa in the penis. However, it lacks a corpus spongiosum and is not penetrated by the urethra. It is folded on itself because of the traction exerted on it by the labia minora. The glans is richly supplied with nerve endings and is highly sensitive to stimulation. In times past the clitoris was regarded as the sole seat of voluptuous sensation. Recent investigations, however, have demonstrated that the entire vulval area is richly supplied with nerve endings and hence susceptible to stimulation.

Vestibule

The vestibule is the lenticular area enclosed by the labia minora. It extends from the clitoris to the fourchette and is perforated by six openings: the urethra, the vaginal orifice, the two ducts of Bartholin, which lead to Bartholin's glands (vestibular glands), and the two Skene's ducts.

Hymen

In virginal women, the vestibule is entirely hidden from view by the overlaying labia minora. When the labia are parted, the floor of the vestibule is seen as a thin membrane surrounding a crescentic or circular vaginal opening. This membrane is the hymen (Fig. 6–6). Hymens differ in shape and thickness. As a general rule, the hymen ruptures at the first coitus, tearing at several points, usually at the posterior edge. The edges of the tear soon scar, and the hymen becomes permanently divided into two or three flaps. Although it is generally believed by the laity that rupture of the hymen is associated with slight bleeding, such is by no means always the case. In rare instances there may be such a profuse loss of blood as to require surgical intervention. Again, the hymen may be so thick and resistant to penetration that surgery is required before coitus can be accomplished.

Bartholin's Glands

These paired glands (Fig. 6–6), also termed the greater vestibular glands, vary in size from that of a pea to a small bean. They lie beneath the vestibule to the right and left of the posterior margin of the vaginal orifice. They secrete fluid that previously had been thought to be of importance in genital lubrication. However, the work of Masters and Johnson has discredited this theory. It is currently accepted that they are vestigial organs associated with creating a scent. In the male, their counterparts are the bulbourethral glands.

Skene's Glands

On the right and left sides of the urethral orifice lie the openings of two small ducts, leading to two small vestigial structures, Skene's glands (Fig. 6–6). Their chief significance is that they represent in the female the counterparts of the glandular elements of the prostate gland in the male, and they are subject to infection. Although they resemble mucous glands, their function, if any, is obscure.

Hormonal Activity In The Sexual Immature Female; Anovulatory Menstruation

The principal hormones active in female sex physiology are as follows:

Name	Symbol	Site of Production
Follicle stimulating hormone	FSH	Anterior pituitary
Luteinizing hormone	LH	Anterior pituitary
Progesterone		Placenta Corpus luteum of the ovary
Estrogens		Follicular cells in the ovary Placenta Adrenal cortex Corpus luteum

When a female child is born, she possesses two ovaries, a uterus, two uterine tubes, and a vagina, as well as a pituitary gland and a hypothalamus. All these organs are active in the sexual development of the female. Even at birth, the uterus and vagina are amenable to stimulation by hormones, for not infrequently one sees a small amount of blood emerging from the vagina of the newborn. This bleeding is due to the influence of the mother's estrogens on the uterus of the newborn child.

During a female's childhood, little FSH is produced because activity of the pituitary seems mainly devoted to the production of growth hormone, and the girl is experiencing the major portion of her total body growth at this time. Usually between the ages of 10 and 13, a sudden spurt in the amount of growth hormone occurs, after which production of this hormone decreases. Between the ages of 8 and 12, FSH is first produced in discernible quantities, and by its action on the ovary that organ begins the production of estrogens. Between the ages of 8 and 12, the girl then begins to show slight breast development, typical female hair distribution, and the beginning of the female habitus in general. As the amount of growth hormone decreases, the amounts of FSH and estrogens increase markedly. Among other actions, the estrogens exert an effect on her bone structure and seal the growing parts of bone. This does not mean that all growing stops, but rather that the major growth has been achieved. The ovaries are also stimulated, and small follicles secreting estrogen appear around individual ova. Thus for the first time the amount of circulating estrogens is sufficient to stimulate the endometrium, and the adolescent menstruates. This event is designated the menarche. Ovulation, however, at this early age, does not occur, and menstruations are designated as anovulatory, that is, bleeding without production of an egg. From ages 11 to 15 menstruation may be highly irregular in amount and frequency without requiring medical intervention. Anovulatory bleeding is characteristically painless.

Hormonal Activity In The Sexually Mature Nonpregnant Female; Ovulatory Menstruation

Sometime during adolescence, by a stimulus as yet undetermined, the anterior pituitary produces LH in sufficient quantity to cause ovulation, i.e., the maturation and expulsion of an individual egg. The hormone progesterone is now produced, and at this time the regular ovulatory cycle of the sexually mature female will begin. This is called the estrous cycle. It will be repeated approximately every 28 days (20 to 40 days being within normal limits), depending on the individual female, for the next 30 or more years.

As previously stated, there are between 200,000 and 400,000 potential eggs in each ovary, and one does not need a computer to realize that if 12 eggs are released per year and the female has 30 reproductive years, the loss of one egg per month will not markedly influence the total number of eggs that are present in the ovaries at any one time. As the female ends the period of reproductivity, the unused follicles begin to degenerate with the result that no reproductive follicles remain in the ovaries of elderly women.

PROLIFERATION OR ESTROGEN PHASE OF THE ESTROUS CYCLE. As mentioned for the anovulatory female, FSH in the sexually mature female continues to activate the follicular cells of the ovary to produce estrogens. These estrogens, as before, have a marked influence on the endometrium. Its glandular components (cf. p. 70) increase rapidly in tortuosity and size, the adjacent connective tissue becomes quite dense, and the blood supply to the endometrium is greatly enhanced. This phase of change in the endometrium is called the proliferative or estrogen phase of endometrial activity. It usually includes the first 11 days of a 28-day cycle but is the most highly variable part of the cycle (cf. Rhythm Method in Chapter 17, Contraception).

SECRETORY OR PROGESTERONE PHASE OF THE ESTROUS CYCLE. When the egg is expelled from the ovary, the major portion of the follicle remains within the substance of the ovary. This follicular mass of cells becomes the corpus luteum, which produces large amounts of the hormone progesterone. Progesterone further enhances preparation of the endometrium for possible reception of an egg mainly by increasing the secretory activity of the endometrium. This phase of change in the endometrium is called the secretory or progesterone phase of endometrial activity. It lasts for another 12 days of a 28-day cycle.

MENSTRUAL PHASE OF THE ESTROUS CYCLE.   As the production of estrogens and progesterone occurs, they have an inhibiting influence by way of the hypothalamus on the production of FSH and LH from the pituitary. If fertilization does not occur, the levels of ovarian estrogens and progesterone fall. With lack of supporting stimulus from estrogens and progesterone, the lush lining of the endometrium sloughs off, resulting in the menstrual flow. This phase of change in the endometrium is called the menstrual phase of endometrial activity. It lasts for the final 5 days of a 28-day cycle.

It is therefore evident that there is a reciprocal action between the ovary on the one hand and the pituitary on the other, with the hypothalamus acting as an intermediary between the former and the latter. Thus when estrogens and progesterone wax in quantity, FSH and LH will wane, and the reverse.

Hormonal Activity In The Sexually Mature Pregnant Female

If fertilization occurs, the normal course of events for the estrous cycle is altered. Beginning with the first day of the cycle, as with the female in whom fertilization has not occurred, estrogens and progesterone will be produced, causing the gradual preparation of the uterus for implantation. If fertilization occurs, the developing embryo will undergo implantation in the lush body of the endometrium between the seventh day and the twelfth day following fertilization. Meanwhile, cells of the embryonic mass have begun the production of chorionic gonadotropin, which is an hormonal substance similar to LH. This hormone prevents the usual retrogression of the corpus luteum into a corpus albicans. Instead, it probably causes the corpus luteum to secrete even greater quantities of progesterone and estrogens, which, in turn, cause the endometrium to continue growth and store nutrients.

Following implantation, formation of the placenta begins. The placenta in time secretes great quantities of chorionic gonadotropin, estrogens, progesterone, and human placental lactogen. The first three of these are essential to the continuation of pregnancy, and probably the fourth is as well, although the importance of the fourth in this regard has not been thoroughly established.

At the time of birth, the placenta is shed. The quantity of hormones derived from it is thus reduced to zero. As discussed under Hormonal Activity and the Mammary Glands, if suckling regularly empties the breasts of milk, a circuit is established that prevents return of the estrous cycle for several months. If suckling does not occur, the usual events of the menstrual cycle will begin again within three or four weeks.

Relationship Of The Sex Hormones To Female Sexuality

There is no question that on the evolutionary scale many primitive animals are receptive to sexual intercourse in a cyclic fashion. The activity corresponds to the estrous cycle, which, in turn, is related to the production of estrogens (cf. Chapter 21, An Anthropological Approach to Sexuality).

This receptivity, however, is not true for the human female. The estrogens to be sure contribute in the early years toward the hormonal milieu that makes a female a female. After that, estrogens contribute to such factors as the firmness of the breasts and the texture of the vagina, but they do not significantly influence a female's receptivity to sexual intercourse. Many women come to the office with a sexual problem inquiring about their hormonal status. The implication is that if the hormones are in some way awry, this malfunction is the cause of their sexual difficulty. Studies have been made on young women who have had their ovaries removed, and they are just as receptive to sexual intercourse before as after the surgery. There does not seem to be a relationship between the products of the ovaries and the sexual desires of the female. In addition, there have been investigations to ascertain the time within the estrous cycle, if any, at which the human female would be most receptive to sexual advances. Although there is a suggestion that she may be most amenable immediately prior to menses, at which time estrogen production is quite low, the findings are far from conclusive.

Menopause

Menopause is the cessation of menses. It is a gradual process, not an abrupt one, involving varying lengths of time, depending upon the individual woman, and usually occurring between the ages of 45 and 50. Both physiological and psychological changes are simultaneously involved.

Marked diminution of the estrogens are responsible in large part for the physiological changes. These include alteration of menstruation, some redistribution of body tissue, particularly fat tissue, some degree of aging, and the characteristic heat flash. This last phenomenon is difficult to describe. Suffice it to say that when a woman has experienced it, she is quite conscious that it has occurred. Administration of exogenous estrogen may help a woman to some degree in sustaining these physiological changes, but it is not wholly ameliorative because it has little or no effect on the concomitant psychological changes.

The psychological changes appear related to the role the woman is playing in her particular society. Television commercials portray sex, beauty, and youth almost as a unit. Realization by a woman that she is "no longer sexy" certainly can play havoc with her self-image. Furthermore, events occur within the family which change the role of the female. Her role as a mother is certainly diminished as the children begin to leave home. Her husband may have reached the zenith of his career, being totally devoted at this point to his business endeavors. He, too, may be undergoing physiological and psychological changes of his own in the male menopause (cf. p. 57).

The remedies for the female during this frequently difficult period are to have the support, understanding, and reassurance of her husband and children. Of assistance also may be a return to work, the finding of some useful outlet for her talents, or a return to academic pursuits interrupted by marriage and childbearing.

References

HELLMAN, LOUIS M., AND J. A. PRITCHARD. 1971. Williams Obstetrics, 14th ed. New York: Appleton-Century-Crofts.
(See also references for Chapter 5).

7

human sexual physiology

Although many of us believe we live in an enlightened era, research on human sexual physiology has in reality just begun. So far as understanding sexual phenomena is concerned, we are just beginning to emerge from the Dark Ages. Although the surface has barely been scratched and the work is far from definitive, certain information is now available. It is important for every well-educated individual to know what occurs in the human body during sexual activity. Four benefits in particular come to mind:

1. Normal physiological values are established for sexual activity.
2. An awareness of the diversity of sexual behavior comes to light.
3. Realization is established that certain sexual responses, such as orgasm, are almost universal among humans.
4. Improvements in sexual techniques, based on this knowledge,

become possible, giving rise to the possibility of correcting or preventing sexual difficulties.

Historical Background

The subject of human sexual response has been ignored throughout the greater part of recorded history. Probably in the caves and huts of early man and certainly in the Victorian parlors of the nineteenth century, such a topic was avoided in conversation. Until recently it has been ignored in scientific investigation.

It remained for Freud at the turn of the century to emphasize the importance of sexual appetites in normal and, more importantly, abnormal human development.

An abortive attempt to do research in human sexual response was initiated by Dr. R. L. Dickinson in the 1920's. His work, however, was too radical for his time and by and large was disregarded by his peers.

During the 1940's, Dr. Alfred Kinsey, a zoologist, began a statistical approach to answer the questions of human sexual behavior. His two volumes, *Sexual Behavior in the Human Male* and *Sexual Behavior in the Human Female*, revolutionized our thinking, transforming our concepts from a nonrealistic, idealistic, puritanical, and virginal point of view to one of realism, which freely admitted the existence of masturbation, premarital coitus, and adultery as commonplace in our society.

A valid criticism of Kinsey's work, which Kinsey himself recognized, is the potential inaccuracy of any interview. That is, there is likely to be a discrepancy between what a person thinks or says he does, or both, and what he will admit to an interviewer. Still, the Kinsey reports more accurately than any previous study analyzed the current sexual practices in the United States and opened the door for evaluation of these practices. In addition, they gave dignity to the sexologist and a sense of inner security to thousands of persons who previously had felt their own sexual practices were running counter to those of the community in which they lived.

Dr. William H. Masters, an obstetrician and gynecologist, and Mrs. Virginia E. Johnson, a psychologist and now Mrs. William H. Masters, took the next logical step. They observed sexual activity in the laboratory and attempted to record sexual activity in a scientific manner.

It is interesting to note that these three historic events—the work of Freud, Kinsey, and Masters, covering a period of 50 years—recapitulate the scientific method as we know it today. Freud hypothesized, Kinsey gathered the data necessary to evaluate the hypothesis, and Masters took the hypothesis to the laboratory and attempted to prove or disprove it.

The Work Of Masters And Johnson

Before we review the work of Masters and Johnson, two important points must be emphasized. First, it is very difficult to study the physiological aspects of sexual intercourse without considering the emotional aspects. Yet the primary focus of *Human Sexual Response* is the physiological data. More attention to the emotions or psychological aspects of sexual intercourse is contained in *Human Sexual Inadequacy*.

Second, one must accept the credibility of the investigators, their scientific attitude, and their complete honesty and integrity in these sexual studies. Prior to undertaking these studies, Dr. Masters had established an excellent reputation in the academic circles of his specialty, obstetrics and gynecology. He was an outstanding leader on infertility and pelvic pain. Attempting research on human sexual physiology, previously considered taboo, required a great deal of courage. Quite like Kinsey, Masters and Johnson sustained ridicule at the hands of their peers and the lay public, but undaunted they followed their beliefs and have made a singularly great contribution to this field. It is only with the attitude of the true scientist, not the thrill seeker, that we can hope to view their work intelligently.

Human Sexual Response

Experimental Participants. The initial subjects employed for observation were male and female prostitutes of St. Louis. However, as word of Dr. Masters' work spread through the academic and hospital circles, educated single individuals and married couples volunteered as subject material. The statistics used in the Masters and Johnson books represent these latter groups.

Methodology. Both Dr. Masters and Mrs. Johnson interviewed each potential participant extensively. A selected group of those interviewed were then familiarized with the laboratory and the surroundings to the point of feeling comfortable and being able to perform in a natural fashion. Hundreds of complete cycles (those terminating in orgasm) were observed and analyzed. Three technics were employed: (1) natural coition in several positions; (2) self-masturbation by both male and female; and (3) female insertion and manipulation of a plastic obturator (hollow sheath) with optical power so that motion pictures could be taken through it with cold light illumination.

GENERAL OBSERVATION. Sexual response is a total body response, whether in the male or female. It is enacted in a series of steplike phases, beginning with excitation, reaching a plateau, culminating in orgasm, and terminating in a period of resolution (Figs. 7–1, 7–2). The male follows a more repetitive pattern, whereas the female shows greater variation in terms of intensity and duration.

Total Female Response

The general mechanisms involved in sexual excitation are twofold: vasocongestion and myotonia. Vasocongestion is simply an in-

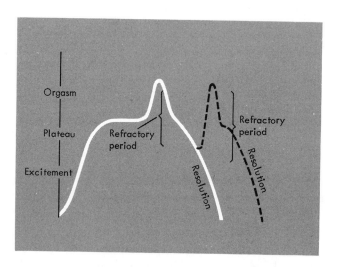

FIGURE 7-1. The male sexual response cycle. (From Masters and Johnson. 1966. *Human Sexual Response.* Boston: Little, Brown. All subsequent figures in this chapter are also from this source.)

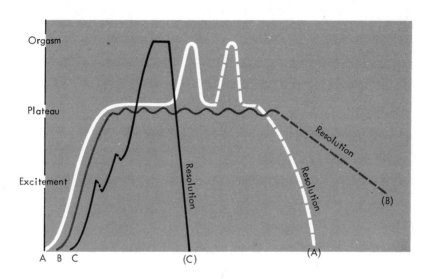

FIGURE 7-2. The female sexual response cycle.

crease in the amount of blood in a specific area, in this case the genital area. A similar phenomenon occurs in eating a large meal, during which there is vasocongestion of the gastrointestinal tract, or in participating in an athletic event, during which there is vasocongestion of the voluntary muscles. At the same time, an extreme myotonia occurs, which in actuality is a tightening of the musculature of the genital apparatus. These two physiologic phenomena, vasocongestion and myotonia, increase in degree during excitation and the plateau phase. With orgasm there is a sudden release of both these factors, resulting in the return of a free flow of blood and subsiding of the muscular tension.

While the sexual act is being performed, certain events alter the total body appearance and activity of the female:

1. The respiratory rate increases. This event, termed hyperventilation, appears late in the plateau phase and lasts throughout the entire orgasmic experience. Peaks as high as 40 inhalations per minute have been recorded.
2. The heart beat increases. Whereas the normal pulse is 70 to 80, the pulse rate during sexual activity may rise to 110 to 180

beats per minute. This phenomenon, termed tachycardia, also occurs in the late plateau and orgasmic phases.

3. The blood pressures rises. The systolic pressure may rise 30 to 80 mm. of mercury, and the diastolic, 20 to 40 mm. That is, an individual with a normal blood pressure of 110/70 during intercourse may have a blood pressure of (140 to 190)/(90 to 110).

4. Generalized sweating may occur primarily in the resolution phase.

Individual Organ Response In The Female

BREAST (Fig. 7-3).   During excitation the nipple responds with erection. Frequently there may be a lag phase in one nipple or the other, as both nipples do not necessarily respond simultaneously. A second physiological alteration develops when the veins of the breast become engorged with blood. This creates a color change in the breast, and it tends to darken. The breast actually increases in size and becomes firmer. (This reaction was described by Dickinson some 30 years earlier.)

In the plateau phase, the areola, or pigmented area surrounding the nipple, becomes engorged and projects forward, embedding the nipple somewhat, thus giving the false impression that the nipple has

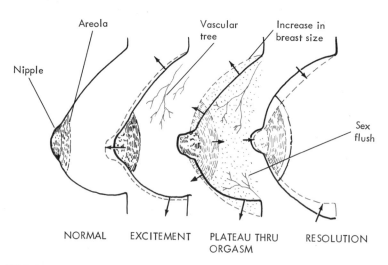

FIGURE 7-3. The breasts in the female sexual response cycle.

regressed. Before the female has reached orgasm, the breast may have increased in size by one-fifth or one-quarter. This reaction is not as obvious in the parturient female, particularly if she has breast-fed her children.

The breast also participates in the sex flush, to be described.

There is no specific breast reaction to the experience of orgasm.

Resolution is heralded by disappearance of the sex flush and detumescence of the areola, although the nipple is frequently still erect. The decrease in total breast size occurs more slowly. Five to ten minutes may elapse after orgasm before the breast returns to its pre-excitation state.

SEX FLUSH. A fine measleslike (maculopapular) rash spreads over the body during the plateau phase, constituting the sex flush. This flush terminates with orgasm. Although the intensity and distribution patterns of this flush vary with the individual, the severity of the reaction may be considered an indication of the intensity of the sexual tension experienced by the individual responding female.

VAGINA. During the excitation phase, the immediate reaction of this organ is self-lubrication. This "sweating phenomenon" was discussed earlier (p. 72). Individual droplets of a mucoid material, resembling perspiration, appear in the folds of the vagina (Fig. 7–4). These coalesce to form a smooth glistening coat for the entire vaginal

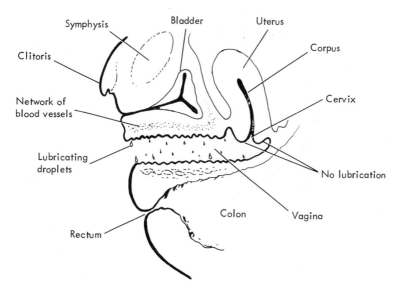

FIGURE 7-4. Schematic representation of vaginal lubrication.

barrel. Simultaneously, the inner two-thirds of the vagina lengthens and widens. The cervix and body of the uterus elevate as sexual tension mounts, creating still more room for insertion of the penis (Figs. 7–5, 7–6). Simultaneously, a distinct color change occurs. The vaginal wall demonstrates a purplish hue, at first mottled and then contiguous. The corrugated vaginal lining flattens, thins, and stretches.

During the plateau and orgasmic phases, characteristic vaginal changes occur throughout the outer two-thirds of the vagina. Marked vasocongestion develops as the lower vagina and vestibule become distended with venous blood. The diameter of the vaginal barrel is decreased in this area and thus, in effect, a platform is created which increases the length of the vagina (Figs. 7–7, 7–8). This has been aptly labeled the "orgasmic platform" in that it reacts explosively at the time of orgasm. Strong recurrent contractions are set in motion. These occur at 0.8-second intervals, and 3 to 5 contractions are usually observed with each orgasmic experience.

Resolution quickly disperses vasocongestion, and the vagina returns to its collapsed unstimulated state (Fig. 7–9).

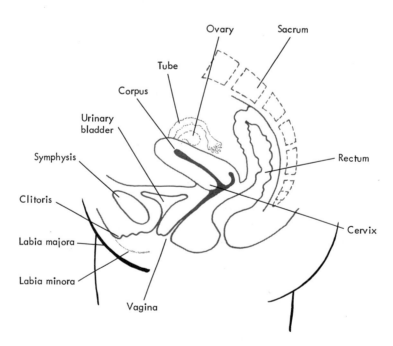

FIGURE 7–5. Female pelvis: normal anatomy (lateral view).

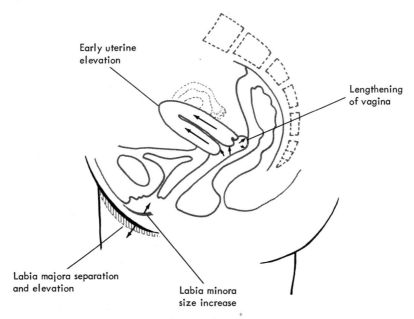

FIGURE 7-6. Female pelvis: excitement phase.

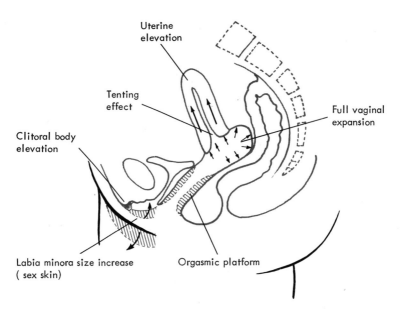

FIGURE 7-7. Female pelvis: plateau phase.

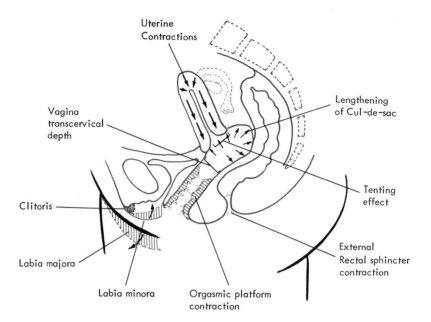

FIGURE 7-8. Female pelvis: orgasmic phase.

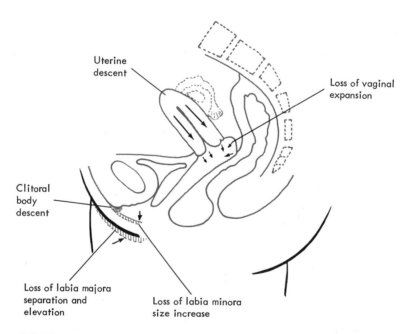

FIGURE 7-9. Female pelvis: resolution phase.

CLITORIS. With any degree of excitation, the glans of the clitoris increases in size. This places the glans in close approximation with its adjoining structures. At times this increase is so slight that it can only be observed with magnification. Vasocongestion occurs in the entire clitoral area, and the shaft of the clitoris increases in diameter.

During the plateau phase of sexual excitation, the clitoris retracts with universal consistency. The shaft and glans withdraw toward the pubic bone deeply beneath the protective clitoral hood or foreskin. This process occurs more quickly with direct manipulation than with other forms of foreplay. In the preorgasm state, the clitoris is not visible. Although no clitoral reaction has been observed with orgasm, it has been observed that the clitoris returns to its normal extended position 5 to 10 seconds after cessation of orgasmic platform contractions. However, resolution in clitoral size takes from 5 to 10 minutes.

LABIA MAJORA. Differences occur in response of the labia majora during sexual excitation depending upon the child-bearing experience of the female. If she has not borne children, when sexual tensions increase, the labia majora become thick and seemingly flatten against the perineum. This displacement may actually be caused by the emergence of the labia minora (see following section). It is an involuntary sexual change, which gynecologically may be considered to remove any exterior impediment to mounting. Once a female has borne children, the labia majora for the most part become markedly congested and seemingly are withdrawn in a lateral fashion, but do not disappear as just described.

LABIA MINORA. The labia minora increase two to three times in diameter during sexual excitation. This thickening actually adds approximately 1 centimeter to the length of the vagina. The expansion also causes the labia minora to protrude through the labia majora. By so doing, the former may cause the lateral movement and flattening of the latter, as described previously.

As with the labia majora, there are vivid changes during the plateau phase, the degree of coloration apparently being related somewhat to the number of children the female has borne. The variations are from a light pink to a very deep purple. Following orgasm, this color change returns to normal. Masters and Johnson state that none of their subjects has been noted to have orgasm without first having these rather dramatic color changes. The labial color change thus becomes an excellent indicator of impending orgasm.

BARTHOLIN GLANDS.   These glands secrete a few drops during the excitation phase and the early plateau phase, but thereafter do not seem to involve themselves in the orgasmic processes.

UTERUS, UTERINE TUBES AND OVARIES.   These structures react with vasocongestion and myotonia to the point of actual pain. One subject, a prostitute, underwent 6.5 hours of coital activity without attaining orgasm. She noted severe pelvic pain, which persisted during the additional 6 hours she was observed. Within 5 minutes after she had had an orgasmic release, the pain and congestion were resolved.

Female Orgasm

Masters and Johnson define orgasm as "a brief episode of physical release from the vasocongestion [distension with blood] and myotonic increment [muscle tightening] in response to sexual stimuli." This can be observed in the female to be a total body reaction with focus in the pelvic region.

This reaction pattern can be interpreted in three realms: the physiological, the psychological, and the sociological. Of these, the only consistent reaction is the physiological one, since it is measurable and reproducible.

Masters and Johnson interviewed their subjects following orgasm. Some described the orgasm as a state of suspension, lasting only an instant, followed by an isolated thrust of intense sexual awareness. Others compared orgasm to the sensation of "bearing down" associated with labor. Still others described orgasm as a suffusion of warmth starting in the pelvic area and extending progressively over the remainder of the body.

Total Male Response

As in the female (cf. p. 84), vasocongestion and myotonia occur in the male. While the sexual act is being performed, the male also undergoes physiological changes. There are respiratory rate and heart beat increases equivalent to those in the female. Blood pressure rises to somewhat higher levels in the male, the systolic elevations increasing by 40 to 100 mm. of mercury, and the diastolic by 20 to 50 mm.

Immediately following orgasm, approximately one-third of the males exhibit perspiration, usually confined to the soles of the feet and palms of the hands, although occasionally also extending to the trunk, head, and neck.

Individual Organ Response In The Male

PENIS.   The essential reaction of penile excitation is erection (Fig. 7–10). The temporal relations of this state may be short or extended. During foreplay, the erection may be partially lost and regained. The male may be subject to psychosexual diversion, that is, asexual stimuli may result in partial or complete loss of erection, despite the continuance also of sexual stimulation.

During the plateau phase (Fig. 7–11), the corona may increase in diameter and the glans demonstrate a mottled reddish-purple color. The latter phenomenon is not a consistent finding.

Orgasm is heralded by the forceful ejaculation of seminal fluid from the urethral opening (Fig. 7–12).

Resolution occurs in two rather distinct stages (Fig. 7–13). First, the penis returns rapidly to a size about 50% larger than its flaccid

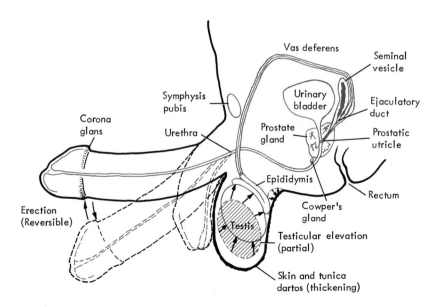

FIGURE 7-10.   Male pelvis: excitement phase.

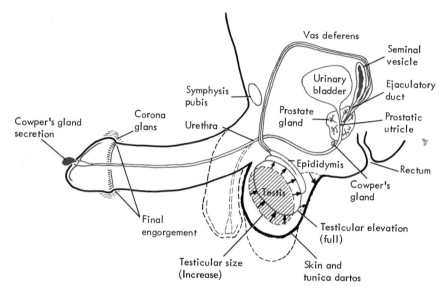

FIGURE 7-11. Male pelvis: plateau phase.

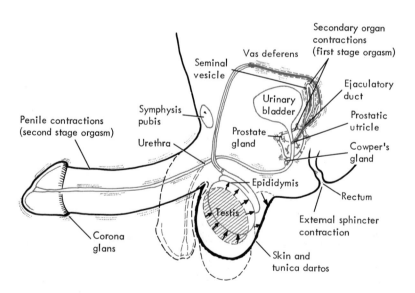

FIGURE 7-12. Male pelvis: orgasmic phase.

state. Second, over an extended period of time it returns to its usual relaxed size. In those cases of prolonged erection, particularly with intravaginal containment, the first of these stages may be noticeably

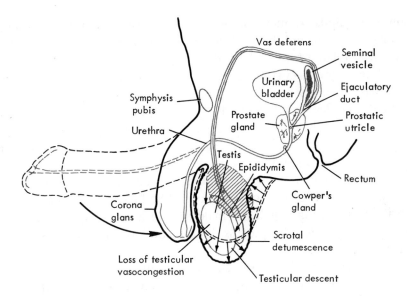

FIGURE 7-13. Male pelvis: resolution phase.

delayed. Asexual stimuli may markedly reduce the time for resolution.

SCROTUM. During excitation, there is a tensing and thickening of the scrotol skin, as well as a decrease in testicular movement. There are no specific changes characteristic of plateau or orgasm, but with resolution the skin returns to its normal state.

TESTES. During excitation, there is a degree of testicular elevation, which may decrease with longstanding foreplay. With plateau the testes increase in size and immediately prior to ejaculation are tightly approximated to the male perineum. This full elevation is characteristic of impending ejaculation. Return to normal size and position occur, following orgasm and resolution.

Male Orgasm

Male orgasm is characterized by ejaculation, which is emission of semen from the penis. This event can be described in physiological, psychological, and sociological terms.

PHYSIOLOGICAL ASPECTS. There may be a pre-ejaculatory emission. This is usually only a small amount of fluid, one or two drops, although occasionally copious. The fluid is believed to emit from

Cowper's glands. It may contain viable sperm. It is not a constant finding and may not be consciously recognized by the male. It is frequently related to a prolonged plateau phase.

The major ejaculation is further divided into two phases. The first phase involves contraction of the muscles about the testes and seminal vesicles, forcing fluid upward and closing the internal sphincter to the bladder. The second phase is characterized by a series of pulsations of the bulbocavernosus muscle with ultimate expulsion of the sperm-bearing semen.

PSYCHOLOGICAL ASPECTS.   Subjects interviewed, following ejaculation, describe two distinct sensations. The first is one of ejaculatory inevitability, during which the male can no longer contain, delay, or in any way control the process. The second is an awareness of the extrusion of fluid.

SOCIOLOGICAL ASPECTS.   In recent years cultural demands have focused on achievement of orgasm for the female. Oddly, in the male the ejaculatory process is accepted as an inevitable conclusion of the sexual union, whereas sociological focus has been placed on the ability of the male to attain and maintain an erection.

References

DICKINSON, R. L., AND L. BEAM. 1931. *A Thousand Marriages.* Baltimore: Williams & Wilkins.

KINSEY, ALFRED C., et al. 1948. *Sexual Behavior in the Human Male.* Philadelphia: W. B. Saunders.

KINSEY, ALFRED C., et al. 1953. *Sexual Behavior in the Human Female.* Philadelphia: W. B. Saunders.

MASTERS, WILLIAM H., AND VIRGINIA E. JOHNSON. 1966. *Human Sexual Response.* Boston: Little, Brown.

MASTERS, WILLIAM H., AND VIRGINIA E. JOHNSON. 1969. *Human Sexual Inadequacy.* Boston: Little, Brown.

8

the relation of fertilization and implantation to genetic engineering

Genetic engineering implies determining the manner by which heredi-
tary factors influence body development and how such factors may be
controlled and maneuvered for the betterment of mankind. Rather
than devote excessive space to detailed descriptions of fertilization
and implantation, for which excellent accounts are given by Patten and
Arey (see references), I have chosen to devote a few pages to the im-
portance genetic engineering can have upon these processes.

Fertilization And Implantation

With some special exceptions, all cells of the human body contain 23 pairs of chromosomes. Of these 23 pairs, 22 pairs are autosomes, or chromosomes associated with the development of general

body structure and function. The remaining pair is the pair of sex chromosomes, mainly associated with development of sexual features of the body (Fig. 8–1). A sex chromosome may be either an X or a Y chromosome. Two X chromosomes are found in each female body cell. An X and a Y are the counterparts found in each male body cell. It therefore follows that each body cell of the female contains 44 autosomes plus two X chromosomes, and each body cell of the male contains 44 autosomes plus an X and a Y chromosome.

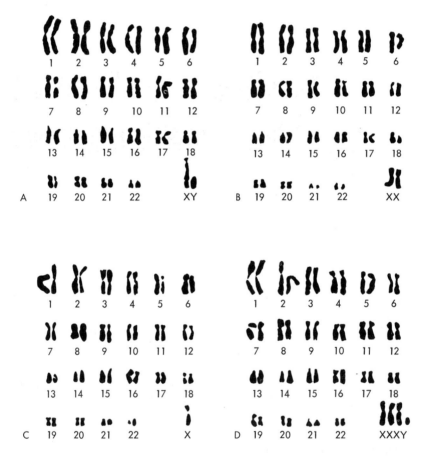

FIGURE 8-1. Human chromosomes. (a) normal male; (b) normal female; (c) XO condition, defective gonadal development; (d) XXXY, an unusual example of Klinefelter's syndrome, the typical Klinefelter pattern being XXY. (From Page, Villee, & Villee, 1972. *Human Reproduction.* Philadelphia: W. B. Saunders.)

Since the fertilized human ovum contains the required 23 pairs of chromosomes, it follows that the sperm and unfertilized ovum must contain half that number. Germ cells within the ovary have the ability by an ingenious method of division to deliver 22 autosomes plus one X chromosome to each mature ovum. Germ cells within the testes similarly deliver 22 autosomes plus either an X or a Y chromosome to each sperm. Sperm are then either X bearing or Y bearing. Union of the former with an ovum produces a female, and union of the latter with an ovum produces a male.

Division and separation of chromosomes occasionally go awry in the formation of new body cells or sex cells. The abnormal presence of one or more chromosomes to a given pair or the absence of one member of a pair generally results in aberrant growth, or function, or both. Both autosomes and sex chromosomes can undergo these abnormal distributions. Thus if an X chromosome has neither an X nor a Y mate, an XO condition exists (Fig. 8–1), resulting in defective gonadal development. Or, if a Y-bearing sperm happens to fertilize an ovum containing an extra X chromosome, an XXY condition exists, resulting in a male exhibiting what is known as Klinefelter's syndrome. This syndrome is characterized by degrees of eunuchoidism and other sexual disorders.

Precisely where the union of the sperm with the developing ovum takes place in the human is a moot question. For years it had been postulated that fertilization occurred in that part of the uterine tube nearest the ovary. Some authorities now contend that it occurs in the uterine cavity, and others specify the peritoneal or body cavity as the site. Depending on the times of ovulation and insemination, it is likely that the site of fertilization varies, occurring anywhere from the periphery of the ovary to the uterine cavity.

Recent investigators have tried to determine whether the vaginal environment can be altered in such a way as to favor the survival of one or the other type of sperm, thus influencing the potential sex of a given infant. The results thus far are inconclusive.

After fertilization has occurred, the resulting zygote divides in geometric progression, delivering 46 chromosomes to each resulting cell, until a hollow sphere of cells, the blastocyst, is formed. It is this phase of human development which becomes embedded in the uterine wall. From this cell complex the new individual arises, as does one-half of its nutritional organ, the placenta. The other half of the placenta arises from the maternal surface of the uterus. The reader who is interested in a detailed presentation of placental formation is referred to the work of Arey or Patten.

New Techniques In Genetics

AMNIOCENTESIS.   Amniocentesis is the puncture of the intra-uterine sac surrounding the developing embryo by way of the maternal abdominal wall and withdrawal of some of the amniotic fluid. This can be accomplished as early as the twelfth week of pregnancy. The fetal triangle is determined by palpating the abdomen of the mother and fetal parts. A pool of amniotic fluid is generally found below the puncture site indicated in Fig. 8–2, around the nape of the neck, or at

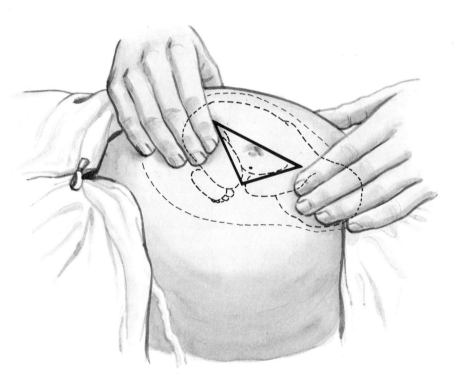

FIGURE 8-2. Determining the fetal triangle prior to undertaking amniocentesis. The black dot within the triangle indicates the site of puncture. (After Greenhill, J. P. 1969. *Surgical Gynecology*. Chicago: Year Book Medical Publishers.

the fundal end of the uterus. After fluid is withdrawn, examination of both the fluid and the cells floating therein can reveal vital information.

From chromatin content of the cells the sex of the unborn infant can be determined. By fluorescent staining of cells the Barr body (Fig. 8-3), designating a female, or the Y body (Fig. 8-4), designating a male, can be determined. The Barr body is larger than the Y body, stains more diffusely, and usually lies adjacent to the nuclear membrane, whereas the Y body is usually centrally located within the nucleus. If there is indication that the child will be male and if his hereditary background indicates that he will be hemophiliac (cf. p. 122) or suffer other serious sex-linked consequences, the developing embryo may be aborted.

Smears of the cells may reveal chromosomal anomalies, which may cause such disorders as Mongolism, defective embryonic development of the gonads, or Klinefelter's syndrome. Here, again, abortion can be performed to prevent birth of a defective child.

Maturity of the unborn individual can be determined from the amniotic fluid by testing for the concentration of creatinine and by

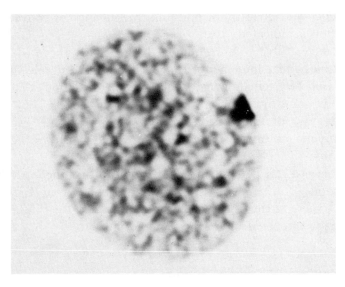

FIGURE 8-3. A cell from the buccal mucosa, showing the peripherally located Barr body, indicating a female. (From the University of Colorado Medical Center by courtesy of Arthur Robinson, Arnold Greensher, and David Peakman.)

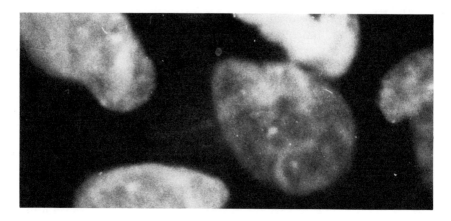

FIGURE 8-4. Cells from the matrix of the umbilical cord, showing two centrally located fluorescent Y bodies, indicating a male. (From the University of Colorado Medical Center by courtesy of Arthur Robinson, Arnold Greensher, and David Peakman.)

determining the sphingomyelin-lecithin ratio (SL ratio). If the former figure is greater than 2.0, or if the latter ratio is greater than 2.5 to 1, the fetus can be assumed to be mature.

The likelihood of Rh disease can be determined by testing for the presence and quantity of bilirubin, permitting corrective steps if malfunction is indicated.

SECURING OVA. A technique has recently been developed whereby individual human ova can be obtained. Suitable drugs are administered to a female which result in superovulation, the production of numerous ova at one time. A laparoscope (cf. p. 206) is introduced by way of an incision in the abdominal wall, and with satisfactory magnification ripe ova can be withdrawn from the surface of the ovary.

These ova can be studied or fertilized outside the body by the introduction of live sperm. Moreover, as reported in the British literature, these fertilized ova can then be implanted within a uterine wall, suitably prepared in advance for the purpose.

The Implications Of Genetic Techniques

What do these developing techniques foretell? First, the physician is faced with the possibilities of taking therapeutic steps prior to birth. As previously mentioned, tests can be undertaken to determine to some degree whether growth of the fetus and its chromosomal complement are normal. If not, therapeutic steps to deliver the fetus prematurely or abort it can be undertaken. This, of course, presupposes the acceptance of such events by the public.

Second, they predict and allow for genetic engineering. The implications here are of grave importance and will require decisions demanding the best of human thought.

Test tube babies, or offspring to order, are within the capability of man. An individual or couple could request the type of child wanted as to sex, degree of intelligence, or general background. Fertilized ova from selected donors could then be implanted in the uterus of the requester and delivered at term. Attempts have been made, with limited success thus far, to grow embryos in media outside the uterus, and if this technique can be perfected, it is reasonable to believe that a child can be produced without the biological mother ever being pregnant.

Genetic engineering poses a myriad of potential moral, social, and legal questions, which future generations will be called upon to solve. The general public may be highly reluctant to allow such investigations to proceed because of inherent dangers. Are we seeking the "optimum man"? If so, who will determine what characteristics are optimum? Would individuals who are less than optimum be destroyed before birth? Were a second Hitler to appear, would he be permitted to engineer a master race genetically?

Legally who would be responsible for a test tube baby? Does the father or mother have any rights, or would the child be considered a product of the state? What would happen to the present constitutional provisions for due process of law, rights of privacy, and rights of the individual?

As yet, society has no solutions for these questions, which exist in theory today but with continued advances in biomedical science will exist in actuality tomorrow.

References

AREY, L. B. 1965. *Developmental Anatomy*, 7th ed. Philadelphia: W. B. Saunders.

GOODMAN, R. M. 1970. *Genetic Disorders of Man*. Boston: Little, Brown.

GREENHILL, J. P. 1969. *Surgical Gynecology.* Chicago: Yearbook Medical Publishers.

PAGE, E. W., C. A. VILLEE, AND D. VILLEE. 1972. *Human Reproduction.* Philadelphia: W. B. Saunders.

PATTEN, B. M. 1968. *Human Embryology,* 3rd ed. New York: McGraw-Hill (Blakiston Div.).

PORTER, I. H. 1968. *Heredity and Disease.* New York: McGraw-Hill (Blakiston Div.).

9

pregnancy

Fetology

Fetology is the study, diagnosis, and treatment of the fetus *in utero*. As elsewhere in the book, the aim here is to emphasize selected practical aspects of the subject presented and to attempt in some instances to stimulate additional thought of perhaps more philosophic nature. For more complete factual coverage of embryology and fetology, the reader should consult the references listed at the end of the chapter.

Arbitrarily, the developing human individual is termed an embryo for the first three months of its development, and from the beginning of the fourth month to birth it is termed a fetus.

GROWTH OF THE EMBRYO AND FETUS. The newly formed individual at the time of union of the sperm and egg possesses all the genetic potentiality it will ever possess, barring mutation. That is, in the single cell created lie the total hereditary potentialities of the human being that will develop. This single cell has a tremendous growth rate, which at least in the earliest cell divisions is geometric. Approximately one week after conception, the embryo, as a cluster of cells, buries itself in the wall of the uterus, there to take up residence until delivery.

The initial zygote, or union of sperm and egg, gives rise to (1) the embryo, which subsequently becomes the fetus, (2) the protecting fetal membranes, which surround the embryo, and (3) one-half of the nutritional apparatus, which is called the placenta. The other half of the placenta is derived from the mother.

Following implantation of the embryo, growth continues at a rapid rate. By the end of the thirteenth week after fertilization, the infant has developed all of the incipient features that characterize it as human. This is significant, inasmuch as from the thirteenth week until delivery there is only an increase in the size of the fetus and maturation of its integral parts. Theoretically, therefore, if we had a mechanical device that could house and nourish the fetus, it could be removed from the uterus and mature to adulthood. In fact, some research is now being undertaken on extracorporeal development of the human individual.

During the first 13 weeks, the embryo is most susceptible to harmful effects of changes in its environment. For example, the virus of German measles is capable of crossing the placental membranes and causing injury to a significant percentage of individuals. Between 16 and 32% of the embryos exposed to the virus have been reported as affected. Also certain drugs, of which thalidomide is the most notorious example, can cross the placental barrier and cause undesirable changes in the configuration of the infant. Excessive dosages of X rays may also cause harmful mutations, although scientists differ as to what constitutes an excessive dose. Certainly a harmful dose is greater than is used in the usual diagnostic X-ray studies in pregnancy.

Following the fourteenth week, the fetus increases in size and weight in a progressive manner that is measurable and discernible. By the end of 20 weeks it weighs about 1 pound, by the end of 28 weeks about 2 pounds, and 3 to 4 pounds by the end of 32 weeks. The chances of infant survival at any given time are directly related to the birth weight. The greater the birth weight, the greater are the chances of survival. There is a myth that 7-month babies do well and 8-month babies do poorly. There is no scientific basis for this erroneous statement. Seemingly, however, it is true that a premature female infant has a better chance of survival than a premature male infant, for reasons unknown.

Certain peculiarities of the fetus make its growth and nutritional pattern unusual. In the first place the fetal circulation derives itself from the umbilical vein, which carries nutrition from the mother to the infant. These food substances are then circulated in the infant's blood, not passing through the lungs, which during this time are unexpanded. The infant's waste materials are then passed by way of the umbilical artery back toward the mother's circulation. In addition, the blood cells of the fetus have the capability of carrying more oxygen than do the blood cells of the mother; therefore, the fetus with less oxygen can nourish itself as well as can the host, the mother.

The mother is well aware of this growth in fetal size. Between 12 and 14 weeks after fertilization has occurred, the uterus can be palpated immediately above the pubic bone. At 16 weeks its crest is halfway between the pubic bone and the umbilicus. At 20 weeks, when fetal movement is usually noted, the crest has reached the level of the umbilicus. Thereafter it grows until it occupies almost the entire abdominal contour of the mother.

GESTATION TIME. Gestation time, the time spent by the infant in the womb from conception to delivery, is estimated as 264 days. However, this is not a fixed figure, and practical experience demonstrates that the normal gestation time is 264 plus or minus 10 days. Since it is frequently impossible to determine the exact time of conception, the general rule used is that the infant will be born 280 days, plus or minus 10 days, from the first day of the last menstrual flow. Physicians use this figure when estimating a date of confinement (EDC).

PHYSIOLOGICAL ACTIVITY OF THE FETUS. The moment at which life is engendered into the embryo-fetus has often been discussed from practical and philosophical points of view in both medical and legal circles. Biologically speaking, of course, life is continuous, and a new individual is created at the time of union of sperm and ovum. From a practical medical standpoint, however, the advent of quickening, i.e., the noting of fetal movement which occurs approximately during the twentieth week of gestation, assigns life to the fetus. The significance of this concept will be considered further in the chapter entitled Abortion.

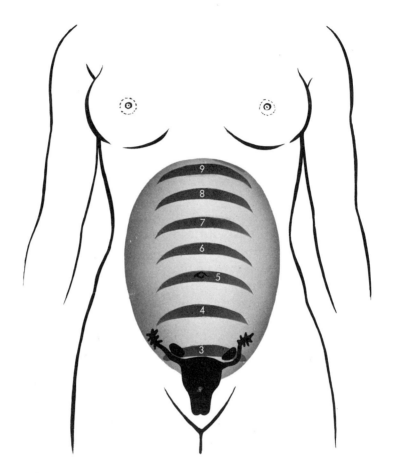

FIGURE 9-1. Various levels reached by the uterus at successive months of pregnancy. (After Birch, W. G. 1972. *A Doctor Discusses Pregnancy.* Chicago: Budlong Press. All subsequent figures in this chapter have been modeled after this source.)

In some states the law requires that an aborted fetus be designated as stillborn if it weighs more than 1 pound or is older than 20 weeks. Those states designate a fetus terminated at an earlier time as an abortion.

Regardless of the arbitrary medical designation of life in the fetus by the end of the twentieth week, there are various other ways of determining life in the fetus prior to that time. Audiometric devices detect the fetal heartbeat by the end of the sixteenth week, occasionally earlier. Brain activity can also be detected during the sixteenth week by electroencephalograms (EEG's).

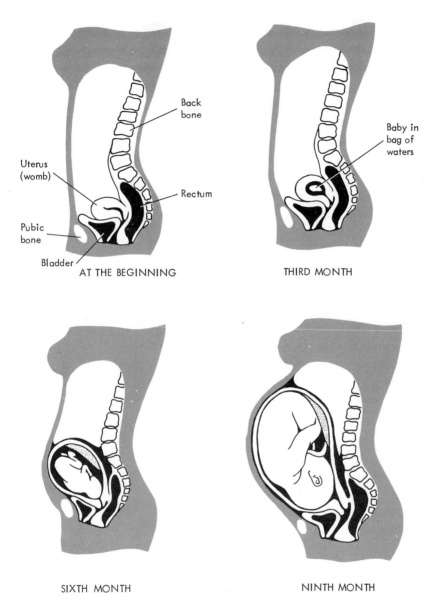

Uterus
(womb)

Pubic
bone

Bladder

Back
bone

Rectum

AT THE BEGINNING

Baby in
bag of
waters

THIRD MONTH

SIXTH MONTH

NINTH MONTH

FIGURE 9-2. Stages of development. (a) at the beginning; (b) third month; (c) sixth month; (d) ninth month.

The mother is quite aware that fetal activity varies. First, the infant does, indeed, seem to demonstrate different degrees of activity at different times. Second, the mother is more likely to complain of

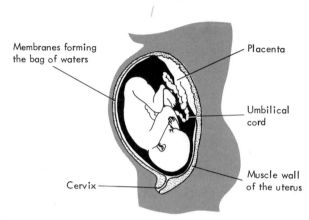

FIGURE 9-3. Full term baby in the uterus.

excessive fetal activity if the infant is placed in such a position as to make its movements felt against the abdominal wall. That is to say that if the infant is positioned with its back to the mother's abdomen, activity of the extremities directed toward the mother's spine will not be as noticeable as they would be if the position of the infant were reversed.

Tests For Pregnancy

At this point it is wise to discuss certain tests commonly used to determine the pregnant state. In former times the physician relied solely on physical findings. These consisted of a softening and bluish discoloration of the cervix, as well as enlargement of the uterus. In 1929, Aschheim and Zondek devised a biological test for pregnancy, which was called the rabbit test. In this test urine from a female early in pregnancy was injected into the peritoneal cavity of a rabbit. If the patient was pregnant, the rabbit's ovaries would become congested with blood. Later variations of the same test used such animals as rats and frogs.

In the early 1960's an agglutination test was devised whereby a drop of urine is placed with a prepared rabbit serum, and if certain characteristic changes occur, one can predict with 98% accuracy that pregnancy has or has not occurred. These tests become accurate 10 to 14 days after the first missed period or approximately 42 days after the last menstrual period.

Physiological Changes In The Female
During Pregnancy

Characteristic changes are noted in the female during the 9 months of her gestation. An attempt will be made to correlate these changes with the rather frequent signs and symptoms associated with this condition.

UTERUS. The uterus increases tremendously in size during pregnancy. We are as yet uncertain if this is merely a change in the size of individual uterine muscles or if new musculature is actually created. The uterus increases from the size of a pear to that of a watermelon. It is obvious that this increase in uterine size accounts for the change in contour of the female. Certain hormonal changes, namely the production of large amounts of progesterone, we believe, keep the uterus from contracting or attempting to expel the fetus prior to the time of delivery. The uterine musculature is arranged in a network of intertwined muscles. This is important because the small blood vessels nourishing the placenta course through these gaps among the muscle spirals. After delivery of the placenta occurs, contraction of these muscle fibers cuts off the blood supply and prevents excessive bleeding. If contraction fails to occur postpartum—that is, during the time after delivery—the uterus is massaged by the nurse or the attendant, and certain medications (oxytocins) are given to maintain contraction.

THE CERVIX. The cervix also undergoes marked change from a very firm muscular organ to a soft mushy structure, which has the capability of dilating once the forces of labor are initiated. The initial changes in the cervix are that it turns bluish and softens. These changes in years past have been traditional medical signs of pregnancy.

THE VAGINA. The vagina increases its elasticity during the course of pregnancy. Circulation to it is markedly increased. Thus this relatively small organ can expand to accommodate the head of a 5- to 10-pound infant.

THE BREAST. During pregnancy, the breast becomes pendulous, and the areola changes from a pink or light brown to a darker hue, depending on the ethnic background of the individual.

METABOLIC CHANGES. To the patient, weight gain is the most significant change. In analyzing this, one notes that the fetus weighs approximately 7.5 pounds, the placenta 1 pound, the amniotic fluid

2 pounds, and the uterus 2.5 pounds, for a total of 13 pounds. The breasts increase in weight about 3 pounds, and the blood volume of the mother is increased by approximately 4 pounds, which accounts for the 20 pounds most often suggested as the ideal weight gain during pregnancy (cf. p. 122).

Carbohydrates and proteins are needed for proper growth of the infant, and these are removed from the circulation of the mother. Certain minerals are also required, such as calcium, copper, and iron; these, too, are extracted from the maternal circulation. Because of its parasitic existence, the infant will remove those ingredients necessary for its own well being regardless of the mother's condition. Studies done when infants were delivered in concentration camps, for example, revealed that the birth weight of infants was not a great deal different from that of their siblings delivered elsewhere, even though their mothers were at times in extremis.

BLOOD VOLUME. To accommodate the increasing need for fetal nourishment, the mother will increase her own blood volume by approximately 30%. If additional iron intake does not occur, this increase in volume obviously decreases the amount of iron per milliliter of blood, as the total iron of the blood must now be distributed to a larger volume. Anemia, therefore, frequently accompanies pregnancy. If the mother has sufficient iron reserve, this anemia will not be significant. On the other hand, if her iron reserves are poor, anemia may occur.

OTHER CHANGES. These are listed only for the sake of completeness. Because of increased pressure on the diaphragm by the enlarging uterus, there is a decrease in pulmonary reserve and the heart is pushed upward and outward, giving the appearance of enlarging in size. Activity of the gastrointestinal tract is markedly slowed, resulting from an increase in the amount of progesterone in the circulation, as well as from crowding by the enlarging uterus. In pregnant females, solids are eliminated between 18 and 24 hours after intake, whereas in nonpregnant females the normal elimination time is but 12 hours. This accounts for the frequent symptoms of gas and constipation during pregnancy. In the excretory system, the ureters frequently dilate. The bladder is temporarily altered in capacity, resulting in greater frequency of urination. Finally, most of the endocrine glands are more active during pregnancy.

RH FACTOR. There is a unique situation regarding a special component of the blood, termed the Rh factor. If a mother's blood is

Rh negative and a father's blood is Rh positive, there is the possibility that the infant produced by them may be either Rh negative or positive. Adverse conditions exist only if the infant is Rh positive. It has been found that a small but significant amount of the infant's blood which has been circulating in the placenta is forced into the maternal circulation at the time of delivery. The presence of the Rh component in the infant's blood causes the mother, who lacks the Rh component, to form an antibody, such as is done by anyone's blood when protein is introduced. No harm will accrue to the infant being born, but if there is a subsequent pregnancy with an Rh positive infant, an injurious reaction may result between the mother and the sibling if an appreciable amount of the antibody has been developed in the mother. In the second or subsequent pregnancies, the antibodies developed in the mother have the capability of crossing the placental barrier, entering the infant's circulation, and causing a disease called erythroblastosis fetalis in Rh positive infants. Anemia and jaundice of the infant are characteristic of this disease. If untreated, the antibody reaction becomes successively more and more severe with each pregnancy involving an Rh positive infant in an Rh negative mother.

This problem of Rh incompatability, however, has been lessened in recent years by the use of a drug, rhogam, which is made up of antibiodies against the Rh positive component. It is given to the mother within 72 hours after the birth of an Rh positive infant. In essence, rhogam coats the foreign fetal blood cells carrying the Rh factor, thus eliminating the formation of antibodies by the mother. Consequently, with subsequent pregnancies there are no antibodies present in the mother which are offensive to subsequent Rh positive siblings.

Parturition

Parturition is the act of giving birth, or labor and delivery. Labor consists of the uterine contractions, which in the initial stages of true labor are responsible in part for altering the character of the cervix and in the terminal stages for forcing the infant through the birth canal to the exterior.

Later stages of pregnancy before true labor starts are characterized by irregular contractions, termed Braxton-Hicks contractions, which have no effect on the cervical musculature. If the pains are of an irregular nature and dilation of the cervix does not occur, the condition is termed false labor. However, when the uterine contractions become regular and increase in severity, they initiate dilation of the cervix; normal or true labor is then said to begin.

To date we have not discovered the factor that causes the onset of labor. Many theories have been postulated, including the possibilities that the uterus is stretched to a specific point and then responds with active contraction or that there is a sudden change in the quantity of estrogen or progesterone, causing the onset of labor. However, we do know that if for one reason or another the physician thinks labor should be started, he can initiate the process frequently by simply rupturing the fetal membranes surrounding the infant and letting the fluid therein leak out.

Use of the drug, pitocin, in very dilute quantities will also cause initiation of labor. Pitocin is a synthetic form of the hormone oxytocin.

Medically, labor has been divided for convenient reference into three stages: the first stage accounts for complete dilation of the cervix, the second stage accounts for delivery of the infant, and the third stage accounts for delivery of the afterbirth (placenta and fetal membranes).

The First Stage of Labor.   The process of labor is essentially the escape of the fetus from the maternal uterus that houses it. The initial step in this procedure is accomplished by dilation of the cervix. By dilation we mean a widening of the cervix to allow the baby's head or breech, as the case may be, to descend into the vaginal canal. Two changes take place within the cervix itself. The first we term effacement, which is the thinning of the cervical muscle. The second is dilation, or the actual widening of the canal to allow egress of the head. Basically the total diameter to which the cervix will widen is 10 centimeters. During labor, as the patient is being examined, the attending physician and nurses will refer to the degree of widening in centimeters, or occasionally, the term "fingers" is employed. That is, the cervical opening is said to have expanded to the width of two, three, or more fingers.

This change in the cervix is brought about by contractions of the uterus. These contractions progress in an orderly fashion, starting at the top of the uterus and working toward the cervix in a squeezing effect which forces the cervix to open. These contractions most often are painful, as discussed in the section Analgesia and Anesthesia (p. 120).

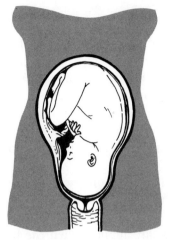

As labor progresses, the cervix becomes thinner and more dilated.

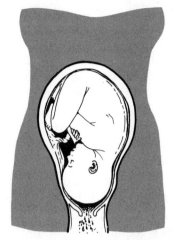

The membranes forming the bag of water rupture.

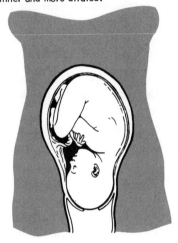

The head molds to the shape of the pelvis as the baby gradually descends in the birth canal.

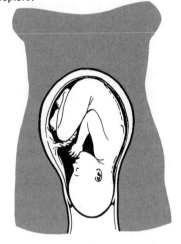

Baby slowly rotates as descent continues.

FIGURE 9-4. The beginning stages of labor. (a) as labor progresses, the cervix becomes thinner and more dilated; (b) the membranes forming the bag of water rupture; (c) the head molds to the shape of the pelvis as the baby gradually descends in the birth canal; (d) baby slowly rotates as descent continues.

The contractions of labor occur at regular intervals, the ideal eventually being a 45-second contraction, occurring approximately every 2 minutes. In early labor these contractions occur 15 to 20 minutes apart, becoming progressively more frequent down to the 2-minute level.

THE SECOND STAGE OF LABOR. After dilation of the cervix has been completed, descent of the infant through the birth canal begins, culminating in delivery. Descent and delivery are considered the second stage of labor and again are accomplished by the forces of uterine contraction, aided by the voluntary abdominal musculature of the female. If little or no anesthesia has been used, the mother can literally push the infant out of the birth canal by contracting her abdominal muscles and bearing down in a fashion similar to moving her bowels.

The head of the infant is delivered either spontaneously or with some mechanical help. If the mother has been anesthetized, she has lost the ability to push the infant out, and delivery by the use of low forceps is required. Low or outlet forceps are applied when the baby's head is visible in the birth canal. Experimental studies indicate that such use of forceps is no more traumatic to the infant than the expulsive force of the mother.

Frequently episiotomy is performed to increase the size of the vaginal opening and permit more comfortable delivery of the head. Episiotomy consists in making a short linear incision in the vulva between the lower portion of the vagina and the anal opening. The significance of this incision is that it prevents laceration of the musculature of the lower portion of the vagina. By episiotomy obstetricians over the years have reduced a number of complications previously associated with delivery.

THE THIRD STAGE OF LABOR. This stage involves expulsion of the placenta and fetal membranes. Expulsion is induced by the aid of drugs like pitocin, as well as by manual application of external pressure. Modern obstetrical management permits removal of a recalcitrant placenta by simply peeling it off by hand.

THE POSTPARTUM PERIOD. The postpartum period is the interval between the end of delivery and the return of the patient to her normal nonpregnant state. Retraction to normal size of the uterus and other bodily parts, which have been expanded during pregnancy, takes approximately 6 weeks. If the patient is breast-feeding, menstruation may not occur until after breast-feeding stops. If she is not breast-feeding, she may well return to a menstrual pattern within 4 to 6 weeks after delivery.

Previously, sexual activity was discouraged for 6 weeks immedi-

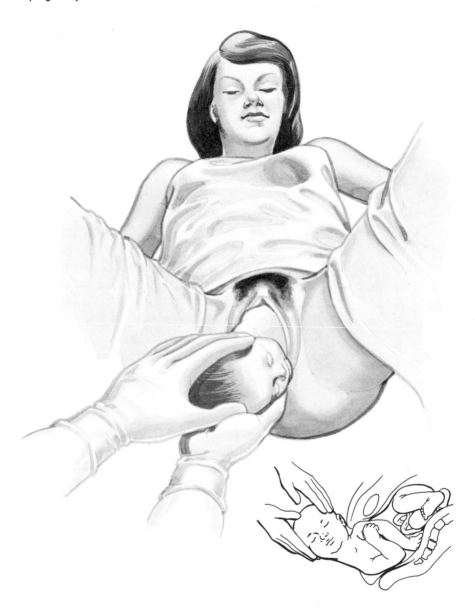

FIGURE 9-5. Emergence of the infant.

ately prior to and after delivery because of the danger of infection. Current obstetrical thinking now places few restrictions on intercourse during this time. The dictum most often used is, "If intercourse is comfortable and the woman feels sexually aroused, she is free to

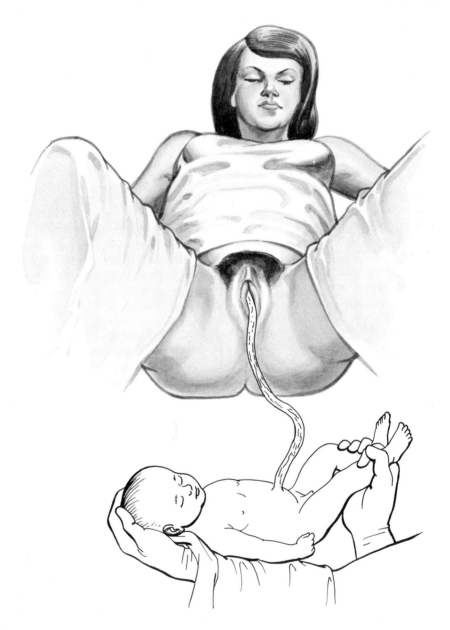

FIGURE 9-6. Birth of the infant. The umbilical cord is still attached.

partake." On the other hand, if intercourse is uncomfortable or dis-
agreeable, she might wait until the cause of her discomfort is resolved.

The Placenta

Until recently little medical attention had been paid to the importance of the placenta. During the past decade, however, studies using sheep have indicated that the placenta is an extremely active organ, playing a substantial role in the development of the infant.

Implantation of the embryo into the uterine wall takes place between the sixth and twelfth days after fertilization. The initial stages of formation of the placenta likewise occur during this time. Growth of the placenta continues until at birth it weighs about 1 pound, is about 1 inch thick at its center, and is about 7 inches in diameter. At the same time the infant is born, the placenta, the fetal membranes, and their contained fluids are expelled as the afterbirth.

Through the placenta pass nutrients from mother to child and excretory products from child to mother. The transportation of nutrients is a very active process, taking place through villi developed by the embryo and bathed in the maternal blood flowing through the sinuses. Exchange of materials in the placenta takes place in one of three ways: (1) gases are transferred by diffusion; (2) certain particles by virtue of their small size pass through the surface of the villi; and (3) the cells of the villi actively select and transfer to the infant's blood a variety of chemicals needed for proper development of the embryo. It follows that the developing individual by way of the placenta is parasitic upon the mother, taking from her in some cases basic chemicals of which she herself may be in short supply. Recent scientific advances indicate that some of these basic chemicals are altered by the fetus and returned to the mother through the placenta to act in an hormonal manner.

The placenta itself is believed also to serve as an endocrinological organ, producing estrogen, progesterone, and other steroids. Recently new tests have been devised that measure the adequacy of placental functioning.

There is no direct interchange of blood between mother and infant, with the possible exception that at delivery a small amount of fetal blood may enter the maternal circulation because of the trauma to the fetal blood vessels at the time the placenta is dislodged from the uterine wall. This is important where Rh incompatability is involved.

Analgesia And Anesthesia

Analgesics are drugs that lessen pain without loss of consciousness by the recipient. They are used, for example, to alleviate pain resulting from heart attacks or kidney stones. They are also used in obstetrics to ameliorate labor pains. The drugs most commonly used are demerol, morphine, and dilaudid. There is no question that in very large doses these drugs have a sedative effect on the unborn fetus as well as on the pregnant female. However, in most modern obstetrical practices these drugs are used in small doses. They are frequently given in association with other agents that complement them. The amounts thus used minimize, if not totally eliminate, respiratory depression in the newborn.

Anesthetics are drugs that produce local or general loss of sensibility. Those commonly available fall into three categories: general anesthetics, conduction anesthetics, and local anesthetics.

With general anesthesia, the obstetrical patient is put to sleep much as are surgical patients. The drug is given quite late during labor in such a way as to be of no harm to the unborn infant.

Conduction anesthesia includes epidural block, caudal anesthesia and spinal anesthesia. These are nerve blocks, similar to those used in dentistry. They eliminate the pains associated with labor without, for the most part, eliminating the process of labor completely. Caudal and epidural anesthetics do not significantly reduce the labor process. Spinal anesthetics can either slow or stop labor. For this reason, a spinal anesthetic is used only during the terminal period of the delivery process. Conduction anesthetics in skilled hands produce relief for millions of women.

Local anesthesia in obstetrics includes the pudendal block and the paracervical block. The most commonly used drugs are xylocaine and novocaine, injected into the cervix to eliminate some of the pains of labor or into the lower vaginal tract to eliminate the pain of delivery or possible episiotomy.

Since 1920, research has been conducted on delivery without the use of drugs. It used to be fairly common practice to give large doses of morphine, and the patient went through labor in what was referred to as "twilight sleep." The drug, scopolamine, was used likewise. By its use the woman completely forgot the entire experience. As a countermeasure against this form of anesthesia, Dr. Grantley Dick-Read devised a natural childbirth method in which the patient is trained to ignore or in some way lessen the pain of childbirth. More recently, the LaMaze method has supplanted the Grantley Dick-Read method. The LaMaze method relies on muscular training during pregnancy and breathing exercises to increase the tolerance for pain by the pregnant female so that she may undergo childbirth without anesthesia or analgesia.

With the increasing popularity of the LaMaze and other methods of natural childbirth, it has become customary in many hospitals to allow the father into both the labor and delivery rooms. The general belief is that this facilitates labor by giving the patient reinforcement during this critical time. In the LaMaze method, the husband plays an active rather than a passive role. He assists his wife with breathing exercises and lends encouragement to her as labor progresses from the first to the second stage.

A new method has recently been devised for monitoring the physical condition of the baby during labor. By it, continuous and simultaneous tracings are obtained electrically of the heart tones of the fetus and uterine contractions of the mother. If the fetal heart rate drops to a dangerous level following a uterine contraction, serious trouble is indicated for the fetus. Delivery should be undertaken immediately, most often by Cesarean section.

Routine Prenatal Care

Tremendous advances have been made in obstetrics by instituting routine prenatal examinations. Because of them, the death rate from pregnancy, as well as serious complications associated with it, has been markedly reduced.

The concept of prenatal care is that an ounce of prevention is worth a pound of cure; early detection of possible trouble can prevent severe complications. On this premise, the patient is seen for a complete physical examination, including her past medical history. Such an examination acquaints the physician with the general condition of the patient and alerts him to possible pathology that may be present.

The initial examination includes an evaluation of the size of the pelvis to determine if it can accommodate an average-sized infant. Blood tests are made to determine the iron content for possible anemia, the type of blood, including the Rh factor (cf. p. 112), and syphilis. Most states require the test for syphilis.

Routine follow-up visits include a blood pressure examination, an examination of the urine for albumin and sugar to see if the patient is developing either kidney disturbance or diabetes, a weight check to be sure she is not accumulating excess fluid, and an evaluation of the increase in size of the infant during the prior month. In later evaluations, in some cases, vaginal examinations are done to determine the condition of the cervix and the nearness of impending labor.

If defects are found, corrective measures are then taken as required.

It had been held for years that a woman should gain only 20 pounds because of pregnancy (see p. 112). However, recent studies done on nutrition have clearly shown that this magic number is no longer relevant. It was felt that if a woman gained too much weight during pregnancy, there would be adverse effects on her as well as on the fetus. This has proven not to be true. Many clinicians, however, still hold to the 20-pound limit for the purpose, I would assume, of the patient's vanity. If a patient has gained, for example, 50 pounds, loses 20 pounds after the pregnancy, and then finds herself 30 pounds over her usual weight, this can definitely adversely affect her psychological makeup. Most clinicians now explain these facts to the patient and find that without serious threats, for the most part, the patient will remain within the prescribed limitation.

General Attitudes Regarding Pregnancy

General attitudes regarding pregnancy have markedly changed over the years as the field of obstetrics has become more sophisticated. Rather than a state of abnormality requiring close supervision, pregnancy today is considered as a state of health. It is true that some difficulties may arise as a result of pregnancy, disease may even intervene, but by and large the pregnant female is probably in as good a state of health as at any other time of her life.

Restrictions, sometimes severe, used to be placed on the female during pregnancy, but the general rule now espoused by obstetricians is one of having the patient do reasonably what she wants but not to overdo.

In the field of exercise, for example, my own stand is that those activities in which an expectant mother is proficient before pregnancy can be continued during pregnancy, but that pregnancy is no time during which to start new athletic endeavors.

Smoking during pregnancy is the subject of much controversy. A 1971 report from the Surgeon General of the United States holds that smoking by the mother during pregnancy decreases the infant's birth-weight, and there is increased incidence of prematurity. The report further states, "There is strong evidence to support the view that smoking mothers have a significantly greater number of unsuccessful pregnancies due to stillbirth and neonatal death as compared to non-smoking mothers."

On the topic of travel, unless there is a problem pregnancy of some sort, most obstetricians now allow travel with the suggestion that if it entails long periods of sitting, the pregnant woman should move her lower extremities appreciably every half-hour.

Common complaints, minimal but annoying, associated with pregnancy include fatigue, backache, heartburn, hemorrhoids, and nausea. With careful and sympathetic understanding on the part of the physician and the family, these symptoms can be treated and rectified.

Medical attitudes regarding sexual intercourse during late pregnancy have recently been liberalized. There appears to be no correlation, for example, between premature birth and frequency of intercourse during late pregnancy. However, the studies of Solberg, Butler, and Wagner indicate that frequency of intercourse generally declines during pregnancy, the decline being greater during the later stages. Frequency of orgasm by the female also appears to decrease at such times as intercourse is undertaken. Women, when questioned, attribute loss of sexual drive during pregnancy to one or more of the following reasons: physical discomfort, fear of injury to the baby, awkwardness of performing coitus, and loss of libidinal interest. This sexual apathy does not appear to be related to the socioeconomic levels, the number of prior pregnancies, or the ages of those females interviewed.

In modern obstetrical practice, restrictions against intercourse during late pregnancy are minimal. The general doctrine is now held that if and when coitus becomes unpleasant and uncomfortable, avoid it. Choice is left to the individual couple.

In the literature there is one reported complication involving those who practice oral-genital activity and blow air into the vagina. Bubbles of air may enter the uterus, penetrate behind the placenta, and enter the blood stream. These air emboli can cause rapid death of the female.

The efficacy of breast-feeding versus bottle-feeding has long been a topic of controversy. The general agreement at this time is that from a nutritional standpoint the infant can grow and prosper despite which type of feeding is used. From a psychological standpoint, it has been assumed that breast-feeding and the cuddling involved with it will offer the infant a better type of psychological nourishment than will bottle-feeding. However, most obstetricians believe a great deal depends on the attitude of the mother. If she would like to breast-feed and if she finds breast-feeding an enjoyable experience, obviously it is ideal for her to do so. However, if she finds the process repugnant and tends to do it only under obligation, one cannot help but assume that the infant will recognize this repugnance. Under those circumstances, bottle-feeding with a great deal of love and tenderness would be more desirable. Furthermore, there are some cases in which allergy of an infant to commercial milk exists. In such cases, breast-feeding is strongly recommended.

Lastly, one of the most important yet often neglected or overlooked benefits a physician can offer in his relationship with a pregnant female is to prepare her psychologically for pregnancy. Certainly the first pregnancy more than others brings out and tests the total psychological reserve of the female. From the very earliest, a young lady is dressed in pink, given dolls, and encouraged to pursue feminine habits leading to motherhood. Pregnancy, therefore, characterizes the fulfillment of a lifetime of psychosocial and in some ways psychosexual development. Because of the many reflections and anxieties that logically and inevitably pass through the mind of the expectant mother, she may exhibit periods of emotional stress, at times going as far as extreme exultation or depression. It is very important in my judgment that during pregnancy the expectant mother should be given every consideration by her husband, family, and attending physician. The last individual, in particular, has spent 12 years of his adult life training to care for problems, major and trivial, that the pregnant female may experience during these unique periods of her life. He can do much to alleviate the stresses of pregnancy. The importance of the husband-wife relationship and the physician-patient relationship during pregnancy cannot be overemphasized.

References

AREY, LESLIE B. 1965. *Developmental Anatomy*, 7th ed. Philadelphia: W. B. Saunders.

HAMILTON, W. J., AND H. W. MOSSMAN. 1972. *Human Embryology*, 4th ed. Baltimore: Williams & Wilkins.

HELLMAN, LOUIS M., AND J. A. PRITCHARD. 1971. *Williams Obstetrics*, 14th ed. New York: Appleton-Century-Crofts.

INGELMAN-SUNDBERG, A., CLAES WIRSEN, AND LENNART NILSSON. 1965. *A Child is Born*. New York: Dell.

LANGMAN, JAN. 1969. *Human Embryology*, 2nd ed. Baltimore: Williams & Wilkins.

PATTEN, BRADLEY M. 1968. *Human Embryology*, 3rd ed. New York: McGraw-Hill (Blakiston Div.).

REPORT OF THE SURGEON GENERAL. 1971. *Smoking and Pregnancy*, Chapter 5 in *The Health Consequences of Smoking*. Washington, D.C.: U.S. Department of Health, Education and Welfare; Public Health Service; and Health Services and Mental Health Administration.

SOLBERG, DON A., JULIUS BUTLER, AND NATHANIEL N. WAGNER. 1973. "Sexual Behavior in Pregnancy," *New England Journal of Medicine*, 288: 1098.

10

psychosexual development

There exists a tremendous variation in adult sexual behavior and appetites. It has long been assumed that this variation reflects differences in childhood development. We term the phenomenon by which a child develops into a mature sexual being as "psychosexual development."

This maturation process involves a physiological as well as a psychological component. Physiological maturation was considered in Chapters 5 and 6. Psychological maturation remains an enigma. At issue are those drives inherent in an individual versus those drives superimposed by his culture.

We do not know what would happen sexually between a male and a female infant if left, adequately nourished, to their own devices on a deserted Pacific island. Yet until that question can be answered, any discussion becomes obviously theoretical. In this light, three *approaches have been advanced to explain psychosexual development: (1) biological, (2) psychoanalytical, and (3) sociocultural.*

All these theories are based on data acquired in one or more of four ways:

1. *Observation of young children or young animals, particularly monkeys (see chapter on anthropology).*
2. *Examination of other cultures (see chapter on anthropology).*
3. *Psychiatric investigation of adults with whom an attempt is made by recall, dream analysis, or hypnosis to recreate childhood experiences and feelings.*
4. *Armchair theorizing—i.e., starting with premises and developing assumptive theories through logical reasoning.*

From this pool of information, research writers selectively choose those data which they feel are most relevant, giving such data preference and special meaning to substantiate their hypotheses.

I emphasize that these hypotheses are theories, not facts, in the scientific sense of the word, although it seems to me that with repeated general use in psychiatric and psychological literature, these theories are frequently treated as facts. The reader may wish to review Chapter 2, Validity, and read the following material in that light.

The Biological Interpretation Of Psychosexual Development

This theory implies, in a sense, that man's sexual activities are programmed from birth and that all man has to do in essence is live out that programming. One may parallel this with the theological position of predestination, in which man's fate is programmed, and if he lives long enough, he will substantiate these basic drives. In this light, it is interesting to note recent observations by Konrad Lorenz on the graylag goose. He noted that there was a critical period immediately after hatching in which the young gosling would follow the first moving object it saw. Most often this object would be the mother, and so the gosling would continue to follow her. However, if a human being were the first moving object seen, the gosling would then follow that human being. There is then a definite reason why half a dozen little geese in single file can be seen following a mother goose, as she ambles down a country road.

To be sure, one cannot evaluate the biological programming of man, but one must admit that a certain amount of it is present. The general consensus is that this programming is not absolute and that man has the capability of altering it during his lifetime. Those who espouse this biological theory more or less base their thinking on the instinctual nature of the sex drive. They would equate the sex drive with hunger or thirst, which are also powerful drives seeking fulfillment. Quite unlike hunger and thirst, however, the sex drive is not an absolute necessity for the individual, although it is an absolute necessity for the species if the species is to continue to exist.

It is then within reason to believe that since man is a vertebrate, his adult sexual behavior is primarily based on biological factors, particularly his genetic and hormonal makeup, which is probably influenced as well by psychological and sociological factors that play on him throughout his life cycle.

The Psychoanalytical Interpretation Of Psychosexual Development

There are many variations of the psychoanalytic theory, but they all have in common an interpretation of the writings of Sigmund Freud. Some accept these writings in toto as sacrament. Others have added wider interpretations of Freud's work or variations of their own. Basically, however, they all describe developmental sexual processes in a sequential pattern and they suggest that adolescent and adult sexual problems have their origin in some distortion of these processes during one or more of the sequential developmental periods. I would like to quote Freud's own words on the topic.

The popular view distinguishes between hunger and love, seeing them as representatives of the instincts that aim at self-preservation and reproduction of the species respectively. In associating ourselves with this very evident distinction we postulate in psychoanalysis a similar one between the self-preservative or ego instinct on the one hand and the sexual instincts on the other; that force by which the sexual instinct is represented in the mind we call 'libido'—sexual longing—and regard it as analogous to the force of hunger, or the will to power, and other such trends among the ego-tendencies.

Ernest Jones clarifies this passage by commenting, "By 'sexual' Freud meant 'sexual' in the ordinary sense, but he widened the popular conception of what things are sexual. The psychoanalytic study of early childhood and the knowledge of adult perversions compelled him to recognize that sexuality has many manifestations besides the simple genital union of coitus. The instinct does not begin in this finished form, the one where it obviously serves the end of reproduction. On the contrary, it has to pass through a rather complicated development before this stage of what Freud termed 'genital primacy' is reached."

Let us analyze this sequential process.

THE INFANTILE (PREGENITAL) PERIOD. Immediately following birth, a child is driven toward his mother by his total helplessness. He derives satisfaction from hunger fulfillment as well as pleasurable experiences from closeness. Obviously, his needs are not always satisfied on demand and he experiences certain frustrations. These, in turn, may cause some anger on his part. This period of infantile sexuality lasts approximately four years. It is divided into phases corresponding to the body need primarily in vogue at any given time. The oral phase, for example, lasts until the child's attention is focused elsewhere. During the time of the oral phase, the child is most dependent, and all his bodily needs are cared for. Primary concern is for feeding, which provides nutrients as well as pleasure. The child will be seen putting everything he can into his mouth, literally exploring with his mouth. His mother exists only as a servant to care for these bodily needs.

From a sexual standpoint the concern is sucking and skin contact, but general excitement is possible and erection does occur as a nonspecific response to pleasurable stimulation.

Whenever the mother initiates toilet training she demands muscular control of involuntary muscle activity. The emphasis at this point is on alimentary (excretory) functions. The child may become more aggressive and difficult to control. He seems to be playing games with his elders in regard to his toilet habits. The genital play during this period is minimal.

Association of this anal phase with a rigid timetable for performing elimination processes rather commonly produces distortions in later behavior and sexuality of the individual. Mechanical-time, clock-oriented, toilet training can help set the stage for a mechanical personality, a personality precise and rigid in the sense of a perfection-oriented adult individual.

A more contemporary view, however, of the same phenomenon is that the mother's rigidity in toilet training is only a manifestation of an overall rigid personality on her part in handling the child. So that it is not the act of toilet training per se, but rather the mother's rigidity that creates a similar situation in her offspring.

Within the first year to year and one-half of development, the child is also expected to undertake certain other complicated muscular activities, which Freud seemingly ignored. The child is expected to learn to walk and talk, and failure in these areas can affect self-image in a deleterious way as quickly as can distortions of genital-oriented behavior. Freud, however, seems to have used sex as a paradigm around which to organize human development and function.

THE OEDIPAL PERIOD. The Oedipal period heralds the beginning of the genital period of development, in that during this time the infant becomes more aware of physical differences of the sexes and more clearly identifies his own gender. These years, roughly from four to six, are characterized by an increasingly intense interest in the genital region. This concept is quite Freudian in thought, and pediatricians of today imply that this intensity may not be quite as great now as it was in the 1890's. This period is also referred to as the phallic phase of development, as autoerotic stimulation of the penis is most frequently involved.

Freud coined the term "Oedipus complex" to describe the child's behavior at this time. The young boy seems to compete with his father for the affection (precursor of genital gratification) of the mother. Still, he has a love for his father and an ambivalent situation develops. The boy usually resolves this dilemma by identifying with his father and sets the father as an ideal. The young female is caught in a similar situation as she first conflicts with, and then models her life after, her mother.

The more contemporary neo-Freudian view emphasizes that this is truly a triangular relationship, involving the parents and the child versus what the child has previously known only as a dual relationship between the mother and the child.

This period of time demands a strong relationship between mother and father. If either parent plays into the fantasies of the child rather than reinforcing the parental team, the child will have difficulties in learning to cope with relationships involving more than one person. One can see here that parental attitudes toward behavior, toward each other, and toward the child may strongly influence the eventual character of the child. I would emphasize that the crux of the problem is the full relationship of child to parent rather than individual acts that may occur between child and parent. I decry the emphasis on a single act because it is so easy to implicate superficially a cause and effect relationship between an act and a subsequent pattern of behavior on the part of the child.

As an example of these interrelationships, let us consider a simplified hypothetical case involving masturbation. To consider this example we must first accept the premise, taken from the deutero theory in psychology, that every act conveys two levels of meaning to others:

1. Information or facts are conveyed.
2. The relative relationship between the two individuals involved in the communication is revealed by the way the communicator talks or acts.

In the example the parent says, "If you don't stop playing with yourself, I'll cut off your penis." At the informational level, the parent is saying the penis will be cut off if the activity isn't stopped. At the relational level, the parent is saying that he or she is the parent, is bigger and more powerful than the child, and therefore has the power to cut off the penis.

Let us look at this quotation again. Who really is in control? By using the phrase "if you don't stop," the parent really is returning control of the situation to the child. Now there are certain unspoken implications to the child in this particular warning. First, there is the implication that the penis can be cut off. Second, there is the implication that some individuals—little girls—do not have a penis. Third, there is the implication that little girls have had their penis cut off. Finally, since little boys as well as little girls have been taught in prior years that girls constitute a somewhat lower social level than boys, the boy will face the possibility of becoming lower in the parent's eyes when the penis is cut off.

Out of this potentially incredible chaos, children somehow are capable of sorting the important meanings and understandings that they must have to communicate and interact with other people.

THE LATENCY PERIOD. Following final resolution of the childhood Oedipal phase is a latency phase that extends to prepuberty. The period involved is usually from six to eleven years of age and is characterized by decreased sexual interest or curiosity as the child begins to explore the wonders of the outside world. The child feels relatively secure in his identification with his similarly sexed parent, as well as with his opposite sexed parent. He expands intellectually and develops peer relationships. Interestingly, the latency period coincides with the legal requirement that the child must attend school and with the consequent social expectations that the child expand his horizons. He is learning both to compete and to cooperate. Parenthetically, this is also the age of participating in such activities as Little League football and baseball.

In deference to Freud, some psychiatrists feel that the child is still intensely aware of his sexuality, but he feels incapable of handling it at this time, so he simply gives the overt appearance of ignoring it. This attitude has been used by some, for example, as an argument against sex education during these formative years.

THE PREPUBERTY PERIOD. This period extends roughly from ages eleven to thirteen as the child is faced with the beginnings of secondary sexual characteristics, such as breast and hair development, menstruation, and voice change.

During this time the child may partially revert to more infantile patterns. He may or may not abandon some degree of cleanliness, neatness, and sociability for dirtiness, disorder, and antisocial behavior. The degree to which he changes is quite variable, but it always seems to be enough to upset the parents, who feel that these behavior patterns are important.

The general consensus is that this change in overt activity is symbolic. Up to this time the parent usually has been authoritarian. The child, for the most part, has accepted this authority. At this point in development, the parent must permit the child increasing autonomy. What the child is really saying by his behavior is, "If you don't permit autonomy, I will reject your authority," a situation that is in itself somewhat of a paradox. Changes of mood are frequent during this time, and the relationship between parent and child may become increasingly testy.

THE ADOLESCENT PERIOD. Adolescence encompasses the years following prepuberty until about fifteen and is really interlaced with prepuberty, depending upon the maturity of a given individual. The term "biological maturity," is now used inasmuch as the individual at this point possesses the capability of procreation.

The concept is proposed that any unresolved infantile sexual conflicts are now reawakened (postlatency), and the increasing genital component of the maturational drive (libido) assumes a central position. Puberty initiates a reworking of the Oedipus complex in an adult genital format. This second time around, however, the adolescent has already formulated a character of his own. He has shared experiences, intellectual as well as physical, and has become integrated with the value system of that particular culture and peer age group into which he was born.

With revitalization of sexuality, the child is again drawn to the parent of opposite sex. However, facing this problem at age twelve or thirteen, the youngster now backs off from sensuous experiences with those closest to him. The scene of a 14-year-old boy refusing to kiss his mother is familiar.

Freudian theory postulates a tremendous upheaval occurring within the adolescent as he tries to manipulate those primitive sexual feelings in the context of his now mature being. However, in recognizing the social changes the adolescent must bring about within himself in trying to stop being a child and learning to be an adult, it seems he has more than enough reason to be in a state of upheaval, with or without the addition of sexual behavior.

We can see that if feelings were poorly handled from ages one to six and during latency, the conflict the adolescent faces between ages eleven and fifteen may be even more unmanageable and may totally overwhelm the emotional capabilities of the young individual.

The adolescent period may be subdivided into early, middle, and late adolescence. Here I would like to quote directly from *Sex and the College Student*, because I think the writing is succinct and effective.

Early adolescence includes the characteristic turmoil associated with the often traumatic physical changes. Rapid mood swings, regression with reappearance of early childhood behavior and dependency, angry rebellion against parents and adults generally, and a tendency to be with members of the same sex are all in evidence at this time. By late adolescence, more comfortable distance from parents is the rule with more acceptance of the young person's own interlife. Already the transition toward an adult way of life is noted with a shift to opposite sex relations, more interest in sexual intercourse than in prolonged foreplay; some progress is noted in selection of career and marriage choices. Rebellion against parents has lost some of its intensity and signs of a friendly, but autonomous, attitude will be evident.

THE ADULT PERIOD. Adult sexual behavior is discussed in Chapter 11, Sexual Intercourse.

The Sociocultural Interpretation Of
Psychosexual Development

Sociocultural interpretation suggests that cultural "nurture," rather than biological "nature," is the primary influence of psychosexual development. The leading advocates of this thesis are William Simon and John Gagnon.

These sociologists refute two basic Freudian concepts. First, they reject that social behavior is the expression of a primordial (libidinal) drive. Second, after admitting that there exists a continuity of sexuality from childhood through adulthood, they refuse to accept the thesis that childhood sexual experiences set the tone for adult sexual behavior.

In place of those Freudian concepts, Simon and Gagnon hold a concept they term "scripted" behavior. This concept supposes that sexual behavior is learned, much as one learns the script of a play. They believe that an individual learns sexual behavior just as he learns other behavior patterns, such as obedience, patriotism, or table manners.

They also describe psychosexual development according to age levels, emphasizing learned behavior.

CHILDHOOD. Childhood experiences affect a number of developmental trends and create body potentialities. During this period, the child's capacity for pleasure and discomfort is developed, as well as his ability to relate to others. These childhood experiences carry no sexual overtones except as they affect the entire individual. They are not expressions of biological necessity, but are rather the earliest form of social learning.

ADOLESCENCE. Adolescence begins when society acknowledges that the individual has sexual capacity. "Training in the postures and rhetoric of the sexual experience is now accelerated. . . . . the adolescent begins to regard those about him (particularly his peers, but also adults) as sexual actors, and can find confirmation from others for this view."

Adolescent changes in boys and girls diverge and should be considered separately. In boys, "the beginning of a commitment to sexuality is primarily genital; within two years of puberty all but a relatively few have had the experience of orgasm, almost universally brought about by masturbation. The corresponding organizing event for girls is not genitally sexual but social: they have arrived at an age where they will learn role performances linked with proximity to marriage."

ADULTHOOD. The authors stress that most individuals in our society are married, so that handling sexual commitments within marriage constitutes the bulk of adult sexual experience. Husband and wife enact the scripted roles society has taught them with approximately one-half of the males and one-quarter of the females acting offstage with another leading lady or another leading man during their marital careers.

Within marriage, sexuality is only one part of a total relationship. The frequency and intensity of the sexual encounter are not governed by the basic biological needs of the couple, but rather by extraneous culture-oriented forms, acting upon the two individuals.

The views of Simon and Gagnon can be succinctly summarized by their statement, "In general, we feel that far from sexual needs affecting other adult concerns, the reverse may be true: adult sexual activity may become that aspect of a person's life most often used to act out other needs."

Conclusion

The redeeming value of any explanation of psychosexual development is that it does systematize in some way the data that have been accumulated, and systematizing these data gives them some relevant meaning. However, at the present time there is no solid foundation upon which to establish any ultimate and generally acceptable theory of human personality development or sexuality. We know too much, yet not enough.

References

COMMITTEE ON THE COLLEGE STUDENT FROM THE GROUP FOR THE ADVANCEMENT OF PSYCHIATRY. 1966. *Sex and the College Student.* Greenwich, Conn.: Fawcett.

ERICKSON, E. H. 1963. *Childhood and Society,* 2nd ed. New York: W. W. Norton.

GAGNON, J. H., AND W. SIMON. 1968. *Sex Education and Human Development*, in *Human Sexual Function and Dysfunction*, ed. by P. J. Fink. Philadelphia: F. A. Davis.

JONES, ERNEST. 1971. *The Libido Theory of Sigmund Freud*, in *Human Sexual Behavior*, ed. by Bernhardt Lieberman. New York: Wiley.

SIMON, WILLIAM, AND JOHN GAGNON. 1973. *Psychosexual Development*, in *Human Sexuality: Contemporary Perspectives*, ed. by Eleanor S. Morrison and Vera Borosage. Palo Alto, Calif.: National Press Books.

11

sexual intercourse

One essential for any book on human sexuality is a discussion of sexual intercourse. Whether to? When to? How to? And with whom?

Each author attempts to answer these questions based on his own readings and experience, and I am no exception. I shall present a format for instruction that works for me and which I have seen work for others. Its redeeming value lies mainly in its pragmatic approach.

Two Types Of Sexuality

On a recent trip to Amsterdam I observed a rather unique situation. The prostitutes of that city displayed themselves freely in store windows in a bedroom setting to allow the customer to see exactly what he was purchasing. The customer agreed to a price; a curtain was drawn; and transaction of the business proceeded.

How does one reconcile this situation with the moonstruck lovers of Eric Segal's *Love Story* or the romance of the nuptial bed?

Biologically the acts are the same. The erect penis penetrates the lubricated vagina. Subsequently undulatory motions on the part of the male culminate in orgasm, usually for both participants. Yet the events are as different as day and night.

In the first example, the act is purely biological. No deep emotional feelings are engendered. Neither partner is particularly concerned with the well-being of the other. It is interesting to note that in present-day society there seems to be an increase in purely biological sexual intercourse. Although prostitution is on the decline, the one-night stand or casual sexual encounter is apparently on the increase. Although this type of sexuality may serve as a safety valve for those caught in a highly tense, competitive and demanding social order, it would seem unfortunate if it served as the only type of sexual experience for a given individual.

The unique quality of the second example lies in the word "love." Love, itself, is an odd and remarkable word. It holds a supreme position in our vocabulary, yet it is just about indefinable. However, the parameters that surround a love relationship are definable. To me, empirically, three of these parameters must be met before I will define a love relationship as such.

The first is that a mutual respect exists between the partners. By mutual I imply that each partner can say, "I like you" or "I love you."

The second is some degree of mutual responsibility or commitment. He or she can say, "I am not ashamed of what I am doing. I am willing to defend my actions, and I am willing to defend you against others about this action should the demand be made."

The third is some element of permanence. From a practical point of view, considering today's mores, this need not necessarily mean " 'til death us do part." Historically, the male has been less committed to this concept of permanence than the female. The female on the other hand, unless under duress, would copulate only with someone toward whom she had a strong emotional attraction, implying some permanence. However, with changing values in our society, one would expect in time that either the male will become more committed to this concept or the female will become less so. The important point is that this sexual love occurs only as a part of an ongoing relationship, rather than as an episode that will end when the sexual encounter is over.

I stress this differentiation because there has been much semantic neglect in the field of human sexuality. Until recently, for example, the vernacular term for sexual intercourse was "making love." Today, in many cases, it has been replaced by "having sex." Are we now talking about the same thing, or were we making love then and having sex now? In discussion or counseling in the sexual area, one must first define precisely what type of sexual intercourse is being enacted, so that analysis of one's motivation may be accurate.

Two Important Addenda To Sexual Love

I feel obliged here to add two important addenda to this concept of sexual love.

First, if the preceding three criteria are met, I believe society should not concern itself with the two humans involved, regardless of the participating sexes.

Second, I refuse to equate an occasional departure from this prolonged relationship, an external fling as it were, with adultery or infidelity, although others doubtless will take issue with me. Casual commitment is really no commitment at all and may have little or no effect on a deep abiding love existing elsewhere at the time.

Some Parameters Of Sexuality

FREQUENCY. If sexual intercourse is undertaken, what should be the frequency? Various authors estimate that the number of times an individual has coitus has been established at 2.5 times per week. This figure, however, represents an average. If one investigates the frequency among individuals in the 20 to 40 age bracket, the number may be 4 times a week, whereas if one investigates the 50 to 60 age bracket, it may be once a week. The magical figure of 2.5 is the average that occurs with married couples. No one, so far as I know, has accurate figures for the single individual.

Within the limits of good health, mental and physical, the frequency of coitus is really unimportant. Frequency should be satisfactory for both members of the couple, and if a discrepancy exists, one would expect a compromise that is not damaging to either partner.

VARIATION.   What variations of sexual behavior should be considered normal? The scope of this book cannot be extended to include the many positions and variations possible to achieve sexual gratification. Orogenital, anogenital, masturbatory, and homosexual experiences have recently received wide attention. *The Sensuous Man, The Sensuous Woman,* and *The Couple* have adorned our best-seller lists. The concept of consenting adults doing what they please within the confines of their own privacy seems to be gaining general acceptance. My only addendum to this dictum is to footnote that nobody should be hurt physically or psychologically.

TECHNIQUE.   We have noted earlier that human sexuality is a learned experience. Thus, as with any other learned experience, one can with practice and study become an expert. Certain areas of the body are erogenous zones, i.e., they respond to sexual stimuli. The degree of response varies considerably from individual to individual, and the preference for stimulation of one area versus another can only be manifested by communication between the two individuals involved. The most superlative technique in one situation may be quite inappropriate in another. I refer the interested reader to *The Joy of Sex* for a sophisticated pictorial handling of this topic. This treatise, subtitled "A Gourmet Guide to Lovemaking," handles lovemaking in the unique fashion of a recipe with emphasis on the variation and fun of intercourse. Although the author stresses the significance of a love relationship, one cannot help but feel that the author is more concerned with performance. In fact, performance, or sexual agility, is the major theme of most sex-oriented books on the market today. It seems the act is becoming more important than the actors. I emphasize again that communication is the essence of any satisfactory sexual technique.

Motivational Aspects Of Sexual Intercourse

The only intelligent way I have found to discuss sexual intercourse truthfully is to ask the question, "What are the motivating factors involved?"

The social scientist supposes that we humans tend to act for some reward or goal, rather than in a haphazard fashion. The motivating force for an act is the anticipation of that reward. The term used by the social scientists to define reward is *effective consequence*. It follows, then, that the greater the reward or goal or effective consequence, the greater the anticipation and, consequently, the greater the motivating force which will encourage us to proceed.

This motivating force is influenced by several factors:

1. The intensity of the goal or reward, as stated.
2. The prior experience of the individual and the prior degree of success in attaining an individual goal. For example, a man goes to a certain bar and picks up a woman with whom he subsequently has intercourse. Simply going to the bar in the future may cause him to become sexually excited. If he is frequently successful in this venture, the very thought of going to the bar may cause sexual arousal.
3. Habituation in which repetition produces diminished reward. For example, if the man in example 2 has visited the bar and had intercourse three nights in a row, he may be less inclined to try again on a fourth night.
4. The realization that one can have both positive and negative factors regarding motivation; that is, one avoids doing something because one is aware of the unpleasant rewards involved. For example, our man contracts gonorrhea from one of his conquests at the bar. He may in the future avoid the bar like a plague.
5. The goal or reward may be fantasized. This factor is highly significant in sexual matters. For example, our man may fantasy an imagined sexual encounter with someone he has met only casually. This may cause sexual arousal when no sexual contact has occurred.
6. Several expectations may arise simultaneously. An individual must categorize and choose the strongest of these. This may be done by addition or subtraction, including several together or eliminating some. For example, our man has $50 in his pocket, with which he can do several things. He can stay home and watch television, thus saving the money. Or he can visit the bar, spending a good portion of the money. Or he can go to a movie, spending only a small part of it.

Sexual Motivations For Intercourse

Based on this motivational theme, there are several goals which we commonly accept as healthy sexual motivations or lust: (1) the pleasurable excitement of arousal; (2) the intense pleasure accompanying orgasm and the relaxation that follows; and (3) the desire for interpersonal relationship, warmth, and concern. I feel that the human being has a definite need for such relationships and that sexual behavior offers a tremendous outlet toward that end.

It follows, therefore, that sexual motivations fall into the same categories and generalities as do other motivating forces. The elements of intensity, prior experience, habituation, positive and negative motivating factors, fantasized goals, as well as simultaneous expectations, are as appropriate, if not more so, for sexual behavior as for general behavior.

This thesis then offers us a rather simplified method for discussing sexual intercourse. From it one can draw answers for why, where, and how intercourse is undertaken. For a more profound treatment of motivation, the reader is referred to Kenneth R. Hardy's *An Appetitional Theory of Sexual Motivation*.

Nonsexual Motivations For Intercourse

Many nonlustful motives contribute to participation in sexual intercourse. The activity thus fulfills a nonsexual need, often a neurotic one. What are some of these motivations?

Some individuals seek intercourse as a method of obtaining love only for himself or herself. There is the girl, for example, who throws herself at men for the sake of gaining their love, the idea being that if a man has intercourse with her, he obviously loves her. The error of this thinking is self-evident.

Other individuals offer sexual intercourse as a defense against loneliness. This reason for undertaking sexual relations is increasing in our current society. Here the individual is in essence selling himself or herself sexually for companionship, believing that this may be the only way he or she is going to get another person to spend a period of time with him or her. The principal danger in this type of relationship, as I see it, is that the experience in time may lessen self-esteem.

Sexual intercourse is sometimes undertaken as a method of overcoming feelings of inferiority. This concept is particularly common among men who have doubts about their own masculinity and try to neutralize this by a long string of sexual conquests. Their idea is that if a man is capable of having sexual intercourse, he proves he is a man. The more sexual conquests he can make, the more manly he becomes in his own mind.

Intercourse as a demonstration of power is a concept held by some. It has been called the battle of the bedroom. It is a means of manipulating another human being, with one person emerging victorious and the other defeated.

Sexual intercourse has also been considered as a manifestation of hostility or contempt. Here is the man or woman who immediately drops his or her partner as unworthy of further consideration after seduction results in a conquest.

Intercourse may be used as a defense against anxiety, which is similar to its use against loneliness. We have the situation of an individual being uncertain about himself or herself and believing that he or she will be less anxious about the external world if he or she has someone else to share sexual relations. It is difficult to think of worldly matters when one is engaged at the height of sexual gratification.

The obsessive health fadist indulges in sexual intercourse at regularly specified intervals, not because he is sexually aroused or desirous, but rather because he considers the activity essential for good health. A closely related variant of this category is "ritual intercourse," which requires sexual activity on a specific night or at a specific time. In addition, some husbands and wives practice what is termed "dutiful intercourse," which is undergone without passion or tenderness simply because the other party may be expecting it.

"Mothering" sexual intercourse is undertaken by some as the expression of a wish to comfort or mother another individual in distress. Some may indulge in sexual intercourse merely out of gratitude for favors that have been given.

Hopefully this presentation will make the reader keenly aware that in the same sense that all that glitters is not gold, so all that seems sexual is not necessarily sexual at all. The individual planning to participate in sexual intercourse might pause and evaluate, if possible, not only his own motivation but the motivation of his partner as well. Should these motivations prove nonsexual, then at least the individual is aware of what is happening before he or she commits himself in an emotional way in a one-sided relationship.

For a more complete analysis of this topic, the reader is referred to the article "The Non-sexual Uses of Sexuality," by Judd Marmor.

The Need For Determining Why Sexual
Intercourse Is Undertaken

Understanding one's own sexual motivation, as well as understanding the motivation of one's partner, is paramount. If a relationship is purely biological, one based on noncommitment, the psychological problems are minimal if the relationship proves unsatisfactory.

However, if one believes that a relationship is of the love or romantic type and involves commitment, then he has made himself extremely vulnerable. He has exposed himself to another human being, not only physically but emotionally. He has said in the words of the popular ballad, "All of me, why not take all of me?" He has lowered his usual self-defense mechanism and said in effect, "This is the real me." Under these circumstances, if the individual is refused or scorned or treated badly, the trauma becomes a psychological one. Moreover, if these circumstances happen repeatedly, the psychological scar deepens. In my experience, people thus damaged frequently become soured on their own self-image, on their own ego, and frequently on the world in general. It seems to me, therefore, that one must tread lightly in becoming sexually involved in the category requiring a commitment, not only for one's own sake, but for the sake of one's partner as well.

Thus, parenthetically we arrive at a situation wherein the most meaningful and gratifying sexual experience is the most dangerous sexual encounter from a psychological standpoint.

Common Problems Which Patients Bring To
Physicians Regarding Sexual Relations

I have stressed that an individual should have some understanding of his own sexual motivations to avoid possible sexual difficulties. Should difficulties arise, however, despite this understanding, the individual should be better able to handle them and to accept outside help. I would like to present briefly the more common sexual problems that patients bring to physicians.

It cannot be stressed too strongly that within the confines of a marriage or an otherwise committed relationship there is no individual with a sexual problem, only a couple with a sexual problem. Masters and Masters repeatedly stress this theme, and I am in full accord. The various problems that follow, therefore, should be read with this thesis in mind.

MARITAL INFIDELITY. Other than the increasing divorce rate, no figures are available to indicate the extent to which our present social system has permitted, and perhaps even encouraged, marital infidelity. Kinsey's figures of the 1940's and 50's are no longer valid for today. With an external milieu geared to appeal to and stimulate human sexuality, what seems to be happening is that complete sexual satisfaction and stability are becoming increasingly difficult within the marital state alone.

For the female, the complexities of our life demand that in the married state she provide the following duties. She must be a housekeeper to meet the standards set by her spouse. She must be an intellectual companion, but at the same time be a sounding board for the trials and tribulations that have confronted her partner during his working day. She must be a satisfactory mother. With the increasing ages of her children and the chores of managing the household, she must also be a chauffeur. In many cases, she must also provide some financial aid to the family, either by working or by being the bookkeeper and treasurer for the menage. In addition, she must serve as a sexual partner. If any of her duties are tedious for her or cause her emotional consternation, there is no question but that such stresses will influence her sexual drives and abilities.

The physician is frequently faced with the "tired housewife syndrome," in which the female is so exhausted physically and emotionally by the end of the day that her sexual appetites are diminished to a point of not being able to enact her sexual role satisfactorily. The economic role she serves in the household is probably the single most important factor in diminishing her sexual role.

Disgust with her sexual function in the home may cause the wife to seek more exciting sexual experience elsewhere. There is little question that such an extramarital affair is more titillating and exciting than the sexual relations within the family bedroom, for by such an affair she can at least temporarily separate herself from all responsibilities except the sexual one.

For the male, ego expression is certainly lacking in today's so-

ciety. Although this is certainly clinically obvious, no statistics exist
for proof. Furthermore, accomplishments from his job may not satisfy
the male drive, which he has been taught our society expects. A man's
boss may be excessively harsh, or his job extremely demanding, so
much so that a male may develop doubts about his gender role.

The easiest way for a male to assure his manliness is to have
intercourse. This can be carried to the pathological point of continu-
ally seeking conquests. There may be a lack of responsiveness on the
part of his wife, and he thus turns to extramarital outlets.

The management of these problems is beyond the scope of the
average physician unless he is specializing in marital relations, possibly
by way of psychiatry. Such difficulties in our society have been taken
over by the clergy to some degree and by the burgeoning field of
marriage counseling. A new type of psychotherapy has evolved for the
couple who are mutually sincere in wanting to resolve such difficulties.
This therapy has been called the encounter or marathon group, in
which a retraining process or sensitizing is mastered. The short-term
results from this type of therapy seem promising, but the long-term
results have not yet been analyzed.

The ultimate solution, if none of the alternatives succeeds, seems
to lie in the divorce courts.

INABILITY TO ACHIEVE ORGASM. For the most part this is a
problem of the female and seems to have developed only recently as
a product of our current social thinking. We do not know, for example, if orgasm was experienced by such women as Cleopatra, Juliet,
or Madame Pompadour. There simply are no data on women of those
times. As recently as 10 years ago, physicians were reassuring their
female patients that orgasm is not a necessity for the female. She was
advised that if love, understanding, and consideration were present
during the sexual act, orgasm was an added fillip, which some women
have the capability of enjoying. The physician could quote that
possibly 70% of women had experienced an orgasm at one time or
another during their sexual lives, that 30% had achieved orgasm much
of the time, and that only 10% had achieved orgasm regularly. However, with the advent of women's liberation and increased coverage
about sexual activities in lay publications and movies, orgasm now
appears to be an innate birthright for the female. If it is not obtained,
it has now fallen into the realm of a problem.

The situation may be improved by improving sexual techniques,
as advised in the book *Human Sexual Inadequacy* by Masters and

Johnson. Or psychiatric help or marriage counseling of both partners may be effective.

FRIGIDITY. Frigidity is a different emotional response from a simple lack of orgasm in the female. It implies not only a disinterest in sexuality but an actual disdain for it. More often than not, the basic roots of frigidity lie either in the intrapersonal relationship of a couple or in previous, often during childhood, maladjustments to sexual experience or gender role.

IMPOTENCE. Impotence is the inability of the male to achieve sexual intercourse, usually resulting from inability to achieve or maintain erection. There are both organic and psychological causes for this condition. The organic causes most frequently encountered are diabetes, thyroid dysfunction, or some neurological defect. The psychological causes are more complex and probably constitute more than 90% of the cases.

The patient with this condition is most often initially evaluated by a urologist, who rules out the organic causes by extensive history taking and testing. If no organic causes are present, the physician assigns a psychological basis to the disorder. Frequently, the simple reassurance that there is nothing organically wrong cures the patient. However, if such assurance does not overcome the difficulty or if a major psychological problem exists, then psychiatric help or counseling may be needed.

There is no question that the incidence of impotence is increasing and that an increasing number of younger men are reporting it. One cannot be certain if this means that there are actually more cases now than there were ten years ago, or if there are more males who are willing to acknowledge this disorder than were willing to do so heretofore. My own thoughts are that both are true; more men are now admitting impotence, but at the same time more men are afflicted with it than previously.

Until recently, the classic description of the impotent male involved a veteran husband who appeared to be tiring of his veteran wife and was no longer able to perform. In many instances, the husband fantasied that if he had a younger partner, the problem would resolve, and to be sure it did in many cases. Now, however, it appears more younger, otherwise healthy, males are reporting impotence, and this condition has been termed "the new impotence."

This new impotence is graphically and carefully assessed by Philip Nobile in an article entitled "What Is the New Impotence, and Who's Got It?" Nobile contends that the reasons for this impotence are related to cultural changes in male and female sexual roles. He points out that whereas previously the Victorian woman who believed herself put upon, frequently reacted to her position with frigidity, the young male of today now may feel put upon as a sexual object and respond with impotence. The theory suggests that the male, facing an aggressive and overassertive female, may psychologically recall his childhood castration anxieties, his consequent fear of the vagina, and thus responds with impotence.

I think it is significant to reiterate at this point that erection, as has been mentioned in Chapter 5, is a complex neurological mechanism and one that functions poorly in an anxious or fearful situation.

PREMATURE EJACULATION. Premature ejaculation is the inability of the male to maintain an erection for a sufficient length of time to satisfy his female partner. There are no strict definitions of the length of time the male must retain an erection prior to ejaculation before one tabs him as a premature ejaculator. The condition is often a problem of the couple, rather than just of the male. The situation is far from hopeless and can be corrected by counseling and suggested therapy, as has been designated in *Human Sexual Inadequacy* by Masters and Johnson. Concentration by both partners is required for correction.

UNACCEPTABLE SEXUAL BEHAVIOR BY ONE PARTNER. There are many modes of sexual behavior. Current thinking defines sexual relations as sexual activity done by two people in private which is not harmful to either partner. If one partner has desires that are unacceptable to the other, the problem may be one of two reasons. First, the partner demanding the specific sexual activity may be unrealistic in his or her demands. Second, it may be that the reluctant partner has unjustified inhibitions, resulting from his or her own previous experience. Therapy requires counseling of both partners in helping the one interpreted as pathological.

Unfortunately, it is the partner who finds the behavior of the other partner unacceptable who more often comes to the physician. The physician, more often than not, then tends to cast an accusing finger at the partner who is not represented in his office. The situation can frequently be helped by counseling. In some cases the idiosyncracy of the offending partner requires adjustment. Much depends on the total interpersonal relations of the couple, and if these are healthy, then one or the other of the partners can well be expected to acquiesce to the requirements of the other.

Frequently, there is a difference in sexual drives between two partners. Often this difference can be adjusted by discussion with the involved couple. However, sexual frequency may be used by one partner as a weapon against the other. Excessive demands or withholding sexual favors may be used as punishment. When frequency is used as a weapon, often deep underlying psychosexual pathology exists, which may or may not be amenable to treatment.

DYSPAREUNIA. This is painful or difficult intercourse for the female. Again, as with impotence, the cause may be of organic or psychological origin.

The most frequent organic cause is lack of lubrication in the female. This may be the result of (1) relatively short and unsatisfactory foreplay, which does not allow sufficient time for lubrication, or (2) birth control pills, which can have a drying effect upon the vaginal tissues. Use of lubricating jellies may remedy the situation.

On the psychological side, if intercourse has initially been painful for the female, the mere suggestion of subsequent intercourse may result in renewed fear of pain, a freezing attitude on her part, and tightening of the vaginal musculature. All of these factors may result in having the second, third, and subsequent sexual experiences becoming increasingly painful. The physician should try to break this cycle by suitable counseling.

INFERTILITY. Handling this problem has become highly specialized. Formerly, the physician examined the female to ascertain if she had the necessary organs for childbearing. He then examined the semen of the male, including a sperm count. If these examinations were satisfactory, he presumed that there was nothing wrong and with continued efforts fertilization would eventually be accomplished.

With the advent of drugs that can cause a woman to ovulate at a specific time and with the development of surgical instruments that permit viewing of the female internal sexual organs, specifically the tubes and ovaries, the specialty has become a great deal more sophisticated.

However, it seems fair to say at present that infertility should not be considered a problem until a couple has had intercourse for a year on some regular basis without the occurrence of conception.

INABILITY TO ACHIEVE HARMONY IN MARRIAGE. Here we are

concerned with factors leading to discord. Among these factors we should list differences in temperament, which lead to constant quarreling and fighting; differences in religious backgrounds; personalities derived from strict versus permissive upbringing; and differing concepts on the rearing of children. These factors usually are antecedents to divorce or marital infidelity. They are extremely important. It should be pointed out to both members of the partnership that such factors can lead to nothing but ill. In our highly complex social order, one cannot tolerate homelife that is constantly erupting. Such activity is harmful in the extreme to the children.

The physician may offer constructive guidelines. Again, the marriage counselor and the clergy are frequently highly beneficial.

OTHER COMMON PROBLEMS. For other common problems, see the appropriate chapters: Abortion, Chapter 19; Sterilization, Chapter 18; Unwanted Pregnancy, Chapter 19; Guidance on the Instruction of Offspring, Chapter 12.

References

BERENSTAIN, S., AND J. BERENSTAIN. 1970. *How to Teach Your Child About Sex.* New York: McCall.

COMFORT, ALEX (ed.). 1972. *The Joy of Sex.* New York: Crown.

GOLDSTEIN, M., AND E. J. HAEBERLE. 1971. *The Sex Book.* New York: Herder & Herder.

HARDY, KENNETH R. 1964. "An Appetitional Theory of Sexual Motivation," *Psychologic Review,* 71: 1. Reproduced in *Human Sexual Behavior,* ed. by Bernhardt Lieberman. New York: Wiley, 1971.

"J." 1969. *The Sensuous Woman.* New York: Dell.

"K," MR. AND MRS. 1969. *The Couple.* New York: Berkeley.

KIRKENDALL, L., AND R. N. WHITEHURST. 1971. *The New Sexual Revolution.* New York: Donald W. Brown.

"M." 1971. *The Sensuous Man.* New York: Dell.

MARMOR, JUDD. 1969. "The Non-sexual Uses of Sexuality," *Medical Aspects of Human Sexuality,* 3: 8.

MASTERS, WILLIAM H., AND VIRGINIA E. JOHNSON. 1969. *Human Sexual Inadequacy.* Boston: Little, Brown.

NOBILE, PHILIP. 1972. "What Is the New Impotence, and Who's Got It?" *Esquire,* 78, no. 4, 95.

RUBIN, I., AND L. KIRKENDALL. 1971. *Sex in the Childhood Years.* New York: Association Press.

SIECUS (authored by various members of the Board of Directors). 1970. *Sexuality in Man.* New York: Scribner's.

SIMON, WILLIAM, AND JOHN H. GAGNON. 1967. "The Pedagogy of Sex," *Saturday Review,* 18 Nov.: 74.

12

counseling young people about sexual relations

This topic is unusually significant in that by proper instruction and guidance at the earlier and younger levels of life, one can hope that the younger generation will avoid the difficulties in their sexual and married relations presented in Chapter 11. This presentation represents a discussion. A discussion by itself implies several different points of view. One can no longer intelligently present sexual relations in terms of absolutes. The era of "thou shalt" and "thou shalt not" is ended. In its place such terms as "encounter" and "confrontation" have been employed.

From the young person's point of view this is a difficult subject to meet. It is brought up most frequently during adolescence, for that time is designated by nature as one of maximum sexual drive. In a society that regards the family as the essential social unit, adolescence is also the time of minimal legitimate sexual permissibility.

This paradox inevitably presents the young with perplexing problems of personal morality.

The parent is no less perplexed in this era of sexual freedom. However, it is certainly justifiable for the parent or teacher to impart to the child or adolescent those values which he himself accepts. The parent or teacher should explain in an intelligent and rational way why he believes in those values. If the argument is convincing, the listener will accept the mentor's point of view on an intellectual rather than on an emotional basis. It is important to present all the information frankly and clearly.

The Pros And Cons Of Adolescent Intercourse

Of the cons we should note the possibility of venereal disease, the possibility of pregnancy, the fears and anxieties that arise in the home and school atmosphere following secretive intercourse, feelings of guilt following secretive intercourse, loss of individual self-respect, and the loss of respect for those who have prematurely indulged in sexual intercourse.

Of the pros we may note that intercourse is a means of relieving frustration. It is a means of expressing mutual love, if such exists. It represents positive proof of gender role. It is expedient in that if an extended sexual relation exists, time is saved, which otherwise would be spent in activities such as dating or flirtations.

Nowadays, the young adult is as cognizant of these pros and cons as is the parent or educator. For the parent or educator to ignore this fact only labels him as uninformed in the eyes of the young adult. If the parent or educator once places himself in this position, very little of what he has to say is going to appear pertinent to the individual with whom he is discussing the subject.

However, certain cogent truisms seem to appear again and again in my practice of medicine. At this point I wish to share them with the reader—indeed, as I have shared them with those adolescents to whom I have been asked to give sexual advice. I present them for the reader's consideration, for although adolescents may be fully informed on the preceding pros and cons, the adolescent, at least in my experience, has not given much consideration, if any, to the concepts embodied in these truisms.

Truisms About Sexual Intercourse

PATTERNS OF INTERCOURSE.   In our society at the present time, it seems fair to say that there is more than one reason for intercourse.

1. Intercourse accomplishes reproduction.
2. Intercourse can fulfill a relationship between two people.
3. Intercourse can be a pleasure-seeking activity.

These several experiences certainly can coincide. However, in discussing intercourse, one might logically ask:

1. What type of intercourse is one considering?
2. What kind of intercourse is someone seeking from you?
3. What kind of intercourse is one trying to avoid?

Frequently, we glibly talk about sexual intercourse without first defining our terms. As Chapter 3 pointed out, semantics is important. Because these types of intercourse exist, it is therefore essential that the parent or teacher on the one hand and the adolescent on the other know just which type of intercourse is being discussed.

THE IMPRINT ON EXPERIENCE AND PERSONALITY.   Although intercourse is genital in nature, one should emphasize that the entire prior experience and personality of each individual are involved. In particular, during the adolescent years, it is impossible for two people to have intercourse without having it affect both participants in one way or another. To be sure, in some cases this effect may be minor, but in all cases a definite experience has been imprinted on the brain cells and on the pattern of personality of the individual's makeup. It becomes in a sense the basis of a habit pattern that may be extremely difficult to break at a later date. It is not surprising, therefore, that some males who are oriented to sexual intercourse only in terms of illegalities, secretiveness, haste, and anxiety, may find themselves unable to perform sexual intercourse satisfactorily in the confines of the marriage bed.

UNIVERSALITY OF INTERCOURSE.   The adolescent should be advised against the possibility of trying to make sexual intercourse his or her specialty. Sexual activity is really everyone's forte in much the same way as eating. In searching for his own identity, more often than not at the college age, the adolescent may elect to choose sexual activity as one area in which he or she excels. The adolescent assumes the posture of a sexual athlete or perpetual flirt. This concept may prove disastrous because of its impact on the later development of the individual. Let me bring this point home by a bit of mathematics.

The present population of the United States is approximately 200 million. Let us assume that half this number are at an age for sexual activity. Therefore, there are 100 million people who are sexually active. Since it takes two individuals for sexual intercourse, there are 50 million pairs who have intercourse. If the average couple has coitus 2.5 times per week, then there are 125 million sexual experiences per week or approximately 18 million sexual experiences per day. It has been stated that the average length of time from the beginning of foreplay to mutual orgasm takes 20 minutes. One can therefore conclude that there are 266,666 sexual acts occurring simultaneously in the United States. Being one of that number hardly makes one unique.

THE COMMONNESS OF SEXUAL EXPERIENCE.   The adolescent, and sometimes the older individual, has the feeling that what he or she is doing sexually is unique. This is particularly true when fear and anxiety exist. One can reiterate that there are only a certain number of sexual activities that one can do, only a certain number of sexual activities one can learn. If one is then truthful and honest with oneself, he or she will realize that vast numbers of people have shared similar tastes, similar behavior patterns, and similar problems in the past.

EVALUATION OF EARLY COITION.   I think it fair to say that early coition cannot be treated in a casual way. When faced with the problems of sexual disharmony, psychiatrists frequently relate the pathology to the early sexual experience of the individual. This does not indicate that early coition causes sexual disharmony. It does indicate that coition, when an adolescent is not mature enough to handle it, certainly can have repercussions in the sexual activities at a later time. The child is father of the man. Early habit patterns may well come back to haunt the individual in his adult life.

REPEATED CASUAL SEXUAL RELATIONS.   A similar argument can be made against repeated casual sexual relationships. The individual who figuratively hops from bed to bed, unable to develop a total relationship with another individual and able to communicate and function with another individual only in a sexual way, has a serious problem related to interpersonal relationships. In most cases, when repeated bed-hopping has become a habit, I have found the hopper notoriously unhappy. He is always looking for new worlds to conquer

and receives little satisfaction from the worlds he has already con-
quered. The psychiatrists refer to this as a Don Juan complex. It is a
pattern the adolescent might well avoid. In this day and age, certainly
the prospects of venereal disease would be enhanced by such casual
sexual involvement.

Counseling Young People About Sexual Intercourse

Having surveyed the usual topics that arise during a discussion
about sexual relations, how should one counsel the adolescent about
undertaking intercourse? Certainly there should be no rigid procedure.
Adolescents, like adults, present too many varied personalities.

There are those counselors and parents who believe young people
should simply be presented with the basic facts about human sexuality and then permitted to make their own decision about undertaking intercourse. I, too, am well aware that adolescents ultimately
will make their own decision on the issue, but I would hope this need
not be exclusively on a trial and error basis. Disastrous results, often
of lifetime duration, occur all too often from erroneous decisions.
Rather, I believe, one should appraise the relative maturity of each
adolescent and proceed accordingly with appropriate directive counsel.
I don't think the counselor or parent need fear expressing his own
feelings in an intelligent and nonpunitive fashion.

Professionally I have found counseling on the basis of age groups
to be quite successful. I realize full well that there may be shortcomings, as a 16 year old may be more mature than a 20 year old. I
therefore present the following method for consideration.

If the individual is younger than 16, I deem it advisable to stress
the emotional immaturity of such an age to undertake the complicated
handling of sexual intercourse. Sixteen is an arbitrary figure, for some
individuals are immature at a later age and some mature at an earlier
one. The individual may argue the point with you, but one can
justify one's position by pointing out other examples of restrictions
placed on the age group, such as driving, drinking, and voting.

If one or both individuals are 16 to 18 years old, my own point of
view is that these years are hardly the time for youngsters to initiate
sexual intercourse. The act and the decisions involved therein require
a great deal of emotional expenditure, time, and energy. These are
formative years for the young male or female. They should be advised
that the foundation for much broader aspects of life should be laid

during this period. Among these aspects are the types of people with whom they expect to establish friendships, the setting of standards that they wish to see in those with whom they develop friendships, and a decision as to the possibility of life's major undertaking and employment. I wish to stress that during these formative years it is highly preferable to consider the total growth and development of the individual among his or her peers rather than to focus on the one-to-one relationship involved in sexual intercourse.

If the individual is older than 18 years, one cannot make any specific recommendation. Young people in this group differ widely. Many are financially self-supporting and no longer dependent on parental funds for support and education. I therefore contend that whether sexual intercourse should be undertaken during this period largely depends on the maturity of the individual. Much depends on the individual's self-reliance and self-esteem. If he or she feels sufficiently mature, sexual intercourse would certainly be acceptable. However, I would advise the young person to go one step further in his thinking than a simple yes or no about intercourse. I would suggest he ask himself, "Why am I having or not having sexual relations, and why is he or she having or not having sexual relations with me?" I would then ask him to consider his answer in light of the previous discussion on motivation (see the motivational sections in Chapter 11).

Having presented the subject matter, the adviser at this point is perfectly justified in stating whatever he happens to believe in his own mind the sexual activity of his offspring or student should be. I think the adviser has the right to say, "I think you should not have intercourse now," and then uphold his point of view in an intelligent fashion. Or, if on the other hand the adviser is more permissive, he might say he has no feelings about the issue or that he approves of sexual intercourse for the offspring or student. If the latter stand is taken, certainly contraception should enter the discussion.

If the subject of sexual relations is presented in this manner, the adolescent knows where he himself stands, and he knows where the parent or counselor stands. Moreover, by now the adolescent should be aware that what he does, how he behaves, and what action he takes will definitely influence his later existence. The cards are on the table. Should problems arise in the future, the avenue for additional discussion remains open. That is about as much as the parent or counselor can do, for when the door closes behind the adolescent as he goes out on his next date, he or she is on his own.

13

gender roles

Each of us is born into a certain set of rules and standards based upon his or her biological sex. Historically, these gender roles have been more or less clearly defined. Masculinity implies one standard of behavior and femininity another.

Recently the subject of gender role has again undergone careful scrutiny. Theoretical arguments have arisen as to which of these rules and standards are basically biological and which are cultural (cf. Chapter 21, An Anthropological Approach to Sexuality).

Practically, these gender role questions—Who am I? What am I? and Where am I going?—are being asked repeatedly in my medical practice, as well as in the classroom. There is overt confusion regarding acceptance of the traditional roles played. Individuals have become disenchanted with these traditional roles, but they are not yet comfortable in their new, but undefined, roles.

Needless to say, the ease that an individual feels toward his or her own gender role reflects in his or her sexual performance.

Categorically there are no concrete answers at this time to the preceding questions. What I have attempted to do in this chapter is to draw from the current literature—which on this topic of gender roles is quite hodgepodge and very opinionated—certain generalities and organize them in some meaningful fashion.

New Truisms

There exist certain obvious physical differences between male and female that are well defined and hardly worth repeating. Differences such as body strength, hair distribution, and body build are not new observations. However, certain new truisms that have appeared in the recent literature are worthy of recognition at this time.

First, there is no question that from the standpoint of orgasmic experiences, a single female can consistently outperform a single male. The male requires a period of resolution following orgasm. With repeated sequential orgasmic experience, this period of resolution increases dramatically in length. The female, on the other hand, may have many repetitive orgasmic experiences and can continue in this fashion until such time as she becomes physically exhausted.

If one concedes that clues about human behavior can be derived from behavior of his anthropoid relatives, then a quotation from the work of psychiatrist Mary Jane Sherfey regarding female apes offers a spirited view.

Having no cultural restrictions, these primate females will perform coitus from twenty to fifty times a day during the peak week of estrus, usually with several series of copulations in rapid succession. If necessary, they will flirt, solicit, present, and stimulate the male in order to obtain successive coitions. They will 'consort' with one male for several days until he is exhausted, then take up with another. They will emerge from periods of heat totally exhausted, often with wounds from spent males who have repulsed them. I suggest that something akin to this behavior could be paralleled by the human female if her civilization allowed it.

Second, the female is equipped with a unique area, totally and singly devoted to sexual pleasure, namely the clitoris; whereas the male penis serves several functions, only one of which is sexual gratification. I am not in a position to analyze the psychological effects of these anatomical and physiological differences, other than to point out that the female can compartmentalize her sexuality, at least in terms of sexual outlet and orgasmic experience.

Third, the adolescent female seems to be less sexually lustful than is the male of similar age. She is more the master of sexual self-control. Although she may use sex in straightforward as well as devious ways, it does not appear that she possesses the sexual compulsiveness of the adolescent male. I emphasize this last point, for the male parent or teacher so often erroneously assumes that the sex drive of his female children or students is identical to his, and the female mentor has the same erroneous assumption regarding her male charges. It is certainly a revelation to many that this difference exists during the adolescent stages.

For the most part, two individuals do not necessarily become amorous simultaneously. The situation is remedied by having the aggressor try to kindle a similar spark in the partner. It is impossible at the moment to suggest which of the two human sexes should be the biological initiator.

Female Gender Role

Certainly nothing has characterized and encouraged the changing female role so much as has the movement referred to as the Women's Liberation Movement. On the surface, this movement has as its objective those rights to which women would appear to be fairly entitled: equal pay for equal work, day nurseries for the children of working mothers, free abortion on demand, and equal treatment under the law, particularly in matters of finance and inheritance. These problems can be solved by changes in our legal framework, such as the proposed Equal Rights Amendment and the recent decision of the U.S. Supreme Court on abortion.

Less frequently mentioned, and yet possibly more significant when one attempts to analyze the basic premises of this women's liberation movement, is that there are two new thoughts created yet left unanswered. Should women's liberation succeed in its attempt to equalize the sexes, what is going to happen to the nuclear family as we know it? Should women's liberation reach its ultimate purposes, exactly what will happen to the male-female relationship as it now exists?

In response to the first question, it is fair to say that the women's liberation movement has raised considerable consternation in regard to marriage as we know it. The greatest concern to women's liberation is that through the institution of marriage a woman seems to lose her identity. Not only does she give up her name, but she gives up her personality and goals for those of her mate. Moreover, she emotionally has appropriated her feelings and achievements to the accomplishments of her mate.

A repudiation of this image is evident. Many women are returning to school and others are joining the work force. Interestingly enough, some women who don't need jobs from a financial standpoint are going back to work seemingly for the purpose of reidentifying themselves with a useful project. Younger women currently in school are pursuing their educations further, and the number of women in medical, law, and other professional schools is increasing markedly.

The followers of women's liberation are asking for a fair share of the marriage relationship and the right to express their views and have them accepted.

There is an interesting feeling as you read literature regarding women's liberation, that although these women are asking for equality, in truth many are demanding superiority. That is, as a woman becomes liberated, she becomes superior to a man, who therefore becomes inferior. Some women attack the male chauvinist pig, the MCP, unmercifully. One wonders whether there will be a men's liberation movement to try to set things again on an even keel. In addition, those women who are tremendously antimale in attitude, suggest developing a society free of all male influence, which in this day and age becomes as unrealistic as trying to create a society free of all female influence. If one were to follow this rationale to its natural conclusion, the only sexual outlets left for the female would be lesbianism, masturbation, or total chastity.

Corollary views are presented in Chapter 22, Sex and the Family. The reader is also referred to the article "Toward the New Chastity," by Midge Decter.

As to the latter question of what will happen to the male-female relationship, particularly as related to sex, I have scoured the literature, and the best answer I can find is one written by Nora Ephron in the

July 1972 issue of *Esquire.* After defining her true commitment to the Women's Liberation Movement, Miss Ephorn agrees that man has a right to ask this particular question. Her answer is a succinct one: "Okay, the answer is, nobody knows what happens to sex after liberation. It's a big mystery. And now that I have gotten that out of the way, I can go on . . ." I must say that I share her straightforwardness. No one can predict what is going to happen in this changing world, and to attempt to do so is folly. I think one can only remain an interested observer.

However, it is interesting to note that the male and female frequently interpret the sexual changes associated with women's liberation in totally different lights. The male world suggests that through the sexual revolution women have gained sexual freedom. This sexual freedom includes the right to enjoy sex, a right that has more or less been denied women through the centuries, and also the right to female orgasm. Males who previously had more or less reserved sexuality for satisfying their own needs have now begun spending a great deal of their sexual time in efforts toward satisfying their mate. In previous generations, it was deemed masculine to make a large number of conquests. Certainly many males still believe this is a masculine trait. Yet others now feel that it is equally, or even more important to satisfy one's partner completely.

To the liberated female this concept of sexual revolution becomes totally unacceptable. She will admit that women have now at least been allowed the pleasures of sexuality, but the thought is immediately added that this new orgasmic experience only further enslaves the female to the male. Her thinking proceeds along this line: Freud described both a vaginal and a clitoral orgasm. He assigned vaginal orgasm as the higher form of orgasm and the type of orgasm to be sought. Vaginal orgasm requires a man's presence in the sexual act and in that sense further enslaves the female. Freud downgraded clitoral orgasm as less desirable, and although Masters and Johnson have refuted this concept and proven conclusively that orgasm is orgasm, be it clitoral or vaginal, this differentiation in orgasmic patterns is still well established in the minds of men and women.

This pattern of "further enslavement" is also complicated by the fact that it places the liberated woman in a rather ambiguous position when a male asks her for sexual favors. Since she now openly enjoys sexuality, it gives her little, if any, reason to say no to participating in a sexual act. To say no is now equated with denying that she enjoys sex, and to deny that is in a sense to admit that there is something wrong with her. She is trapped by her own freedom practically as well as theoretically.

Male Gender Role

As recently as ten years ago, it would have been easy to list those characteristics assigned to the human male as virtuous simply because he was male. Such terms as courage, guts, aggression, forceful, and manly were self-explanatory. Today, however, questions arise as to whether these characteristics are truly inborn in the male, or only fashioned by our society. Even more devastating is the question as to which of these traits are desirable, and which may prove to be destructive to the individual or society. Such terms now are developing as awareness, sensitive, warm, and loving, and the male society is having some difficulty dealing with them. If you identified a robust male ten years ago as being a beautiful person, you might well have suffered bodily harm.

This uncertainty about the role and responsibility of the male truthfully permeates all stages of male development. The male child is being raised, for the most part, in a female society. That is, almost all his training through the first ten years of his life is female oriented. His mother has primary responsibility, and his teachers for the most part are female. Thus a standard is being set for a male child by females, many of whom are now uncertain of their own gender role. It will be interesting to see how, for example, males fare who are raised by aggressive advocates of female liberation.

The adolescent male is bombarded with questions regarding his system of values. The Vietnam War annihilated the responsibility of many adolescent males for serving in the Armed Forces. It made them contemplate whether the war was good or bad and obliged them to decide exactly where such attributes as national loyalty and courage fit into their realm of thinking. Questions have also been raised as to whether the material affluence and influence, which their parents held in such high esteem, are truthfully worthwhile standards for life's activities. In like manner, for the first time, homosexuality raises a choice for the adolescent male in that it has become, if not completely

acceptable socially, at least socially recognizable. Whereas homosexuality in the past could have been dismissed as unimportant, it
now becomes a matter of choice and judgment.

The mature adult male is bombarded by woman's changing attitude and is often frequently less certain of his own position. Although primarly this uncertainty affects the male-female relationship,
it can be even more unsettling because the male historically has gained
a great deal of his ego-strength in many instances from that relationship. If ego-strength no longer comes from the male-female relationship,
it will have to come from a new and as yet unrecognized source.

References

DECTER, MIDGE. 1972. "Toward the New Chastity," *Atlantic Monthly*,
230, no. 2: 42.

EPHRON, NORA. 1972. Editorial, in *Esquire*, 78: 42.

RUDY, ARTHUR J., AND ROBERT PELLAR. 1972. "Men's Liberation," *Medical
Aspects of Human Sexuality*, 6: 84.

SHERFEY, MARY JANE. 1972. *The Nature and Evaluation of Female
Sexuality*. New York: Random House.

14

masturbation

Historical Background.   From Biblical times, masturbation has been an activity of concern. In Genesis it is related that Onan had the misfortune of losing his older brother. Custom at that time provided that if a deceased brother had no heir, a living brother should impregnate the widow to preserve family lineage for inheritance and social purposes. Onan was instructed to impregnate his sister-in-law. For reasons unknown to us today, Onan chose not to fulfill this obligation, and at the last moment he withdrew and spilled his seed upon the ground. For this he was struck dead by the Lord. Since then, Biblical scholars have equated onanism with masturbation and inferred that to masturbate was to bring down the wrath of the Lord.

The puritanical stance probably reached its height with an extreme fanaticism against masturbation in the latter part of the 1800's. A tremendous amount of guilt and anxiety was engendered against

*the activity. Since that time, modern science has absolved the mastur-
bator of any major consequences. We certainly no longer accept that
masturbation causes insanity, stunted growth, hair on the palms,
acne, or fear of reprisal from the Divinity. However, a certain degree
of guilt and shame remains unnecessarily associated with the act.*

Definition

Masturbation can be defined as self-stimulation to orgasm. This
definition excludes haphazard handling of the genitalia during childhood, which some writers have equated with masturbation. It also
excludes mutual masturbation, whether homosexual or heterosexual.
It narrows the activity to the act an individual performs in the confines of his own privacy to achieve orgasm. It is by definition a normal
aspect of psychosexual development.

Number Of Masturbators

How many people masturbate? Reports on the number of individuals who masturbate vary. Studies of masturbatory activity, as
previously defined, indicate that 95% of all men masturbate to
orgasm sometime during their lives, and 40 to 70% of all women do
likewise. Discrepancy in figures for women represents discrepancy in
interview techniques. It is probable that in the future an increasing
number of women will masturbate as a result of the change in attitude
brought about by women's liberation and as wider dissemination of
sexual knowledge makes women aware that orgasm by masturbation
can be more readily achieved than was thought possible heretofore.

Frequency Of Masturbation

How often do people masturbate? The number of times per day
varies widely, and the variation is greater among females than among
males.

Among males, there are individuals who never masturbate. There
are individuals who masturbate two or three times in a lifetime.
Kinsey states that some boys and older youths masturbate 2 and 3
times per day, averaging 20 or more times per week over an extended

period of years. Older men masturbate with decreasing frequency. Masturbation has its greatest frequency at 15 years of age, which is 2.5 times the rate for men who are 30 and 4 times the rate of men who are 50. Although there are no recent figures on the rates of masturbation, it is likely that the figures just stated are as accurate today as they were when they were published in 1948.

For women, Kinsey states that the average single woman masturbates once every 2.5 to 3 weeks. The average for married women is once a month. Variations among women, however, are great, some women averaging 14 or more times per week up to 10 to 20 or more times per hour.

Mechanism Of Masturbation

In the male, masturbation is performed predominately by grasping the penis with the hand and stroking up and down in a manner similar to that accomplished by coital activity. Occasionally, extraneous objects, such as stockings or underclothing, are used to grasp the penis. This latter behavior is designated as a fetish.

In the female, the act is most often accomplished by digital manipulation of the clitoris or general handling of the vulvar area. On occasion breast manipulation alone will lead to orgasm. More refined techniques include a vibrator of various types, which is placed either in contact with the genitalia or on the hand which then is placed in contact with the genitalia. Dildoes are also used. There are penis-shaped objects, made of various materials such as hard wax or rubber, which the female manipulates in the vaginal and vulvar area.

As with heterosexual activity, motivation for masturbation falls into two categories: sexual and nonsexual.

Sexual Motivation

RELIEF FROM SEXUAL FRUSTRATION. The adolescent male probably most commonly practices masturbation. He is rather strictly instructed to avoid heterosexual activity, yet he is faced with substantial internal hormonal change. He experiences frequent erection, fantasizes freely on the opposite sex, and has nocturnal emissions. Masturbation becomes a handy way of relieving these frustrations.

In adult life as well, when heterosexual intercourse is not available for one reason or another, masturbation becomes a compelling activity for relieving sexual frustration.

MASTURBATION FOR PLEASURE.   There should be no question in anyone's mind that masturbation can be a pleasurable experience. When practiced for this reason, it cannot be condemned, and for the most part I think it is well condoned. Some physicians and scientists are now pointing out that masturbation is a valuable means of learning to accept one's own body and how it responds to sexual stimulation.

MASTURBATION AS A FANTASY RESPONSE.   The implication here is that the male or female fantasizes sexual relations when such are neither available nor permissible. Masturbation as a fantasy then serves as a healthy outlet for pent-up emotions.

Nonsexual Motivation

Several situations can be considered as nonsexual, and therefore perhaps unhealthy, motivation for masturbation.

MASTURBATION AS REBELLION.   If masturbation is undertaken as an overt act of rebellion, most frequently against parental or other authority, it is unwise. The trouble in tying a sexual act with a nonsexual motivation lies with the effect it may have on the later sexual life of the individual. If the individual turns to sexual relations only at times of rebelliousness, he certainly is not likely to be an ideal lover.

MASTURBATION AS AGGRESSION.   The second nonsexual motivation, quite similar to the first, is to use masturbation to show aggression. We have here the individual who when thwarted in his everyday activities turns to masturbation as a means of reestablishing his self-assurance. Again, the possibility is very real that an undesirable pattern of behavior will be established, which will be detrimental in his later sexual life.

MASTURBATION AS A WITHDRAWAL MECHANISM.   A nonsexual motivation exists for the individual who masturbates within the confines of his own water closet as a result of removing himself from society and group activity. Shy or overly sensitive individuals risk potential hurt in group environment. This is particularly true of adolescent years, during which a great deal of cruelty can be encountered. Rather than suffer such hurt, the individual who withdraws and masturbates as a result of so doing has an emotional problem and probably a rather serious one.

MASTURBATION AS AN EXCESS. No one has clearly defined what excess masturbation is. It would seem to me that excess would be that degree of masturbation which would interfere with the everyday life style of the individual; that is, he would have to alter his plans and activities to compensate for masturbatory activity. The individual who feels compelled to leave the classroom or business meeting (if that situation provokes anxiety) to visit the bathroom and masturbate is in this category.

Summary

Masturbation remains a delicate subject for some to discuss. We are still perplexed as to how children should be educated about it. The growing child should be informed of the universality of the activity and that there is nothing vile or sinful about it. Modern science has dispelled the many deleterious concepts formerly associated with it. With the passage of time one can expect that even the delicacy of discussing the topic will disappear.

15

homosexuality

The topic of homosexuality has received wide attention and discussion in current literature. Not too many years ago the subject was almost taboo in polite society, the subject of derision among comedians, and infrequently encountered in scientific literature. However, a more realistic approach has recently been undertaken to try to understand the magnitude of homosexuality, its cause, and the motivations for it as a preferential sexual practice.

Before attempting to evaluate the milieu of homosexuality, the reader must appreciate that homosexual relationships are not significantly different from heterosexual relationships. Some are casual, fleeting; others are sincere and enduring. It is significant to point out that there is no such thing as a homosexual act. Sexual activities of the homosexual can be and are performed by many heterosexuals; it is only that with the former the sexes are the same, and with the latter the sexes are different.

The usual picture that one conjures in one's mind when the subject of male homosexuality is raised is that of an effeminate man—effeminate in voice, speech, mannerisms, and appearance. This individual is pictured as constantly looking for other homosexuals, hoping they will identify themselves in some way, and then engaging them in a homosexual encounter. One fancies such an individual as driven in a seemingly uncontrolled and compulsive fashion, at times even exhibiting inappropriate behavior, offensive to the population in general. In truth, this pattern of behavior is not dissimilar in many respects from some of the casual heterosexual relationships one sees advancing toward culmination in a variety of surroundings in today's society.

It is true that examples of the type of homosexual just described do exist and are not figments of the imagination. However, it is equally true that they constitute but a small minority of the male homosexual community.

At the other end of the spectrum is the homosexual with outward appearances and mannerisms as masculine as any of his heterosexual counterparts. Only recently has he begun openly to announce his sexual preference. This individual may be a professional man, community leader, business executive, or just an ordinary male citizen who for the most part prefers male sexual companionship. He may be married to a woman and have children. His homosexual relationship may be casual or enduring, quite similar to the relationships of heterosexuals. These individuals often lead a double life in that they maintain an outward heterosexual mode of life but devote some of their time, if not indeed a great deal of their time, to the homosexual subculture.

The majority of homosexuals fall between these two stereotyped individuals.

Study of the female homosexual, the lesbian, is somewhat more difficult in that there is little known about the number of such relationships and less written of lesbian practices than of male homosexual practices. There are certain aspects, however, of a lesbian relationship that do seem clear. First, the relationship is more often enduring than casual. The roles assigned within the lesbian relationship are often more clearly defined, one individual taking the more active, the other the more passive, role. This is not totally unexpected in a culture that has emphasized female passivity sexually and fosters the female in a love relationship, as opposed to the male, in whom *promiscuity and aggression have been encouraged. Second, lesbians are more discreet, and in that way better accepted in our society. Two women living together, for example, are not usually singled out as being offensive to the community, whereas two men living together might be considered an "odd couple."*

Definition

In defining homosexuality I prefer to differentiate between the adolescent type and the adult type. Overt adolescent homosexuality or homosexual tendencies seem to be a rather natural part of adolescent psychosexual development. Whether an adolescent engages in homosexual acts is not at issue, as during this phase of development an adolescent may find sexual activity with those of the opposite sex to be difficult and unwieldy, and an adolescent may feel more comfortable in the company of similar-sexed individuals. As the time between the onset of puberty and the undertaking of heterosexual exploration and activity has been and is being reduced, there may be less psychological need for homosexual thoughts. This adolescent homosexuality may or may not lead to adult homosexuality; obviously, for the most part it does not. When homosexuals are queried as to the time they first realize they are homosexual, the usual response is that of late teens or early twenties. Rarely is the discovery made during young adolescence.

An adult homosexual is an individual who is sexually motivated by preference to members of the same sex, such preference usually to involve overt homosexual relations, but not necessarily. A person can be homosexual in his erotic motivations, yet be inhibited about actually having homosexual relations.

Situational homosexuality results from an artificial environment but should be mentioned for the sake of completeness. Here members of the same sex are chosen as sexual objects because of their availability in the absence of members of the opposite sex. Environments such as jails, military installations, and ships constitute situations wherein this type of homosexuality may prevail. Studies indicate that in most cases the situational homosexual returns to heterosexual practices when the restricting environment is reversed.

Sexual Methods

In the male homosexual, sexual satisfaction is usually obtained by oral-genital contact (blowing), anal-genital contact (buggery in British terminology; sodomy or pederasty in American terminology), or mutual masturbation. Of these, the oral-genital act seems to be most favored and commonly used. I again stress that all of these activities can be and actually are performed by heterosexuals and are not confined to homosexuals.

The female homosexual receives her sexual satisfaction in somewhat similar ways, either through oral-genital contact, mutual masturbation, frottage or rubbing the pudenda of one individual against the pudenda of another (described as rubbing swords together), or by the use of dildoes (penile substitutes). The last method is probably portrayed more in pornography and actually less used than the others.

Incidence

Although the actual measurable frequency of homosexuality is not easily determined, there is no question that there are more homosexuals than we previously supposed, and that the number is increasing. This increase is due to several factors. First, the subculture of homosexuality has begun to surface with the advent of various gay movements, so that people are willing to admit their homosexual preferences. Second, both social and legal sanctions against homosexuality have been decreasing, so that those individuals who had been latent homosexuals, that is, homosexuals with desires but who did not engage in active homosexuality, are now asserting their homosexual preference. Third, it has been shown that with urbanization and concentration of population, the practice of homosexuality increases.

The third factor needs additional comment. Both the male and female roles are less easily defined in concentrated urban populations, and individuals may become more confused as to their sexual roles. If one accepts the thesis that clues to human behavior can be found in experimentation with animals, then investigation of crowded rat populations is revealing. When rats are crowded into small areas, the incidence of homosexual behavior increases rather dramatically. Decreased fertility results, and behavior may become psychotic, accompanied by hostility and territorial fights. However, the percentage of human homosexuals in urban populations may be somewhat higher than for the general population, for homosexual males in particular tend to establish themselves in urban communities to minimize detection and maximize contacts.

For actual figures, the statement most frequently quoted is by Kinsey. His statistics indicate that 37% of all American white males have had at least one homosexual experience leading to orgasm. This percentage includes the exploratory homosexuality of adolescents, all of whom I do not believe should rightly be designated as homosexual. Other authorities estimate that between 2 and 10% of American males are exclusively, or primarily, homosexual. The 2% figure is perhaps the most generally accepted by contemporary authors on the subject.

The number of lesbians in the American population is even more of a guess. Further sexual research will be necessary before we truthfully know the magnitude of the lesbian population.

Etiology

THEORY OF BIOLOGICAL ORIGIN.   There are two generally held theories on the etiology of homosexuality. The first advances a biological basis for the preference and suggests that a child is either born with homosexual tendencies or attains them because of some hormonal imbalance. Extensive genetic studies have failed to reveal any type of chromosomal derangement in the homosexual, and to most observers this genetic basis has little appeal. Recently, it has been suggested that abnormal testosterone levels can be found in homosexuals, but this work has not been substantiated and is still in a state of flux.

A team at the Reproductive Biology Research Foundation in St. Louis under the aegis of R. C. Kolodny analyzed plasma testosterone and semen in 30 young homosexual men. The scientists found that 15 totally or almost totally homosexual subjects had male hormone levels sharply lower than the levels determined for 50 heterosexual controls and the remaining homosexuals with some heterosexual leanings. Sperm scores were also much lower among the exclusively homosexual males. To locate the endocrine abnormality, the St. Louis scientists took a new set of measurements, analyzing plasma luteinizing hormone levels and follicle-stimulating hormone concentrations in the same 80 men. The results were inconclusive. Some homosexuals exhibited primary testicular dysfunction, some showed a central disturbance in the pituitary gland, and others seemed to have a hypothalamic defect.

THEORY OF PSYCHOLOGICAL ORIGIN.   Psychological or emotional interpretation of the etiologies of homosexuality originated before Freud and have undergone a rather steady metamorphosis to the present day.

Classic Freudian psychiatry defines the origin of homosexuality as the failure of the normal resolution of the Oedipus complex. In this situation the boy does not identify himself with the father as a sexual male, but rather identifies himself with the mother as a sexual female. The theory implies that the child fears castration by the father for the child's libidinous interest in the mother. The male child then renounces this interest and at the same time renounces the aggressive male role in favor of the more passive female role. He thus identifies himself with the mother and becomes homosexual in his attitude. This altered activity occurs early in the child's life, probably during the ages of 3 or 4. Freud classically hinges all these causative events on the dictatorial father as he knew him in the Victorian period.

A later modification of this theory places responsibility for the child's homosexual activity on both the mother and the father. The homosexuality appears to be a result of the interpersonal relationship of the parents, as well as their relationship with the child. This situation is best described by Bieber.

. . . In comparing 106 male homosexuals in psychoanalytic treatment with 100 heterosexuals in treatment, certain clusters and themes of parental attitudes and behavior were found to be typically characteristic of the homosexual case histories. Significant statistical differences were found between the homosexual and heterosexual patients, particularly in items tapping parental interaction and influence.

The modal type of mother of the homosexual was overly close, overly intimate, possessive, and dominating; she was overprotective as well as de-masculinizing. She spent a great deal of time with her son and generally favored him from childhood on over other siblings. She demanded undue attention and solicitude from this boy. She encouraged an alliance against the father and frequently openly preferred son to husband. Puritanical and sexually frigid, she interfered with her son's heterosexual interests in childhood and adolescence, yet she herself tended to be seductive with him. Overly concerned about illness and physical injury, she babied him and hindered his participation in normal activities and the rough and tumble of boyhood, presumably out of concern for his welfare. In a few cases, the mother was seemingly detached, rejecting, and overtly hostile, but the majority had formed a possessive, controlling, inappropriately intimate relationship with the son. There were instances where mother and son occupied the same bed far into the boy's adolescence or where the mother exhibitionistically exposed her nudity.

Salient attitudes to such a mother included submissiveness, overeagerness to please her, and a fear of displeasing or hurting her. These sons usually felt admired and accepted by the mother; in turn, they admired and respected her. Consciously, few homosexuals hated or feared their mother; they turned to her for protection and sided with her in family quarrels.

The father was usually detached, unaffectionate, and hostile to this son, whom he minimized and humiliated and with whom, in most cases, he spent very little time. Rarely his father's favorite, usually his least favored child and scapegoat, in the large majority of cases the homosexual hated and feared his father and lacked respect or admiration for him.

Thus, the parental constellation most likely to produce a homosexual or a heterosexual with severe homosexual problems was a detached, hostile father and a close-binding, overly intimate, seductive mother who dominated and minimized her husband.

OTHER VIEWS. Some decry the need for any discussion related to the etiology of homosexuality. According to Dr. Ralph Blair, Director of New York's Homosexual Community Counseling Center (HCCC), the whole question of etiology is irrelevant. In Joan Solomon's article, "A Long Gay's Journey into Light," Dr. Blair is quoted as stating, "It's a nonproductive issue at this stage. It's also nonproductive if you're talking about heterosexuality. The only reason that no one questions heterosexual development is that heterosexuality is the assumed routine expectation. That's the way the world is, people think." He points out that in various parts of the world at various times throughout history "you find that homosexual behavior in animals and human beings is much more frequent and natural than a lot of people have recognized."

The question may be more important than the answer. As psychiatrist Martin Hoffman of the Mount Zion Hospital and Medical Center in San Francisco frames it, "Why does a person become sexually excited when confronted with a particular kind of stimulus? If the question is asked in this way, it can be seen that heterosexuality is just as much of a problem as homosexuality, in the scientific if not in the social sense." And it would require an answer we don't have, he says, because people are so diverse, their sexual orientations are so complicated, and their sexual object-choice often quite fluid well into adult life.

General Discussion

Intellectually, we have seen in as short a period as the last ten years attitudes toward homosexuality run the gamut from perversion to deviation to variation to personal preference to normal behavior.

Most recently, the avant-garde sociologists and psychiatrists state that homosexuality is not an illness. They contend that homosexuality is not a malady but represents normal behavior on the part of some of our citizenry. I think it appropriate to quote Judd Marmor on this point. In his article "A Moral Dilemma," he states, "The real issue behind the question whether or not homosexuality is a mental illness is neither a medical nor a somatic one, but a moral one. Both exclusive homosexuality and exclusive heterosexuality are uniquely human patterns. There is no more justification for labeling the former as a mental illness than there would be for labeling the latter as such."

In the remainder of that review, Dr. Marmor makes a comparison of homosexuality and left-handedness. He states that both of these are variants from the general population, and that in each case the afflicted individual has some difficulty adapting himself in our current social order. As we have found, it is unwise to attempt to change the handedness of an individual, so Dr. Marmor suggests it is not appropriate to change, or attempt to change, the sexual preference of an individual.

He emphasizes, in fact, that many vertebrates, including infrahuman primates, display patterns of homosexual behavior from time to time, even though heterosexual partners are usually preferred. Although such behavior tends to be more frequent in the absence of heterosexual partners, homosexuality is also displayed even when heterosexual opportunities exist (see also Chapter 21, An Anthropological Approach to Sexuality). The fact is, moreover, that both exclusively homosexual and exclusively heterosexual behavior are unique to humans, who alone in the animal kingdom have set up absolute, psychological barriers of anxiety and guilt toward ambisexual behavior.

The classic study refuting the disease hypothesis was published in 1957 by the U.C.L.A. psychologist Evelyn Hooker. She administered a battery of psychological tests to 30 nonpatient homosexuals and 30 matched heterosexual controls. She then submitted the results for analysis to several of her colleagues. The judges found no evidence that the homosexuals were more pathological than the controls, nor were they able to distinguish in any way between the two groups. Dr. Hooker concluded that there is no inherent connection between homosexual orientation and clinical symptoms of mental illness. She affirms, "Homosexuality as a clinical entity does not exist. Its forms are as varied as those of heterosexuality. Homosexuality may be a deviation in sexual pattern which is in the normal range, psychologically."

To be sure, many psychiatrists still advocate that homosexuality is a disease state. In their defense it must be stated that most homosexuals who go to psychiatrists for help are frequently neurotic, maladjusted, or have some basic emotional conflict. Yet, it must also be added that most heterosexuals who seek psychiatric help—and certainly heterosexuality is not pathologic—fall into this category. Bieber very explicitly expresses the classic psychiatric opinion toward homosexuality in the following quotation. "From a theoretical point of view, I conceive of two distinct categories, heterosexual and homosexual. Heterosexuality is part of a normal, bio-social development, while homosexuality is always the result of a disordered sexual development. The two categories are, therefore, mutually exclusive and cannot be placed on the same continuum."

Psychiatrists like Bieber place their emphasis in therapy on attempting to convert the homosexual to a heterosexual role. In this attempt, to be truthful, they have failed miserably. Even the best studies indicate only a 27% success. It has at last become obvious that the homosexual does not necessarily want to become heterosexual. It has even been postulated that most homosexuals would refuse a pill that would convert them to a heterosexual state, were such a pill to exist.

Although one cannot deny the neurosis of some homosexuals, the homosexual outlet somehow or other must offer psychological rewards. There must be something positive in homosexuality, for were there no such rewards, the homosexual would obviously revert to heterosexual practices (cf. the topic Motivation in Chapter 11, Sexual Intercourse). To me, the various rewards, which might seem to be separate, can easily be tied together. On one hand, homosexuals as a group gain strength by figuratively "thumbing their noses at society," and there is little that society can really do about it. The homosexual mockingly states, "I am going to do my thing, and if you don't like it, let me alone. I am right and you, society, are wrong." Although society has historically taken a strong stand against this type of aggressive and antisocial behavior, little has been done to alter it.

Second, on a more individual basis, the homosexual, who feels emotionally uncomfortable in his everyday dealings with males, can gain some element of control by taking these men down sexually. This situation is similar to a heterosexual relationship wherein an inadequate female can derive ego-strength through provoking male sexual conquests, in which the female by this provocation actually keeps control of the relationship. In both instances cited, one notes individuals or groups asserting themselves and, in a sense, gaining the upper hand by controlling males through sexual means. Using opposite gender roles, the female homosexual uses the same psychological pathways.

Facets Of Homosexuality

I am not in a position to moderate all the aforementioned opinions regarding the normality or abnormality of homosexuality. The literature is divided, and each author can argue effectively for his own viewpoint. I prefer to list certain facets of homosexuality that I have gleaned from the literature and from my medical experience regarding the homosexual, and then to let the individual reader decide whether this information is sufficient to consider the condition of homosexuality as a pathological one. We are truthfully faced with a moral judgment, not necessarily a scientific one.

1. Male gay relationships most often begin as sexual relationships and then may or may not develop into more meaningful relationships if there is actual substance to the encounter. Frequently, when such meaningful relationships develop, one or both partners may attempt to find their sexual fulfillment outside the developed relationship. A similar relationship exists in the heterosexual world but is not so pronounced as that found in homosexuality.

2. The homosexual appears more preoccupied with his homo-

sexuality than a heterosexual appears occupied with his heterosexuality. That is, in all his daily activities the homosexual is
constantly aware that he is a homosexual. We are uncertain
if this is inherent in the homosexual preference or if it is
forced on the homosexual by society, much as preoccupation
with a major minority factor is forced upon other minority
groups. Certainly the society reminds the homosexual of his
homosexuality frequently. It also threatens by exposure to
deprive him of such stalwart features of daily living as his job,
friends, family, and even life.

3. Studies indicate that self-masturbation is still the most common mode of sexual expression of the homosexual. This
phenomenon may or may not be true in heterosexual relationships. I doubt, however, that one can infer from this that
homosexual relationships are not entirely fulfilling. More
likely, homosexual relationships are not as readily available,
for one cannot recruit a homosexual relationship with the
freedom that one can recruit a heterosexual one.

4. I suggest that somehow or other there is a compulsive component, relating at least to male homosexuality, that is not
necessarily found in the heterosexual population. It is difficult
to explain this compulsion and to understand it. Yet the
homosexual who engages in oral-genital contact in a public
restroom, for example, seems driven to behave in this particular manner beyond the simple needs of sexual gratification.
Indeed, the individual who is the fellator is not obviously re-
warded by the experience, and yet it may well be that he is
the one who initiated it. The idea arises that the fulfillment of
the compulsion is reward enough in itself.

5. Seemingly, a higher percentage of homosexuals display emotional impairment and instability than heterosexuals. Again,
whether this is a component of homosexuality or is simply a
by-product of the social stigma associated with homosexuality
is unknown.

References

Bieber, I. 1967. *Homosexuality*, in *A Comprehensive Textbook of Psychiatry*, ed. by Alfred M. Freedman and Harold I. Kaplan. Baltimore:
Williams & Wilkins.

ELLIS, ALBERT, AND ALBERT ABARBANEL (eds.). 1967. *The Encyclopedia of Sexual Behavior.* New York: Hawthorn.

HOFFMAN, MARTIN. 1968. *The Gay World.* New York: Basic Books. Also in paperback, New York: Bantam, 1969.

HOOKER, EVELYN. 1957. "The adjustment of the male overt homosexual," *Journal of Projective Technique,* 21: 18.

KARLEN, ARNO. 1971. *Sexuality and Homosexuality.* New York: W. W. Norton.

MARMOR, JUDD. 1972. "A moral dilemma," *International Journal of Psychiatry,* 10: 114.

MAUGHAM, ROBIN. 1971. *The Wrong People.* New York: McGraw-Hill.

MURPHY, JOHN. 1971. *Homosexual Liberation.* New York: Praeger.

SOLOMON, JOAN. 1972. "Long gays' journey into light." *The Sciences,* 12: 6. New York: New York Academy of Sciences.

part three

Sex and Society

16

the problems of overpopulation

In 1968 Dr. Paul Ehrlich published a dramatic book, The Population Bomb, which summarized in everyday language what ecologists and demographers had been saying before in more scientific terms. His thesis was simple. There simply are too many people, and there are going to be many many more people. Overpopulation, of course, is the result of sexual intercourse without satisfactory control of fertilization.

Modern medical science contributes substantially to this phenomenon of overpopulation by upsetting a delicate balance of nature. As long as the ratio between life and death had remained in some degree of equilibrium through the centuries, the doubling of the population had been held reasonably in check. Doubling time by definition means the time it takes to double a population. In the centuries before Christ, the doubling time of the world's population *was 1000 years. From 1850 to 1930 it was 80 years, and from 1935 to 1970 it has become 35 years. Medical science disrupted this ratio in two ways.*

First, more healthy babies are being born and kept alive than ever before. Improved prenatal and neonatal care has significantly increased the number of live births from an increasing number of pregnancies.

Second, by proper nutrition and by control of diseases through suitable medications, medicine has kept more people alive for longer periods of time. Both aspects of the population equilibrium have been altered in diverse ways:

$$\text{birth rate} \uparrow - \text{death rate} \downarrow = \text{population} \uparrow$$

Obviously the number of people has increased.

The consequences of this increasing population and their effect on the environment are by now obvious to all reasonably intelligent people. The possibilities of war, famine, and disease as corrective elements to this overpopulation are anticipated.

The only other remedy that might prove adequate is that of birth control. Here, interestingly enough, modern medicine is also active in providing some degree of hope. However, neither the science of medicine nor that of psychology has presented a satisfactory way of motivating the people of underdeveloped nations to use birth control methods. We talk about an increasing world population, but we often fail to make the distinction between what is happening in the populations of the so-called developed nations as contrasted with what is happening in the underdeveloped nations of the world. Let us consider the latter first.

Underdeveloped Nations

One should point out at this juncture that the political structure of the world is still basically competition in power and wealth. The population of a nation is truly a political factor, important in the balance of power both in home and foreign affairs. Since there is no true family of nations, each nation still controls its own birth rate. Emissaries of birth control, who have gone to such underdeveloped nations as India, are frustrated by the almost lack of purpose found within the governmental bodies and the people of these nations toward birth control.

A second comment about the underdeveloped countries is that in dealing with them we have to change some of our basic concepts. For example, we speak of optimal density, implying that an appropriate number of people per square mile would maintain some semblance of order in the world. However, when one considers that one American child consumes 25 times as much as one Indian child, the implication might be held that it would be legitimate for the population of India to be 25 times as dense as that of the United States.

A third comment is that most underdeveloped nations would have to change their basic moral concepts to allow effective contraception to come into existence. In nations where it is highly desirable socially to have large families, it is difficult to introduce birth control.

Developed Nations

Now let us consider the developed countries, for there is no question that the birth rate in them is declining. In the United States we have reached the point of zero population growth, a phenomenon not even considered possible by Dr. Ehrlich in 1968. Not only the United States, but countries of eastern and western Europe have similarly shared this marked decline in population. The reasons are several.

IMPROVED CONTRACEPTION. Unquestionably, improved contraception has aided individuals who do not want to have children to remain free of this responsibility. Liberal abortion laws have also contributed to this change in Japan and the countries behind the Iron Curtain and are beginning to have some influence in the United States and western Europe as well.

CHANGE OF MOTIVATION. Of even greater significance, probably, is a change of motivation. People now find it fashionable in the United States to have two children or less. It is socially acceptable to have small families under the concept that fewer people means the good life for those now living and for future generations. In the eastern European countries, late marriages and limited housing have contributed to this change of motivation. Late marriages also affect total population in a subtle way by increasing the time between generations. For example, if a couple has its first child at age 40 and that offspring has its first child at age 40, there is little likelihood all three generations will be alive simultaneously. If, however, one substitutes age 20 for age 40, the likelihood is that the grandparents will live to see and enjoy their grandchildren with more people in the world at a given time than before.

In the everyday practice of medicine, two rather striking phenomena are now evident. First, many couples come to the office saying they would like one child of their own and in the future would like to adopt a child of the opposite sex. They are not discouraged if this second child is from a poverty or minority group. There are many requests for children of those backgrounds.

Second, we find couples who desire no children at all. They feel that they have a solid relationship and that there are enough children without their begetting more. The couples are quite happy without them. Certainly such couples are not numerous, but five years ago they were almost nonexistent.

CHANGE IN FAMILY STRUCTURE.   The dynamics of many families, at least in the western world, demand that its members work to produce income. This income in turn, it is supposed, should bring enhanced happiness and greater social prestige. However, to accomplish this effectively, the family has altered itself from a three-generation to a two-generation structure in which the grandparents, and perhaps aunts and uncles, have been in many cases dismissed from the unit. In a sense, the families have thus done away with their weakest members. The question remains whether in time the unit will, in a manner of speaking, also do away with the children, i.e., the children will be raised outside the single family unit.

CHANGE OF WOMEN'S ROLE.   The role of women has changed precipitously in the last several years. Whether due to women's liberation or the deleterious economic impact of inflation on the family finances, women are taking a greater part in the production of wealth of the developed countries. This leaves the female member of a couple with the choice of being a good mother by devoting all of her energies to a maternal role or of being a good mother because she also has a full-time job. These days we are thus able to hear such a comment as, "Isn't it wonderful how her children are raising themselves and doing such a beautiful job!"

The female has the alternative, of course, of having no children at all.

Epilogue

I present this chapter to emphasize the dichotomy of what is happening in these two separate regions, developed and underdeveloped countries. This dichotomy is usually not explored; rather, emphasis is placed on the total population of the world. In later world struggles and ideological encounters, the nations with the heaviest populations, developed or underdeveloped, may well carry the greater influence.

For more thorough coverage of the potential consequences of this regulated population control, the reader is referred to Alvin Toffler's dramatic volume, *Future Shock*.

References

EHRLICH, PAUL R. 1968. *The Population Bomb*. New York: Ballantine.

MEADOWS, D. H., et al. 1972. *The Limits to Growth*. New York: Universe.

TOFFLER, ALVIN. 1970. *Future Shock*. New York: Random House. Also in paperback, New York: Bantam, 1971.

17

contraception

The creation and distribution of effective contraceptives have altered the sexual practices of the present generation more than any other factors. The ability of both partners to enjoy coitus without fear of pregnancy has created an entirely new attitude toward sexuality, both within and outside of marriage. The eventual outcome of this so-called "sexual revolution" remains to be determined, but its existence cannot be denied by even the most naive among us. It is therefore of paramount importance that the well-informed individual famaliarize himself with the methods of contraception currently available. In particular, he should know their effectiveness and potential drawbacks. He should be able to evaluate new contraceptive methods as they are discovered and have a set of criteria against which he can evaluate their effectiveness. He should be able to choose from the methods available the most effective method for a given set of circumstances.

Finally, he should be cognizant of the impact contraception is likely to have on control of the world population and of the tremendous political and social problems that can occur as a result of the effect of contraceptives on the population explosion (see Chapter 16).

History Of Contraception

To view modern methods of contraception in a satisfactory light, we can benefit from a brief review of the history of contraception. The earliest reference to the subject is in an Egyptian papyrus of 4000 years ago. The method prescribed was the insertion of a plug, similar to our current diaphragm, into the vagina prior to intercourse. The plug was made of seaweed, crocodile droppings, beeswax, or cloth.

Greek philosophers of 2400 years ago advocated the use of contraceptives to stabilize the population of the Greek city-states. Although the Greeks used infanticide as one method of population control, they also used a spermaticide consisting of a mixture of honey, vinegar, and lemon juice. Sperm were rendered ineffective for fertilization by the acidifying action of the vinegar and lemon juice and by the immobilizing action of the honey.

In the Talmud the ancient Jews of 1800 years ago described placing a sponge in the vagina prior to coitus as a method of contraception.

In Roman times a condom made of animal membranes was used, and more often than not worn by the female as a lining of the vagina.

The condom for men became popular in the 1500's. Again, it was made from animal membranes. Following the invention of vulcanized rubber in 1844, which gave rubber greater elasticity and durability, the condom as we know it today was perfected.

Throughout history mention is made of the insertion of cervical plugs, which were similar to intrauterine contraceptive devices (I.U.D.) used today. Often they were made of gold and silver. The first such devices made of synthetic materials were described in the early 1920's.

The pill had its origin in the early 1950's, following research by Doctors John Rock and Gregory Pincus.

Criteria For Perfect Contraceptive

If the perfect contraceptive existed—and to date it does not—five basic factors would have to be met:

1. It would have to be 100% effective.
2. It would have to be so simple that even the most ignorant could use it effectively.
3. It would have to be perfectly safe, i.e., it could not cause any deleterious side effects.
4. It should be immediately and completely reversible in case pregnancy should be desired.
5. It should be inexpensive to manufacture and distribute.

How well each of the currently employed methods meets these criteria will be discussed under each of the methods presented.

Nonappliance Methods Of Contraception

COITUS INTERRUPTUS. This simple type of contraception requires only that the penis be withdrawn from the vagina prior to ejaculation.

In evaluating the success of a method of contraception, we use the number of women out of 100 expressed as a percentage who become pregnant after using the method for one year. Of those women using coitus interruptus, 16.8% have become pregnant. This relatively high failure rate is attributed to two factors.

First, there is frequently in the male an inadvertent pre-ejaculatory emission derived from Cowper's glands (see p. 51). This emission is primarily intended for lubrication. However, the fluid may contain active sperm. The male, not realizing that this pre-ejaculatory emission has taken place, may withdraw after it has occurred, leaving viable sperm deposited within the vagina.

Second, the sperm that are frequently deposited on the vulva are still active and may ascend into the vagina, causing pregnancy.

When this method is evaluated against the criteria for the perfect contraceptive, one would have to say that it is relatively ineffective, somewhat difficult to use, and would ensure pregnancy if the method were stopped. It is difficult to use because it requires a great deal of self-control on the part of the male, as well as careful timing by both partners. Neither of these conditions characterize the enthusiasm of adolescence and youth, by whom this method is frequently used with frequent tragic failure.

THE RHYTHM METHOD. This method is based on the assumption that ovulation occurs 12 to 14 days after the onset of the past menses. This figure, although not infallible, is fairly accurate, being based on temperature graphs, hormonal studies, and biopsies of the endometrium. The premise is also made that the egg is viable for approximately 24 hours and the sperm for 48 hours. Thus the usual timing for users of this method is to abstain from coitus from the tenth through the sixteenth day of the menstrual cycle on the theory that fertilization can take place only during this period of time. The time can be extended for those couples who are very serious about avoiding pregnancy or contracted by those couples who are less concerned about pregnancy.

The efficacy of this method has been calculated by Tietze at a 14.5% rate of failure and by Westhoff at 34.5%. The importance of the rhythm method is not its degree of efficiency but the fact that it is the only contraceptive method sanctioned by the Roman Catholic Church. It thus affects a considerable part of the American population.

There are three reasons for the relatively low efficiency of the rhythm method. First, sperm are now thought by some to be viable for more than 5 days. Second, there is some evidence that a few women apparently ovulate at the time of coitus; others may experience more than one ovulation between menses. These ovulatory phenomena should not be surprising because they also occur elsewhere in the animal kingdom. Third, and possibly most important, one cannot predict with certainty when ovulation will occur. It is recognized that a female generally ovulates 14 days before the next menstrual flow. Since the menstrual cycle may vary in length, the time of ovulation cannot, therefore, be predicted with absolute accuracy in advance. The rhythm method may, however, be made more effective by use of a temperature graph or daily surveillance of the cervical mucus with litmus paper, both or either of which can be used to pinpoint ovulation more closely.

The reader who wishes to study the rhythm method in detail is referred to the book *The Truth About Rhythm*, by I. E. Georg.

Appliance Methods Of Contraception

CONDOMS. (Fig. 17–1). Condoms are also called rubbers or sheaths. The condom is a tubular sac made of latex rubber or animal membrane. Condoms vary in price, depending on the thickness of the membrane and degree of sensitivity afforded. Some are lubricated,

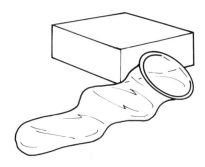

FIGURE 17-1. The condom. (From *A Guide to the Methods of Postponing or Preventing Pregnancy* by permission of the Ortho Pharmaceutical Corporation.)

others are not. Sperm deposited within the sac never come in contact with any part of the vaginal tract. The condom is a highly effective contraceptive, and when used with some form of contraceptive jelly, it prevents fertilization over 90% of the time, or conversely, with less than a 10% failure rate.

When compared with an ideal contraceptive, the condom is relatively easy to use and does not require any type of medical supervision. It is not overly expensive; when properly cared for, it may be reused. Between uses it should be tested for leaks by filling it with water. There are no deleterious side effects. It is an immediate and perfectly reversible type of contraception.

However, the condom has two disadvantages. First, it reduces sensation for the male. Second, it may generate a feeling of unnaturalness, for it is usually donned at the time of heightened sexual excitement.

Despite these disadvantages and the availability of newer forms of contraceptives, the condom is still extensively used and may well be the most popular method employed in the United States. The condom has a secondary benefit in that it will protect the wearer from contracting venereal disease. It is under this pretext that it is sold in certain states and certain other parts of the world.

THE DIAPHRAGM. (Fig. 17–2). The diaphragm is a flexible shallow dome made of thin rubber or latex and provided with a flexible thick lip at its circumference. The lip or ring is composed of hard rubber or a metallic coiled spring encased in rubber. The diaphragm comes in varying diameters. It can be bent for insertion into the vagina. Initially it must be fitted by a physician or paramedical person to cover the

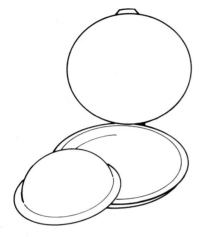

A. The diaphragm

B. Posture for insertion

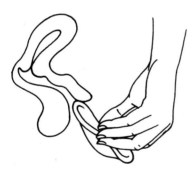

C. Insertion of the diaphragm

D. The diaphragm
in position

FIGURE 17-2. The diaphragm. (a) with container; (b) posture for insertion; (c) insertion; (d) in position. (From *A Guide to the Methods of Postponing or Preventing Pregnancy* by permission of the Ortho Pharmaceutical Corporation.)

mouth of the cervix, as the size and position of the cervix vary from woman to woman. Presence of the diaphragm if it is properly fitted will not be noted by either participant during coitus. Effectiveness of the diaphragm is increased if a spermacidal jelly is placed around its edge. With proper and vigilant use, the diaphragm has proven to be a highly effective form of contraception with some studies reporting a

failure rate as low as 3 to 6%. The generally accepted failure rate for
this form of contraception, however, is higher than these figures.
Although it has no serious side effects, it is more expensive than the
condom, but, of course, it can be used over and over again.

Compared with the ideal contraceptive, the diaphragm has certain drawbacks. First, it is not 100% effective. Second, it is not necessarily simple to insert. Third, it requires fastidious care, which frequently is unappealing to the female. Prior to the newer methods of
contraception, however, it was very popular and probably was the
most commonly used contraceptive device among the upper classes of
American citizenry.

THE INTRAUTERINE DEVICE OR I.U.D. (Fig. 17–3). This device
is also called the intrauterine contraceptive device (I.U.C.D.) or loop.
Since the early sixties there has been renewed interest in an old form
of contraception, that is, the placing of some foreign body in the
uterine cavity to prevent pregnancy. In antiquity, gold or silver stem
pessaries were employed. These rare metals did not cause irritation or
infection in the user but obviously were not within the means of the
mass population. In 1929, Graafenberg developed a firm ring of woven
silk and another of stainless steel for insertion into the uterus for contraceptive purposes. These devices fell into some disrepute in the
United States because their use at the time was accompanied by a
high incidence of infection and occasional uterine perforation at the
time of insertion. Dr. Graafenberg renounced his discovery in the early
thirties after he left Germany and came to the United States. However, his students in Israel and Japan continued using the method
and perfected it. In the early 1960's a polyethylene plastic device was
invented which was supple and which effectively reduced the complications mentioned.

Intrauterine devices come in many shapes, including loops, bows,
rings, and springs. They are impregnated with radio-opaque material
so that they can be observed on radiographs. Frequently a string,
usually of nylon, is attached to the device and allowed to hang in the
vagina so that the user, by feeling the string, can be assured that the
device is correctly retained. One can easily gather from the foregoing
comments that the I.U.D. must be inserted by a physician or paramedical person and checked on occasion to ensure its correct
placement.

Although the mode of action of the I.U.D. is undetermined, two
theories have been advanced. The first is that the device causes some

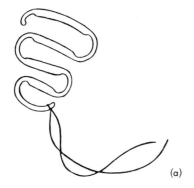

(a)

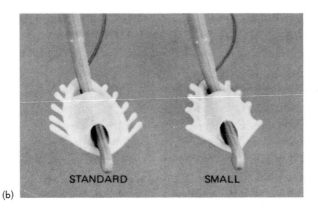

(b)

STANDARD   SMALL

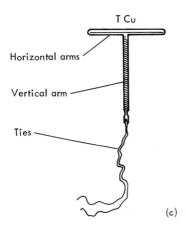

T Cu

Horizontal arms

Vertical arm

Ties

(c)

FIGURE 17-3. Intrauterine devices. (a) Lippes loop; (b) Dalkon shield, standard size (left) and small size (right), with inserting rods; (c) Copper T.

change in the endometrium, or lining of the uterus, which prevents implantation of the fertilized ovum. The second theory is based on studies of uterine motility. With the loop in place, rhythmic contractions progress through the uterine tubes and uterine cavity. These contractions propel the developing egg through the tubes and uterus more rapidly than would otherwise be the case, so that when the sperm meet the egg, the latter is too immature for fertilization to occur.

The devices are reported to be efficient from 96 to 98% of the time; i.e., the failure rate is 2 to 4%. The use of an I.U.D. is relatively simple, inasmuch as the only responsibility of the wearer after the device has been placed in the uterus is to ascertain its presence by palpating its attached string within the vagina. Its insertion, however, requires the service of a physician or paramedical person. The device is relatively inexpensive. The major expense involved is for the service of insertion, but for those who are financially hard pressed, such organizations as Planned Parenthood provide the device and insertion at reduced cost.

There are, however, certain disadvantages. First, the uterus can by contractions force the device out of position and into the vagina. This occurs more often among women who have never borne children. This disadvantage has been overcome somewhat by using devices of different sizes, a larger size for a woman who has borne children and a smaller size for one who has not. Second, a patient with an I.U.D. in place may experience abnormal bleeding, manifested by either excessive bleeding at the time of menstruation or continuous spotting during the month. Third, infection is not unknown but is relatively rare. Fourth, incidents of perforation at the time of insertion can occur.

Approximately one-third of those women who use an intrauterine device will, for one reason or another, request its removal within a two-year period after installation. Most of these requests result from bleeding problems.

A new device, the Copper T (Fig. 17–3), has recently been employed, which seemingly reduces the side effects of the earlier I.U.D. It is called the Copper T because of the presence of a thin copper wire. It is easy to insert, is not expelled with the frequency of other I.U.Ds, and has a lower incidence of pregnancy. It has recently been discovered that Graafenberg's original I.U.Ds also contained copper.

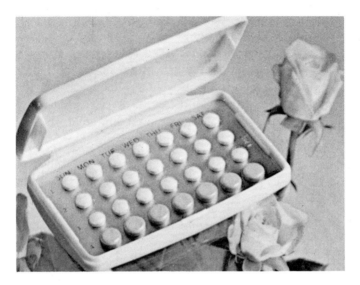

FIGURE 17-4. The pill.

THE PILL (Fig. 17–4). The history of the pill is fascinating, because it is both recent and dynamic. Following the discovery of the hormones estrogen and progesterone, the concept was developed that if sufficient amounts of them could be administered to a female, the process of ovulation would be affected. When estrogen was introduced alone, it caused many bleeding irregularities. Until recently, progesterone was so expensive to produce that its use was impractical. However, the work of Professor Russell Marker revealed that progesterone could be obtained inexpensively from the Mexican plant *cabeza de negro*. When it became commercially available, Gregory Pincus, a biologist, and John Rock, a gynecologist, devised a method of using it as a contraceptive. Their original study began with women in Puerto Rico in 1953, and although their technique has been slightly varied since then, it has been basically similar since its inception.

The pill is a hormone, estrogen, or a combination of the hormones estrogen and progesterone. Various types of pills exist, but they can readily be divided into two groups. The first group are termed combinations. They combine progesterone with small amounts of estrogen. Enovid, Norinyl, and Ovulen are examples. The second group are called sequentials. Each consists of two separate types of pills, given at different times of the month. The first 15 pills contain pure estrogen, and the last 5 or 6 pills of a given cycle contain both estrogen and progesterone. Ortho-Novum, S-Q, and Oracon are examples.

The mode of action, whether combinations or sequentials, is the same. The pill acts in an inhibitory way in the feedback relationship between the ovary and pituitary gland (see p. 78). Secondary changes also occur in the cervix, cervical mucus, and lining of the uterine cavity. One would anticipate that if one gave the appropriate hormones to a female, the uterine lining would proliferate and become thick. The opposite occurs. The membrane becomes very thin and appears almost atrophic.

It is generally believed that hormonal inhibition of ovulation prevents pregnancy, but secondary effects, namely, an alteration of the endometrial lining and a change in the cervical mucus, are also important. These secondary changes, which are also contraceptive, permit increasingly smaller amounts of the hormone to be used, yet maintain efficiency of the pill. Recent research has been devoted to finding a minipill, the smallest amount of progesterone that will effectively inhibit pregnancy. One such pill, Micronor, is already commercially available.

It is interesting to note that manufacturers of the pill have deliberately tried to simulate the female cycle by causing bleeding every 28 days. It was felt initially, when the pill came on the market, that to gain acceptance for the pill the effects would have to be as nearly "natural" as possible. The bleeding that does occur during use of the pill is, however, not true menstruation. Cessation of use of the pill causes the bleeding because the administration of estrogen is stopped. Accordingly, one could, if one chose, cause this bleeding every 20, 35, or 40 days or otherwise, according to choice. However, all the pills currently on the market are constituted on the supposition that women prefer to bleed every 28 days in a cyclic manner.

The pill, then, is for all practical purposes 100% effective. It is relatively inexpensive to produce. With changes in packaging it is simple to take. Many packages now contain 28 pills, and one is taken per day. The woman, of course, must be motivated to take the pill daily (see the section on motivational aspects, Chapter 18). Furthermore, some degree of intelligence is necessary to follow directions properly. This last factor limits full effectiveness in countries with a high percentage of illiteracy.

The contraceptive effect of the pill is generally reversible by cessation of its use. However, reversibility is an area of some concern. On occasion, a patient who has been on the pill for several years will stop its use and not be able to become pregnant. She is convinced that failure to become pregnant results from prolonged use of the pill. Statistically, however, her chances of becoming pregnant under such circumstances are as likely as they would be by cessation of any other method of contraception. It is important to note that if the pill did cause a problem, the problem would entail continued lack of ovulation. Several drugs are available that actually cause ovulation and can be administered to counteract possible failure to ovulate.

The pill, however, has not yet been accepted as the ideal contraceptive agent. The reason is simply that the pill is a drug. It causes changes in the body chemistry, just as any other medication would do. Aside from the contraceptive effect, two other reactions of import can occur.

First, and of lesser importance, are minor side effects. The pill may cause nausea or occasional vomiting. Some patients note a gain in weight, although this gain is not statistically proven. Other patients have irregular bleeding, rather than bleeding at the expected time of menses. Psychological side effects have been reported, such as depression, headaches, and occasional lack of libido. Yet some patients, on the other hand, report an increase in libido. It is difficult to evaluate these psychological side effects, because they are intimately tied in with the motivation of the women to take the pill. The more strongly motivated a woman is, the fewer side effects she seems to experience.

Second, and of greater significance, is an idiosyncrasy to the drug. In some women there is an irritation of the lining of certain blood vessels, perhaps of an allergic or enzymatic nature, although exactly how this irritation comes about is undetermined. The major danger of this irritation is the formation of blood clots, which transferred to other parts of the body cause catastrophic effects. There is indication that estrogen rather than progesterone is the cause of this idiosyncrasy. Accordingly, over the years manufacturers have decreased the amount of estrogen in their contraceptive pills. However, females who have this problem are quite rare. English literature reports possibly 3 deaths per 100,000 women who take birth control pills. This contrasts with approximately 0.3 deaths per 100,000 women who have the same complication without taking birth control pills. However, even the 3 deaths are significantly lower than the 10 deaths per 100,000 women which are associated with pregnancy. As yet no

test can determine which women will react adversely to the pill. It is
hoped that some simple skin test or other procedure will be developed
in the future, which could be used to indicate those few women who
react in this tragically adverse fashion. Personally, I feel the pill at the
present time is the best contraceptive agent, particularly in those cases
of a strong desire to avoid pregnancy.

FOAMS AND JELLIES. (Fig. 17–5). These chemicals are spermati-
cides, killing the sperm on contact. The major advantage in their use
is that there are virtually no side effects. An occasional woman may
develop an irritative or allergic reaction to any of these agents. Other
problems, such as bleeding or expulsion, are nonexistent. The disadvantages are ineffectiveness and the need to apply one or another of
the agents before each coitus. A failure rate of 5 to 10% must be
accepted. Coitus must also be anticipated, as these chemicals must be
introduced a sufficient length of time prior to the act to allow full
formation of the matrix for sperm destruction.

THE VAGINAL DOUCHE. Many women in many parts of the
world still hold that if they douche immediately following coitus, they
can prevent pregnancy. This may be true in some situations, but the
fact remains that the douche has a failure rate of 31%. The method

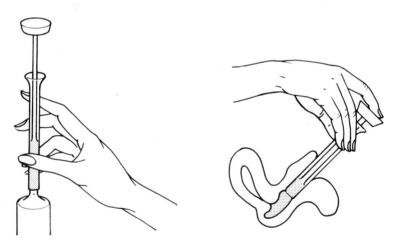

A. Filling the applicator   B. Application of the jelly

FIGURE 17-5. Vaginal spermicides, foams, and jellies. (a) filling the applicator;
(b) application of the jelly. (From *A Guide to the Methods of Postponing or
Preventing Pregnancy* by permission of the Ortho Pharmaceutical Corporation.)

has the additional disadvantage of requiring immediate action following coitus, a time generally conducive to relaxation.

References

GEORG, I. E. 1962. *The Truth About Rhythm,* transl. from German version by Ed Gallagher. New York: Kennedy.

HAVEMANN, ERNEST. 1967. *Birth Control.* New York: Time-Life.

18

contraception (continued): sterilization

By modern medical procedures, both the male and female can be sterilized surgically rather easily. Both husband and wife should realize that such surgery represents a permanent form of contraception. Although individual instances have been reported in which the procedure has been reversed and fertility restored, one should never adopt this method of contraception with the possibility in mind of reversion to fertility. In other words, if an individual, married or single, is certain that under all subsequent circumstances he or she no longer wishes to have a child, this method of contraception is permanently and irrevocably effective.

The Operative Technique In The Male: Vasectomy

The male is sterilized by severing the two vasa deferentia (Fig. 18–1). This procedure effectively blocks passage of the sperm from

improving their lot through contraception. Moreover, they spread misinformation regarding contraception, particularly the unnaturalness of using something to interfere with nature.

This concept of unnaturalness is not confined to the poor alone. Some people of higher economic level also believe that Mother Nature will somehow provide for all, and that if you meddle with Her, rather severe consequences may result. They fail to see, apparently, that Mother Nature herself, through famine, disease, and conflict, can employ harsh and devastating methods with dire and ruthless consequences which enlightened men can avoid.

RELIGIOUS BELIEFS. As is well known, certain religions, particularly the Roman Catholic Church in Europe and America, have forbidden the use of certain forms of contraception. The influence of the Church, however, seems to be on the wane. But, here as with the poorer groups of all faiths, it frequently seems that two, three, or more children are acquired before the parents are willing to go against the doctrines of the Church by employing contraceptive methods.

TEENAGERS AND YOUNG ADULTS. Currently contraceptive information is available from several sources: the school, the family physician, and local organized groups, such as Planned Parenthood and birth control clinics. Yet somehow the message just doesn't get across. Many teenagers and young adults seem to feel that using a contraceptive is, in essence, preparing for coitus, and in that sense the act itself becomes unspontaneous and planned.

One is also impressed with the denial by these young people. Common when interviewing them are such statements as, "I cannot understand how it happened!" and "I just put the possibility of pregnancy out of my mind." Dr. K. E. Bauman has stated that 60% of the unmarried university students at the time of first coitus used no "reliable method of contraceptive control" and "about 40% subsequently used nothing or an unreliable technique." Other studies not restricted to university studies suggest that 75% used either no contraceptive or an unreliable method.

Interestingly enough, use of contraception has not statistically increased promiscuity in our teenage population. The female will not be promiscuous just because she is on the pill. What has been ascertained is that if a couple is having intercourse, they will have it more frequently if a contraceptive is available and used.

One is also impressed that the individual, whether boy or girl, who comes to the physician or Planned Parenthood for contraceptive advice, is rarely virginal. Some sexual encounter has usually occurred before advice is sought.

Epilogue

I deem it important to emphasize that if the possibility of intercourse is present, knowledge of contraception and a contraceptive method should also be present. Furthermore, if a coital situation arises for which an individual has not planned, the only sensible thing to do is to avoid coitus until contraceptive methods can be obtained. In my estimation it is more important, particularly for the teenager, to be aware of the information in this paragraph than to be aware of the mode of action of any individual contraceptive agent.

For those wishing to read in depth on the subject of the psychological aspects of birth planning, attention is called to the publications listed as references.

References

POHLMAN, EDWARD. 1969. *The Psychology of Birth Planning*. Cambridge, Mass.: Schenkman.

SANDBERG, EUGENE C., AND RALPH I. JACOBS. 1972. "Psychology of the misuse and rejection of contraception," *American Journal of Obstetrics and Gynecology*, 110: 227.

19

abortion

There is no subject relating to human sexuality on which there has been such a complete turnabout in attitude as on that of abortion. Ten years ago abortion was illegal, immoral, and poorly performed. Abortion was attacked by the law, the Church, and public indignation.

Those who are financially well-to-do have always had access to responsible abortion. Over the past recent decades, reasonably qualified physicians were available to perform the operation under secretive circumstances. Following the Second World War, many pregnant women traveled abroad to have abortions performed by qualified individuals. However, those economically less fortunate were either destined to have additional children or run the risk of exposing themselves to unskilled hands, often with consequent disastrous results.

Almost overnight this picture has changed. In certain states abortion on demand is now legal, and in others the restrictions have been very much lessened. A Gallup poll taken in June 1972, for example, showed that 64% of the public, including a majority of Catholics, at that time believed the decision to have an abortion should be left solely to the wishes of the patient and the judgment of her physician. A similar poll taken just four years earlier, in 1968, showed that only 15% of the individuals queried favored such a radical policy. This change in public opinion on a moral issue is unprecedented. The procedure of abortion itself has also changed and is now being performed by highly skilled physicians, who have markedly refined the operative techniques and significantly reduced the complications.

As a backlash to the liberalization of abortion, a group known as the "Right to Life" has emerged. They base their campaign primarily, as they see it, on the immorality of abortion and claim they are protecting the right of the unborn child.

Incidence

It is impossible to say at the moment how many abortions are being performed in the United States. A report of 1958, edited by Mary S. Calderone, postulated that there were as many abortions being performed as there were live births. It was suggested that one million abortions a year were being performed, but this figure is presumptive because there were no records and the procedure at that time was illegal. The magnitude of the problem, however, can be appreciated by noting that during the first year of legalized abortion in New York, 262,807 legal abortions were reported, of which 159,969 were for nonresidents of that state.

Regardless of the actual number of abortions being done, there is little or no question that as the liberalization of abortion laws has increased, the number being done and reported has significantly increased.

Who Seeks An Abortion?

From my own clinical experience I categorize those seeking abortion into four rather distinct groups based on age and marital status. The first group comprises females 16 years old and younger.

These youngsters are, for the most part, quite surprised to find themselves pregnant, although they are aware that intercourse may lead to pregnancy. Many of them, to me at least, seem to be very confused about what being a female entails and how they should deal with sex and life in general. For the most part, I think the term promiscuous for these youngsters is quite inappropriate. In many cases the pregnancy resulted from a first coital experience. These girls are vaguely familiar with contraceptive techniques, but their knowledge is frequently fragmentary, and they are also not aware as to where these contraceptive services can be obtained. I find most of them unable to handle the situation of pregnancy. Many of the instances of late abortion, that is abortion beyond the twelfth week of pregnancy or fourteenth week following the last menstrual period, occur within this group. There are two reason for this: first, the young women, despite the fact that they may miss a period or two, do not think they are pregnant or fancy that they are not pregnant; and second, members of this group are most hesitant to tell their parents that they might be pregnant and thus expose themselves to parental anger and disdain.

The second group comprises females from 16 to 20 years of age, who are often students at senior high school or college. They are a great deal more blasé about being pregnant and have already realized that abortion is their only out. For the most part, these individuals handle the abortion situation quite well. They seemingly have few regrets. These females are very much aware of contraceptive methods and in many cases have used some modified or haphazard form of contraception. They frequently state that they have used a modified rhythm system, although their information about the system is frequently faulty. In talking with this group, I am impressed about the lack of responsibility of the male regarding contraceptive techniques. Most of these young women do not blame the male directly for the pregnancy but, more or less, accuse themselves for not using a contraceptive. Interestingly enough, although repeaters do occur in this group as in any other, this one lesson is often sufficient. These patients do not return for second, third, or fourth abortions, except for pathological individuals who perhaps subconsciously want to be pregnant.

The third group to my way of thinking is possibly the most tragic group of all. It comprises women recently divorced or widowed.

These women, following the accident of their singleness, frequently are determined to lead a celibate existence. These women are well-informed about contraceptives and for the most part used them effectively during their married years. As a result of celibacy they find themselves unprepared so far as contraception is concerned at the time opportunity for coitus arises. Among the divorced women, the offending male is frequently the former husband; the woman in hopes of a reconciliation succumbs to his sexual advances. The women in this group frequently have suffered emotionally from the death or departure of a husband, and the circumstances of pregnancy cause an additional tremendous emotional upheaval. They dread consequences of bringing an unwanted and, in essence, illegal child into the world.

The fourth group represents married women who more often than not already have children and who are not anxious to have more children at this specific time. Occasionally one sees a married woman wanting to abort her first pregnancy. Circumstances for wanting to avoid pregnancy are frequently economic or socioeconomic, for the parents do not feel they can afford additional children and raise them according to the standards they have set as desirable. Other parents, although they are financially able to support additional children, do not feel themselves emotionally able to undertake the rearing of an additional child in a household already established. Frequently the patients in this fourth group are over 30 and many are over 35. Many of these married individuals have become pregnant through some manner of contraceptive failure. In this group contraceptive failure seems more frequent than in any of the other three groups. It is also painfully obvious that these women are faced with the most difficult decision of any of the groups. They know that they could have this child, that there is a father and a mother to care for it, and that there is an established family into which the child can be born. They realize that they have had children before, have raised them successfully in most cases, and probably could do it again. The question therefore arises about their selfishness in wanting an abortion. Counseling this group is difficult because of this existent feeling of guilt. Many of these patients choose to have the child and then, following delivery, seek some permanent form of sterilization for one partner or the other.

Statistics from New York following the first year of legalized abortion in that state parallel these clinical findings. Out of the 262,807 legalized abortions, 25% of the patients were in their teens,

10% were 17 years or younger, 55% were single, 14% were widowed, divorced or separated, and 31% were married.

Methods Of Abortion

The method chosen for doing an abortion is strictly related to the duration of the pregnancy. The longer the pregnancy, the larger the size of the uterus, and hence the more difficult the procedure becomes for expelling the contents.

If a pregnancy is less than 12 weeks in duration, i.e., 12 weeks from the point of conception or 14 weeks from the last normal menstrual period, that pregnancy can be evacuated by a procedure termed a "D&C" (dilation and curettage). The cervix is dilated, and the contents of the uterus are removed by instrumentation. Formerly, these contents were removed by curettage, i.e., actually scraping the lining of the womb with a sharp instrument, a curet. However, with the advent of mass abortion, a more sophisticated method has been devised by which the products of conception are removed by suction from the uterine cavity through a plastic tube that has been introduced into the uterus (Fig. 19–1). This second method is by its very nature less traumatic to the uterus.

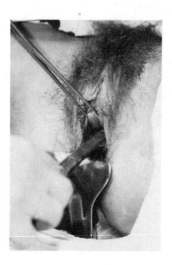

FIGURE 19–1. Suction technique for therapeutic abortion. "Grasping forceps" hold the cervix. A plastic tube, bearing the products of conception, has been inserted through the vagina into the uterus with suction applied.

There is discussion and controversy about the need for anesthesia and the types of anesthetics required to do this procedure. In most clinics if the patient is less than 10 weeks pregnant, suction can be performed under local anesthesia, i.e., an anesthetic applied directly to the cervix. From 10 to 14 weeks of pregnancy, many advise the use of general anesthesia. However, individual differences are significant, as a patient who has borne children previously is easier to dilate than one in whom the pregnancy is the first.

More recently, dilation of the cervix has been accomplished by use of a "laminaria tent." This "tent" is a stick of dried seaweed about 2 inches long and 0.125 inch in diameter (Fig. 19–2). When placed in the cervix, the tent absorbs water from its surrounding environment and expands to a diameter of 0.25 to 0.5 inch. This expansion produces a nontraumatic and uniform dilation of the cervical opening. The time required for dilation is 8 to 12 hours.

If pregnancy lasts longer than 14 weeks, removal of the fetus

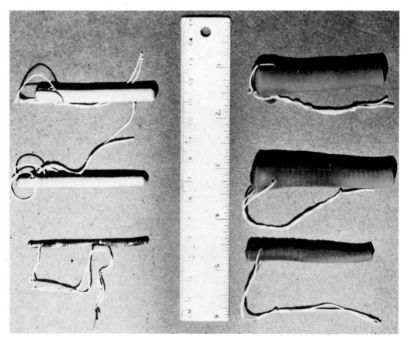

FIGURE 19-2. Small, medium, and large laminaria tents before and after hydration. (From *Obstetrics and Gynecology*, Vol. 39. 1972. New York: Harper & Row.)

becomes more difficult. Formerly, a hysterotomy, a miniature Cesarean section, was performed. However, this procedure has fallen into disfavor. More recently, a method has been developed that introduces a concentrated saline solution into the pregnant uterus. This solution irritates the uterine musculature, causing contraction of the uterus and subsequent expulsion of the fetus, usually 24 to 48 hours after introduction of the solution. Institutions using this technique usually allow the patient to leave the clinic, following introduction of the solution, and to return at the onset of labor. This technique is most easily performed after the sixteenth week of pregnancy; thus many institutions seeing a patient at 14 weeks will suggest that she return 2 weeks later to undergo the procedure.

A new technique for abortion, not yet commercially available, has been described using prostaglandin, a hormonal substance derived from human semen as well as from other body tissues and fluids. In the early 1930's it was first demonstrated that human semen contained a factor that caused contraction of smooth (involuntary) muscles and also reduced blood pressure. The name prostaglandin was proposed for the unidentified substance. Little additional work on it was done until 1962 to 1966, during which period S. Bergström in Sweden isolated and identified six primary prostaglandins. (More than double that number are now known.) These substances were actually found in all reproductive organs, but their highest concentration was found in seminal fluid. In 1969, these substances were first used in an attempt to induce labor in humans with varying degrees of success. More recently, they have been used to induce premature labor, or, in essence, an abortion. They have been introduced into the patient in several ways. In some cases, they were given intravenously or orally. In others, they were injected directly into the amniotic fluid. Until recently, the side effects of using this drug and the concentrations required made it impractical for clinical use. However, refinements, assiduously pursued by the Upjohn Company, indicate that it will soon be commercially available and that it should dramatically alter the management of the midtrimester abortion. There is speculation that eventually it may also be used for early abortion.

Mention should be made of the morning-after pill, a subtle form of abortion. Here a high dose of estrogen is given within 24 hours after coitus. This estrogen influences the lining of the uterus in such a way that it will not accept the fertilized ovum, essentially aborting it.

In nonprofessional hands, many bizzare methods of abortion

have been attempted. Some amateurs dilate the cervix with a catheter, pessary, or other blunt object in hopes of initiating labor. Others have introduced such agents as concentrated soap solution or diluted acid into the uterine cavity with the intent of killing the embryo and thus causing its expulsion. Still others have used a darning needle to penetrate the cervical opening and tear the fetal membranes in hopes of causing labor and ultimate expulsion of the embryo. It is obvious that these primitive methods may cause severe sequelae and in the past have frequently been catastrophic to the mother.

Complications

Three serious potential physical complications are associated with abortion. To be sure, the method of abortion as well as the qualifications of the individuals performing the abortion determine the frequency with which these complications may occur.

The first is hemorrhage, which can occur at the time of the abortion or after the abortion if the uterus has not been completely emptied. This can be of such severity as to exsanguinate the mother. Hemorrhage can be internal into the abdominal cavity if the uterus has been ruptured or torn, or external into the vaginal canal if the uterine wall is seriously traumatized.

A second complication is infection, which is directly related to the degree of sterilization attained at the time the abortion is performed. Lack of adequate precaution against infection can lead to eventual sterility of the patient or even result in peritonitis and death.

The third physical complication is rupture of the uterus. The use of suction techniques has possibly increased the likelihood of this complication. If the uterus is ruptured with the instrument being used, part of the adjacent bowel may be sucked into the instrument and also traumatized.

Dr. Christopher Tietze, Associate Director of the Population Council, the world's leading group in dissemination of contraceptive advice and devices, has compiled statistics on complications resulting from abortions done in the state of New York after its government liberalized the law on abortion. He states that from legalized abortions 1 woman in 20 had minor medical complications, and 1 in 200 had serious complications. As might be expected, his figures show that the later the pregnancy, the higher the risk of complications.

Tietze's study and others have led to the suggestion that an abortion should be performed as early in the course of pregnancy as possible.

The skill of the aborter also comes into play. The record of safe abortions in New York City, for example, improved from 4.6 deaths per 100,000 abortions in the first year of legalized abortion to 3.5 deaths per 100,000 abortions during the second. These figures in turn are significantly lower than the figure of 27.8 deaths per 100,000, which was reported from Great Britain for the first year after the British law on liberalized abortion was enacted.

Another complication, nonphysical in nature, may arise, namely the emotional consequences following abortion. This complication is difficult to evaluate. Long-term studies on this subject are currently being done. The consensus of specialists is that adverse emotional consequences are far less than expected. Most women, in truth, handle the situation quite well. To be sure there are some women who are emotionally unstable to begin with, and an abortion may well be the precipitating factor for an adverse psychological response.

Unquestionably, however, the complications of childbirth exceed those of abortion, and the death rate from childbirth is statistically higher than that from abortion.

Religious Attitudes Toward Abortion

It is fair to state that for the most part the Jewish and Protestant attitude toward abortion is one of general disenchantment with the procedure but one that is malleable depending on circumstances. Many leaders of the Jewish and various Protestant faiths appreciate that there are circumstances in which abortion appears to be the only way out of a very difficult situation. This group also recognizes that abortion is certainly not a chosen form of contraception but rather is indicative of contraceptive failure. These groups are making concerted efforts in the field of sex education and contraceptive education for their young people.

The Roman Catholic view at this time is a rather fixed one. The *Code of Ethical and Religious Directives* for Catholic hospitals, for example, clearly states: "The direct killing of any innocent person, even at his own request, is always morally wrong. . . . Direct abortion is the direct killing of an unborn child, and is never permitted, even when the ultimate purpose is to save the life of the mother." However, exception is made for indirect abortion. Herein, if a situation such as cancer exists and a procedure such as surgery or radiation of the pregnant uterus is required to save the life of the mother, an abortion may occur as an indirect result of therapy. Under these circumstances the abortion is condoned.

Legal Aspects Of Abortion

Prior to January 1973, each state had a code of law devoted to the subject of abortion. In general, it was held that abortion was a crime and those committing it were subject to criminal offense. In like manner, any woman who had an abortion performed was also subjecting herself to potential legal punitive measures. The only general exception to this rule was abortion performed to save the life of the mother. Under such circumstances in most states, several doctors or a committee were required to concur on the decision to do a therapeutic abortion.

In April 1967, the State of Colorado altered its laws regarding abortion to include the standard of the American Law Institute, which suggested that pregnancies could be aborted if they resulted from incest or rape, if the mother's physical or mental health was jeopardized, or if the child might be born deformed or defective. Other states followed this lead, and in July 1970, New York adopted the nation's most liberal abortion law, which allowed abortions on demand if the doctor and the patient agreed. The only limitation was that the abortion had to be accomplished within the first 24 weeks of gestation.

Up to that time, there was no Federal involvement on the question of abortion, although President Nixon did go on record as not condoning the operation. On January 22, 1973, The United States Supreme Court rendered a historic decision when it reviewed abortion cases from the states of Texas and Georgia. Mr. Justice Blackmun writing for a majority of seven judges stated that the right of privacy "is broad enough to encompass a woman's decision whether or not to terminate her pregnancy." The Court then specifically held that "the word 'person' as used in the 14th Amendment, does not include the newborn." The fetus has no constiutional rights; although after viability, the fetus "presumably has the capability of meaningful life outside the woman's womb. . . . If a state is interested in protecting fetal life after viability, it may go so far as to proscribe abortion during that period of time, except when it is necessary to preserve the life or health of the mother."

The Court laid down several basic principles:

1. For the first trimester, that is for the first 12 weeks of gestation or 14 weeks from the last menstrual period, the decision for an abortion must be left to the medical judgment of the pregnant woman's attending physician.

2. For the 12 to 14 weeks subsequent to this first trimester, the state in promoting its interest in the health of the mother may, if it chooses, regulate the abortion procedure in ways that are related to the mother's health. There is no consideration given to the unborn fetus.

3. After the fetus becomes viable, that is after the twenty-sixth to twenty-eighth week, the state, in promoting its interest in the potentiality of human life, may regulate and even prohibit abortion except where it is necessary in appropriate medical judgment for the preservation of the life or health of the mother.

The Court further stipulated that "the state may define the term 'physician' to mean only a physician currently licensed by the state, and may proscribe any abortion by a person who is not a physician as so defined."

In reviewing the Georgia case, the Court added certain other nuances, namely that a hospital committee is no longer needed to decide if an abortion can be performed. This remains the prerogative of a licensed physician and the patient. The state may not demand that the abortion be performed in a hospital accredited by the Joint Commission on Accreditation of Hospitals. It also invalidated the Georgia requirement of residence. However, the Court did say that the state may require that abortions be performed in a licensed hospital after the first trimester with the thought of protecting the mother.

In no way has the Court interfered with the freedom of those who are opposed to abortion. They may continue to act on the basis of their personal convictions, but the decision in effect prohibits them from imposing their views on others.

What effect the decision of the U.S. Supreme Court will have on abortion laws of the individual states is somewhat in doubt, except that at the moment all state laws prohibiting abortion are in essence unconstitutional. Cases that were pending at the time the decision was announced will now be decided along the lines designated by the Court.

Morality Of Abortion

Volumes have been written and endless discussions have been undertaken on the morality of abortion. Under careful scrutiny this verbiage really boils down to one question: Is abortion taking a life?

From that point on, the question changes from a moral one to a semantic one, for there is no adequate generally accepted definition of what constitutes life, and there is even less agreement as to when life begins. Whichever answer one chooses for his definition of life and its beginnings then becomes, as pointed out in the chapter on Validity, an opinion or an attitude, not a scientific fact.

Those who advocate the "Right to Life" position espouse that life begins with conception—that moment when sperm and egg unite. However, if one has had the opportunity of viewing the union of human egg and sperm, it becomes increasingly difficult to dignify this moment with the term "life." Both egg and sperm are individually very much alive prior to this union. They are both active, mobile, functioning cells. Once sperm penetration has occurred, no dramatic change is noted. I believe one can only say that once union has occurred, the potential for a new human life has been created.

Yet, if one refutes this concept—that life begins with conception—one is truly hard put to find any other satisfactory definition; other definitions become even more arbitrary. Does life begin when the embryo's heart begins to beat? Does life begin when brain waves can first be detected in the embryo? Does life begin at 20 weeks when fetal motion is first detected by the mother? Does life begin at 28 weeks when for the first time the fetus might survive outside the maternal environment? The more one contemplates, the more obvious the dilemma becomes and the less resolved.

For my own point of view, I have chosen to avoid the debate and accept in its place the philosophical concept of "the quality of life." If the birth of a child will make life less desirable for a woman, then she has the right to have an abortion to insure the quality of her own life. Or if a child will be born into a situation wherein it is unwanted or unneeded, or if it will be merely a burden to society or a potential problem within the society, then the quality of life for that unborn child is very much in question. Although the unborn child does not have the decision whether or not to be born, certainly the mother does.

I shall not try to defend the opinion because it is scientifically indefensible. I very much respect the opinions of those who have a different attitude from mine. I appreciate their point of view. I hope that they will appreciate mine as generously.

References

CALDERONE, M. S. (ed.). 1958. *Abortion in the United States.* New York: Harper and Harper.

HALL, ROBERT E. 1970. *Abortion in a Changing World.* New York: Columbia University Press.

KUMMER, JEROME M. (ed.). 1967 *Abortion: Legal and Illegal.* Santa Monica, Calif.: Jerome M. Kummer, M.D., P.O. Drawer 769.

NOONAN, JOHN T., et al. 1970. *Morality of Abortion: Legal and Historical Perspectives,* with an introduction by John T. Noonan, Jr. Cambridge, Mass.: Harvard University Press.

REITERMAN, CARL (ed.). 1971. *Abortion and the Unwanted Child.* New York: Springer.

20

venereal disease

In recent years interest has been rekindled in the field of venereal disease (VD). A generation of doctors, health educators, and public health personnel, trained in the immediate post-World War II period, studied VD only for historical value. Currently we are again faced with VD as a ravaging disease.

It is superfluous to suggest the many reasons why we should concern ourselves with venereal disease. It is appropriate to suggest two that might not be immediately obvious: (1) to bring the subject of VD out of the shadows, thus permitting free discussion of it so that individuals afflicted will recognize the symptoms, seek medical help, freely name their confreres, and cooperate in its eradication, and (2) to refrain from the absurdity of using VD as a threat in the hope of eradicating adolescent promiscuity, rather than presenting it as a real consequence with appropriate knowledge as to its prevention and treatment.

226

The term "venereal disease," as commonly applied, includes those five diseases transmitted by sexual contact. Syphilis and gonorrhea will be discussed in some detail. The other three will be mentioned only for completeness, inasmuch as they are not often encountered. For more complete coverage of venereal disease, the reader is referred to the book of Brown et al., Syphilis and other Venereal Diseases.

1. Syphilis is a chronic infectious disease caused by Treponema pallidum, a spirochete consisting of 8 to 12 tightly arranged coils.
2. Gonorrhea is an acute or chronic infectious disease caused by Neisseria gonorrhoeae, a gram-negative intracellular diploccus.
3. Chancroid is an acute or chronic infectious disease caused by the bacterium Hemophilus ducreyi. It is characterized by a soft ulcer, which arises at the point of contact, and enlargement and ulceration of the neighboring lymph nodes.
4. Lymphogranuloma venereum is a genital infectious disease caused by a virus. Diagnosis is established by a subcutaneous skin test, the Frei test. It is characterized by an initial lesion at the point of contact, followed by regional lymph node enlargement and, at times, systemic involvement.
5. Granuloma inguinale is a disease of the lower socioeconomic groups, manifested by chronic ulceration at the point of contact. It is caused by the bacterium Donovania granulomatis, which is nonmotile and gram-positive. Donovan bodies can be found in biopsy specimens, authenticating the disease.

Syphilis

HISTORY.   It has been postulated that the origin of syphilis can be traced to a free-living organism that developed into the pathogenic organism *Treponema pallidum*. Where this first occurred in the world is a moot question. On this subject there are two theories: the pre-Columbian theory and the Columbian theory.

The pre-Columbian theory is based on the belief that syphilis existed in a nonvirulent form in Europe before Columbus and became virulent only coincidently with Columbus' historic voyage. Those who support this view hold that there are Biblical quotations that suggest the disease, although the actual symptoms of the disease are not reported. Somewhat refuting this argument is the fact that syphilis has been called the "great imitator" in that it frequently manifests itself subtly as other diseases do. It is quite possible, therefore, that other diseases described during Biblical times are being mistaken as syphilis by modern authorities.

The Columbian theory is widely held, possibly because of its romantic appeal, although certain facts strongly support it. This theory postulates that syphilis, probably in a nonvirulent form, existed on the American continent prior to the time of Columbus' first visit. According to Dr. Diza de Isle, the men of Columbus' vessels introduced it into the port city of Barcelona in 1493. The theory further holds that prior to that time syphilis was unknown on the European continent.

Soon thereafter King Charles VII of France, using Spanish mercenaries of which Columbus' crew were probably a part, invaded Italy to seize the throne of Naples. One must understand that the armies of that day were accompanied by female camp followers. These girls, of low political allegiance, plied their trade to friend and foe alike. This particular campaign was, apparently, characterized by a minimum of fighting and a maximum of debauchery. By the spring of 1494, a plague attributed to syphilis attacked the French army and forced its retreat from Italy.

Syphilis in local chronicles was then said to have appeared in France, Germany, and Switzerland in 1495, in Holland and Greece in 1496, in England and Scotland in 1497, and in Hungary and Prussia in 1499. These statistics belie those who claim sexual promiscuity is a problem only of the "beat" generation. Interestingly enough, the Italians called it the French disease, the French called it the Italian disease. The English called it the French disease, and the Prussians called it the Polish disease.

In the last few years of the fifteenth century and the early part of the sixteenth century, syphilis existed in plague proportions, and thousands died, primarily because of the pathogenicity of the syphilis spirochete during the second stage of development of the disease.

Sometime during the sixteenth century the pandemic quality of the disease lessened. Syphilis either lost its virulence, or its host (man) became more resistant.

Prior to 1909 available therapy was painful, dangerous, and relatively ineffective. The most popular treatments were as follows:

1. Use of mercury, applied either locally to the lesions or taken internally. Since the effects did not seem to be dose related, the dose was frequently increased to the point at which the patient succumbed to mercury poisoning.

2. Fever therapy, which followed two separate modes. One was to inoculate the victim of syphilis with either malaria or typhoid fever to obtain a high temperature. Not only did this not cure symptoms of syphilis, it frequently resulted in death of the patient from the complications derived from this newly acquired disease. The second method was to place the patient in a box with only his head exposed. The temperature in the box was then raised to 106°F and the patient kept there until he could no longer tolerate it. The 106°F temperature was critical, and if it was overshot in any way, the patient literally and figuratively roasted to death.

Research in the early part of the twentieth century by Paul Ehrlich, a German bacteriologist and pathologist, led to the discovery of arsphenamine in 1909 for treatment of syphilis and yaws. Arsphenamine was also called salvarsan, Ehrlich's 606, or just plain 606, because the drug was the six hundred-sixth experiment conducted by Ehrlich. The major problem with arsenicals, however, was that the procedure required multiple injections over an extended period of time. Although the injections were extremely painful, this proved to be effective therapy in certain stages of the disease.

From 1938 to 1947, tremendous strides were made in limiting the disease by initiation of a mass screening technique in which unsuspecting carriers were identified. In addition, contacts of known carriers were traced and treated. The highest incidence of reported cases was in 1947.

The advent of penicillin produced the first effective cure in the treatment of syphilis and reduced the incidence of the disease markedly. However, it equally reduced vigilance in following up the contacts of new cases and totally broke down the intricate public health procedures required in control of the disease. Hospitals, for example, no longer required a serology test for syphilis on all admissions, and some state legislatures found premarital examination for syphilis was archaic. Physicians also became careless in reporting new cases. Today vigilance is being restored in an attempt to eliminate this dreaded disease.

CLINICAL MANIFESTATIONS. Syphilis, if untreated, passes through four distinct stages:

1. An incubation stage, which lasts about 3 weeks. During this stage there are no signs or symptoms of the infection.
2. A primary (chancre) stage, which lasts from 1 to 5 weeks. This stage is characterized by the appearance of a sore at the

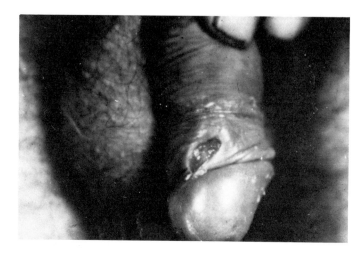

FIGURE 20–1. Penile chancre. First stage of syphilis. (Courtesy of J. Barkoff, M.D.)

site of contact and inoculation, or near by (Fig. 20–1). This lesion looks like a small open ulcer with a red beefy center and pearly raised borders. It is painless. It may be accompanied by enlarged lymph nodes in adjacent areas.

The chancre may appear externally, as on the glans of the penis or on the labia majora or minora, or internally, as on the tongue or tonsils or wall of the vagina. It may arise as the result of intercourse, kissing a person with a syphilitic oral lesion, or by the performance of fellatio or cunnilingus. If anorectal penetration has occurred, the chancre may arise at the lip of the anus or internally on the wall of the rectum.

3. A secondary stage, which appears from 2 to 10 weeks later and lasts from 2 to 6 weeks. It is characterized by the appearance of a rash, resembling measles, except that the individual spots do not itch (Fig. 20–2). Each spot, however, is loaded with spirochetes, making this stage the most highly contagious one. Occasionally, lesions of the secondary stage assume a bizarre form (Fig. 20–3).

4. A latent or quiescent stage, which lasts from 2 to 20 or more years. Among untreated individuals, about 50% recover spontaneously, their own body mechanisms apparently defeating

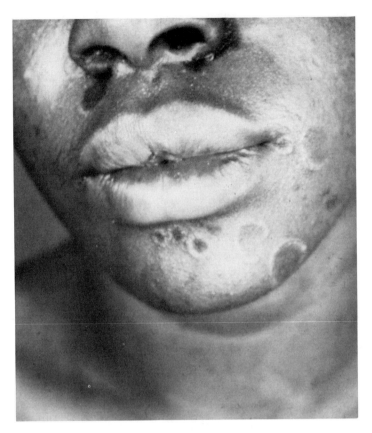

FIGURE 20-2. Typical annular lesions representing the second stage of syphilis. (Courtesy of J. Barkoff, M.D.)

the disease; about 25% are asymptomatic with positive serology but the disease well controlled by the body; and about 25% develop serious sequelae in time, the disease being uncontrolled by the body. These sequelae involve life-shortening degenerative changes, centering principally in the nervous, skeletal, and cardiovascular systems. Initially the infected individual may not be aware of these changes, but if the disease remains unchecked, it may lead to eventual paresis and ultimate death.

During this stage of the disease, the blood of the individual is contagious, but the sexual secretions are not. If for any reason

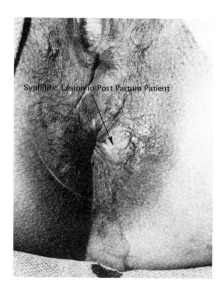

FIGURE 20-3. Syphilitic lesion adjacent to the anus in a postpartum patient. Second stage of syphilis. The vaginal orifice is shown at the top. (Courtesy of C. J. Eaton, M.D.)

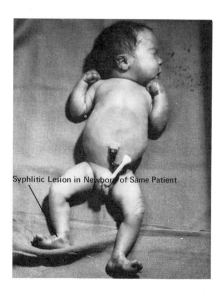

FIGURE 20-4. Syphilitic lesions in the newborn infant of the patient illustrated in Fig. 20-3. Note macerated areas of the skin of the hands and feet. (Courtesy of C. J. Eaton, M.D.)

blood is taken from a syphilitic individual for storage, the usual blood banking procedures commonly employed render the blood sterile.

Generally in stages two and three, the external manifestations of the disease will be readily apparent. Occasionally, however, the chancre may be but the size of a small pimple and go unnoticed, or the rash may be mild. A safe precaution for those who are sexually active under conditions of possible exposure is to have a test for syphilis performed at regular intervals.

TESTS FOR SYPHILIS. Current tests for syphilis are (1) the darkfield test, (2) the Wasserman test, (3) the *Treponema pallidum* immobilization test (TPI), and (4) the fluorescent treponemal antibody test (FTA), the last three of which are serological tests. One or more of these are undertaken if the physician suspects syphilis as a result of standard medical procedures, i.e., a history of the symptoms of the patient involved, his history of sexual exposure, and a general physical examination.

The darkfield test employs a special type of microscope, whereunder live spirochetes, taken from samples from primary and secondary lesions, appear as luminescent or silvery coils on a darkened background. The presence of the corkscrew-shaped organisms spiraling through the fluid examined is suggestive of syphilis.

The Wasserman test is a serological blood test, which becomes positive 1 to 2 weeks after the appearance of the primary lesion, i.e., 4 to 5 weeks after the disease has been acquired. Although highly suggestive that syphilis is present, this test is not absolute proof of syphilis, inasmuch as certain other diseases may give a positive Wasserman reaction, resulting in what is termed a "biological false positive."

The Wasserman test is less expensive to perform than the other two serological tests. It is therefore the method employed for mass screening, undertaken for such purposes as issuing marriage or beauty operator licenses, prenatal blood testing, or selective service induction.

TREATMENT. The treatment of choice is penicillin, given in adequate dosages, depending on the stage of the disease. This treatment is almost 100% curative. If the patient is sensitive to penicillin, tetracycline-type drugs may be substituted.

PERSONAL PREVENTIVE MEASURES. It is essential to remember that outward manifestations of syphilis may not be evident. For the individual, prevention requires discretion, a reasonable degree of self-control, and knowledge of the external indications of syphilis. Contact should be avoided with sexual partners who are suspect.

Treponema is very sensitive to ordinary soap and water or other aseptic techniques. If one is uncertain of the sexual background of a partner, thorough washing of exposed parts, oral, anal, or genital, is quite effective if done soon after sexual contact, and the sooner the better. A thorough douche employing some soaplike derivative is recommended for the female and such individuals as are anally active.

External washing, of course, does not rid the urethra of organisms that may have entered. Ejaculation tends to flush out the urethra in the male, and urination by either sex following coitus is helpful. And for those who are anally active, use of lubricants and voiding by defecation are helpful although far from assured prevention.

A condom so far as genital or anal contact is concerned offers excellent protection. There are those, however, who steadfastly maintain that full sexual satisfaction is prevented by use of a condom. There is also the inconvenience of donning a condom immediately prior to intromission of the penis, and some contend that there is psychological trauma as well. Overall, however, one might well *insist* on use of a condom if the reliability and credibility of the sexual partner is problematical.

Current experiments are being made on foams and jellies that are both contraceptive and lethal to venereal organisms. Research is currently being conducted on VD vaccines for both syphilis and gonorrhea. None of these methods, however, is as yet successful or available.

Individuals, therefore, who are sexually active with other than reliable sexual partners, are advised to have tests made periodically for venereal disease regardless of other preventive procedures employed.

Gonorrhea

HISTORY. The history of gonorrhea is not as exciting as that of syphilis, but it is equally interesting. Although medical historians do not agree, some believe that the venereal character of gonorrhea was known to the early Jews and was described in Leviticus XV as a "running issue" out of the flesh. Galen in 130 A.D. gave it the name "gonorrhea." Its contagious nature was determined in 1376. John Hunter in 1767 believed and taught that gonorrhea was a symptom of syphilis. His strong belief was intensified after he inoculated himself with gonorrheal pus from a patient with concurrent syphilis and developed both diseases simultaneously. In 1860 Phillippi Pricord unraveled this misconception and clearly differentiated the two diseases.

CLINICAL MANIFESTATIONS. Infection is acquired following sexual intercourse with an infected person. Infection following anorectal coitus is common in homosexual relations. Rare epidemics have occurred in children's wards or nurseries, following inadequate nursing or sterilization techniques.

Clinical manifestations in the male are straightforward, developing within 2 to 5 days following infection. The victim initially complains of a burning sensation in the urethra and discomfort on urination. Within 24 hours he becomes aware of a puslike discharge from the penis. This infection may spread upward along the entire length of the urethra and associated structures. It may cause epididymitis or eventually invade the prostate. With repeated or untreated attacks of gonorrhea, the urethra may become constricted. Similarly, the sperm ducts may become blocked, resulting in sterility. Severe prostatic infection may also occur.

Clinical manifestations in the female are more complicated. In the acute stage of the disease, many women do not realize that they are infected and only become aware of the condition when they are examined as named contacts. Other women, however, notice symptoms of an abnormal vaginal discharge and painful urination within 2 to 5 days after infection. Occasionally the Bartholin glands become involved. If the infection ascends into the uterus and into the tubes and ovaries, it is designated as "acute pelvic infection." The symptoms are those of a peritonitis, namely malaise, severe pain, fever, and chills. With repeated attacks of gonorrhea or prolonged infection, the end of the uterine tubes may become sealed and pregnancy becomes impossible. In some cases large abscesses form that endanger life and require surgical removal.

DIAGNOSIS. Microscopic examination of the pus taken from the site of infection provides the method of diagnosis. Obtaining a sample from the male urethra is a simple procedure, but obtaining one from the female cervix requires a physician. It is also advisable to take anorectal samples from either sex when gonorrheal infection is suspected; the procedure is again relatively simple, although care should be taken to avoid contaminating the sample with feces.

A positive medicolegal diagnosis requires that the gonococcus be cultured from the initial sample taken.

TREATMENT. The drug of choice in the treatment of gonorrhea is also penicillin. However, with the advent of resistant strains, in some cases other antibiotics must be used, such as spectinomycin.

PERSONAL PREVENTIVE MEASURES. The major problem with gonorrhea is that 80% of the women who harbor this noxious disease are asymptomatic, i.e., show no manifestations of the disease. Only by clinical tests can the infection be determined in these individuals.

In the male the disease is revealed by a urethral discharge and painful urination. Prostitutes are well aware of this revealing discharge and in essence will milk the penis prior to sexual activity, refusing intercourse if indications are positive.

Anal infections of either sex may be either asymptomatic or characterized by soreness. It is now advised practice to examine urethral, vaginal, and anal samples whenever tests are undertaken for gonorrhea.

There are also rare but increasing reports of gonorrheal pharyngitis.

As with syphilis, thorough washing is not to be disdained, although soap and water are not as lethal to the gonorrheal organism. The same lavage methods as advocated for syphilis are advisable for gonorrhea (see p. 234).

Here, again, the condom is a very effective form of prevention with the same objections, of course, as stated for syphilis.

Individuals who are active with other than reliable sexual partners are advised to have tests made periodically.

Untreated gonorrhea may lead to blood-borne gonorrhea or gonorrheal arthritis.

Public Health Measures For Control And Eradication Of Venereal Disease

Education of the entire population, from the lowest rungs of society to the highest, is the keystone for the control and eventual eradication of venereal disease. The first step in this educational program is to alert the population about the initial signs and symptoms of the disease. This can be done by strategically placed posters in public restrooms, by neighborhood meetings in local public health facilities, and by special conferences held under the auspices of the YMCA, YWCA, schools, or churches.

The second step is to make medical stations easily accessible to all suspecting individuals, even guaranteeing anonymity of the individuals if necessary. Sexual intercourse or body contact of other nature are far and away the most probable means of transmitting syphilis and gonorrhea. Every individual suspecting that he has venereal disease should be made to realize he should reveal his sexual background and contacts without fear of recrimination in any form. Teenagers in particular should know that treatment is available at local clinics free of charge and without knowledge of the parents. The infectious diseases department of any regional public health office or hospital can inform the inquiring citizen where venereal disease clinics are located. Most Planned Parenthood clinics routinely provide the opportunity for venereal disease cultures to be taken from those individuals who seek contraceptive advice.

Preaching moral behavior should be avoided as an effective means of curbing the incidence of venereal disease. For the mass population such preachments are simply not an effective approach.

Syphilis can be controlled and eventually eliminated from society because it is a curable disease. Feasible steps to be taken are as follows:

1. Improved methods of reporting incidence of the disease.
2. Prompt treatment of infected individuals.
3. Thorough interviewing of the patient for sex contacts. Re-interviewing is desirable and necessary.
4. Rapid investigation of social associates of the initial patient and of his or her sexual contacts. Such "cluster associates" tend to be active sexually in ways similar to the initial patient. The examination of such groups of individuals reveals with surprising frequency many individuals who are otherwise unaware that they carry syphilitic organisms.

Gonorrhea, although potentially less dangerous than syphilis to a human, is the more intractable disease. First, the individual afflicted with the disease does not build up an immunity to it. The individual can, therefore, easily be reinfected even after adequate treatment. Second, there is no simple test for gonorrhea. Taking a culture requires a physician's supervision and accurate diagnosis frequently requires the aid of a trained technician. In addition, the accuracy of the culture does not approach the nearly 100% accuracy of serological tests for syphilis. Third, the common antibiotics that formerly had proven themselves so effective against gonorrhea have produced mutant resistant strains. When such strains are encountered, which do not yield to the usual therapy, other newer antibiotics are employed.

Eradication of gonorrhea requires a different approach from that commonly employed. Recently, a 2-minute serologic slide test for gonorrhea has been devised, which identifies asymptomatic infected carriers. Its reliability and value for mass screening are still under scrutiny. Medical science, also, is still searching for a serum or vaccine which will render an individual resistant to this noxious disease.

It has been postulated that the diseases of syphilis and gonorrhea could be controlled if there were a national VD Day, in which any individual who could possibly have sexual intercourse would receive antibiotics simultaneously within a 24-hour period. The nation as a whole would refrain from sexual activity during that time. This concept is presented for its novelty rather than its practicality.

More feasible, especially with gonorrhea, would be concerted effort in eradicating the disease from segments of the population in which the incidence of the disease is known to be very high. Specifically, these groups are teenagers, homosexuals, and some lower economic groups. Cultures might be taken from teenagers, for example, during routine physical examinations at school or camp. Thorough enlightenment of the homosexual community would be enhanced by publication of medical articles pertaining specifically to them on venereal diseases in newspapers and journals of wide circulation, as well as in underground homosexual newspapers. Examinations for venereal diseases should be made a routine procedure for all patients attending county hospitals or public health centers, where many of the lower economic groups go for medical treatment.

All such procedures will require the vigorous aid and financial backing of an enlightened community.

References

Brown, William J., et al. 1970. *Syphilis and Other Venereal Diseases.* Cambridge, Mass.: Harvard University Press.

Roberts, Richard N. (ed.). 1971. "Syphilis," *Clinical Symposia*, Vol. 23, No. 3. Summit, N.J.: Ciba Pharmaceutical Products.

21

an anthropological approach to sexuality

It is advantageous at this point for the reader to consider the basic animal nature of man's sexual drives. In Chapter 1, it was explained that sexual behavior in man is a learned response. This theme was further developed in the chapter on psychosexual development. Yet, we must recognize that man, Homo sapiens, has a basic sexual nature that has evolved from his animal ancestry through a series of primitive societies to its present state.

Fortunately, the science of anthropology, among other responsibilities, has concerned itself with the evolutionary development of man's basic nature. Many such anthropological studies have been published. Until recently, sexuality was not considered a separate discipline of anthropology but was mixed with studies of general cultural patterns, customs, traditions, and behavior in a given group. Ruth Benedict's Patterns of Culture is an excellent example of a composite study of primitive societies.

Ford and Beach have synthesized the sexual behavior of animals and man in a single book, Patterns of Sexual Behavior. *Much of the information in this chapter is derived from their book, supplemented by additional information published in recent years.*

Anthropological Techniques

To gain insight into modern civilized man's sexual behavior, anthropologists have taken three avenues of investigation. They study the sexual behavior of mammals lower than man, paying special attention to the closest kin of man. They make a comparative study of societies of man, paying special attention to the primitive societies. They glean information from the historical ruins and writings of man.

MAMMALIAN SEXUAL BEHAVIOR.   Among some mammals, particularly the more primitive forms, sexual behavior is hormonally controlled. Intercourse occurs only at such times as conception is possible. It is mediated by the hormone estrogen. With evolutionary sophistication, cortical control in the brain comes into play, until in the human female the process of sexual activity has little, if any, relationship to the hormonal status of an individual female.

COMPARATIVE SEXUAL BEHAVIOR OF SOCIETIES.   Ford and Beach surveyed 190 human societies, most of which are considered primitive by our Western standards. They were located in many parts of the world. The authors stress that no one society is characteristic for all *Homo sapiens.* They emphasize that a cross-cultural approach must be used to verify any general behavioral pattern in man.

HISTORICAL RUINS AND WRITINGS.   In essence, this topic has been covered in the chapter devoted to the historical background of sexual mores and customs. However, material from written sources in the past probably reflects only one aspect of the sexual activities of a society, the aspect of the upper social and economic classes, for probably what was written during those times was the product of the intelligentsia.

Conclusions Derived From Anthropological Studies

There seems to be a common mammalian pattern of sexual behavior, including *Homo sapiens.* Many of the behavioral patterns that occur in certain human societies can also be found among apes, monkeys, and on occasion among lower mammals. Primates, which include man, regularly exhibit the following sexual activities: sex play in childhood, self-stimulation, homosexual behavior, and foreplay.

SEX PLAY IN CHILDHOOD. Sex play among adolescents occurs in many species of primates other than our own. The frequency, variety, and completeness of prepubertal sexual reaction tends to increase from the lower mammals to the higher. The amount and variety of such behavior is directly related to evolutionary development; the more advanced is the species, the more extensive and varied is the sexual play prior to maturity.

There seems to be a human tendency for some degree of sexual activity to occur in immature persons long before they are capable of fertile coitus. Different societies treat these sexual manifestations in different ways. In some, sexual play is strongly discouraged, even forbidden. In others it is encouraged.

Among apes, sex play of a more sophisticated nature, simulating mounting, is noted at an earlier stage of development than in man.

SELF-STIMULATION. Manipulation and stimulation of one's own sexual organs can be regarded as basically mammalian. Such activity seems to have its origin in the licking and manipulation of the genitalia by lower mammals, presumably for the purposes of cleanliness. In apes and monkeys, masturbation is found much more frequently in the male than in the female, in whom it is relatively rare.

Human societies vary widely in their attitudes toward masturbation. Some societies encourage masturbation during childhood, whereas others strongly condemn it. Adult masturbation, for the most part, is ridiculed. Among humans, as also among apes, masturbation is more common in the male than in the female.

HOMOSEXUAL BEHAVIOR. Homosexual behavior is never the predominant type of adult sexual activity. Heterosexual coitus is the dominant sexual activity in the majority of the adults in every human society. However, homosexual behavior of some sort is found among human beings in most societies. Again, it is more common in men than in women. The frequency seems to be a factor related to the size of the group studied.

Homosexuality is also found among apes, where immature animals indulge in many homosexual manifestations. Following puberty, however, there seems to be a decrease in such homosexual play. In apes, also, the phenomenon is more common among males than among females.

FOREPLAY. It is evident that many elements of the human heterosexual coital pattern are determined by heredity. For example, the male erection and ejaculation are basically present in all animals. Similarly, the tendency to respond to rhythmic stimulation of the genitals or a thrusting movement of the pelvic region is a fundamental reaction in the mammalian repertoire.

In many mammalian species, application of the male's mouth to the vulvar and clitoral areas of the female is common. The forefeet or hands assist in this stimulation.

Among human societies, there is always some element of foreplay. In modern American society, studies have shown that the social stratum of the individual frequently is related to the degree of variations employed in the foreplay, the lower social classes being somewhat less imaginative.

Basic Concepts Common To Human Societies

There seem to be certain basic concepts, universal in man, which societies have adopted from their own experience and learning.

There is a universal prohibition against primary incest, that is, incest between parent and offspring or between siblings. This is in marked contrast to subhuman species, wherein parents and progeny freely interbreed. Some social learning has apparently made this concept significant for man, and one might teleologically expect that it was significant in the preservation of the family as a nucleus, as well as in the avoidance of genetic disorders.

There appears to be a taboo against intercourse with a menstruating female in most societies. The reasons for this are not immediately self-evident, but one might postulate that menstruation at an early point in man's evolutionary development had some mystical significance.

It seems that man, by his very nature, has some tendency toward forming a nuclear family, or certainly a tendency toward some form of community living. Apes, monkeys, and other primates also exhibit a pack phenomenon and rarely live independently, unless one of their number is ousted for some reason from the group.

Conclusion

It is appropriate at this point to imply that because a phenomenon is natural does not justify it as being necessarily correct or desirable for modern living. Man "au naturel" is certainly not man as we see and know him in today's society and might well be a rather unpleasant fellow at best.

The lesson to be gained by observing man in this natural light is to note what tremendous effects culture, learning, and society have placed, and are placing, on his basic nature.

References

BENEDICT, RUTH. 1961. *Patterns of Culture.* Boston: Houghton Mifflin.

FORD, C. S., AND F. A. BEACH. 1951. *Patterns of Sexual Behavior.* New York: Harper & Bros, and Paul B. Hoeber.

MORRIS, DESMOND. 1969. *The Human Zoo.* New York: McGraw-Hill.

22

sex and the family

Historically, sexual responsibilities have been assigned to the family unit. These include what might be called "permissible sexual activity," that is, sexual activity within a marriage, and sexual training of the young. Even extraneous sexuality is described in terms of the family and marriage. Thus we refer to such affairs as extramarital intercourse and premarital intercourse.

Obviously the family has other functions, such as social, economic, and disciplinary activities, but in the following discussion, because of the subject of this book, consideration of these other functions will be subordinated to the sexual aspects of the family.

Initially we shall observe the traditional American family as it existed on the frontier in the late 1800's and early 1900's. We do this because this is the family that so many of us remember with affection and nostalgia, just as we look back on the old family doctor or the

244

corner grocery store. This belief of what a family used to be is inten-sified by modern communications, particularly television, in which an attempt is made to show this family structure as ideal.

We shall then analyze the family as it exists today with the problems that confront it, its successes, and its shortcomings. Finally we shall take a look at the family of the future and try to get some idea of the direction in which this social institution is heading.

The Traditional American Family

The typical American family of yesteryear was a self-sufficient rural unit. The economic basis for the family was agricultural, and the success of a given family depended on the full cooperation of its members.

Emphasis was on material and practical things. Marriages were frequently economic arrangements, thereby joining one farm with another. Mate selection also centered on such practical considerations as a sturdy constitution, good working habits, good cooking, and good breeding stock. Marriage frequently did not take place until a maiden had proven she could become pregnant.

In such a self-sufficient, cooperative, and extremely practical social unit as this early American family, there developed a unity, based on economic ties and personal loyalties. From this unity the purpose and meaning of family life truly emerged.

This family was characterized by the following:

1. The responsibility of the individual to fit the family's needs. The family came first and the individual came second. To disobey was considered selfish or ungrateful or inconsiderate of the rest of the family.
2. Being an autocratic unit, governed by a single authority, who made considerable demands. From this authority there was no recourse, neither within the family unit nor within the legal courts of that day. The authoritarian figure demanded immediate obedience and allowed little personal freedom.

The major function of sexuality in those times was procreation. Large families were considered financially beneficial. Extramarital affairs were not condoned other than in a brothel. Moreover, the head of the household had too much responsibility within the family to tie himself down with a deeply involved sexual relationship outside the family. The sexual practices of young girls were closely regulated, as daughters represented an economic benefit; they were condemned if they became pregnant out of wedlock by an undesirable individual who would not be an asset to the family. However, once an engagement was announced, a great deal of sexual freedom was permitted.

The change of this family to the family of today was primarily accomplished by two factors.

1. A shift of population of major proportion from a rural to an urban environment. This was accompanied by a decrease in living area per individual. In such a situation, additional youngsters were regarded as economic hinderances rather than assets.

2. Certain sociohistoric changes. As presented by Lantz and Snider in their book *Marriage*, along with the development of democracy on a national scale, democracy developed in the home. With it secularism and humanism were born within the family unit.

This new family, then, exhibits different characteristics from the old-style family. For example, family control now is predominantly based on democratic individualism. Authority, which was associated with the desire to be right, has become more rational. The family is now an association of equals, and family members are treated as human beings with inherent dignity of their own. It is this family that we shall attempt to analyze as it exists today.

The Family Of Today

The family of today exists as a unit of a mother, a father, and two or three children. Gone are the grandparents, aunts, and uncles of former years, who now live apart from this unit. The family lives, for the most part, in an urban or suburban area and is characterized by financial and materialistic affluence. Yet it frequently seems incapable of getting ahead financially because of the constant demands for newer and better material objects.

The family appears to be faced with three major problems: (1) divorce, (2) the role played by each individual within the family, and (3) child rearing.

DIVORCE. Nation-wide, two out of five marriages end in divorce.

In the most avant-garde areas, such as California, possibly two out of three marriages end in the courts. The younger the ages of those individuals engaging in marriage, the more likely they are to wind up in the divorce courts. We are here faced with a dichotomy. The religious leaders, philosophers, and moralists of our society, and seemingly a high majority of people with whom one talks, feel that this horrendous divorce rate represents a real blot on the state of marriage. They contend that divorce is evil, that it represents a failure, that it leaves both partners damaged, and that it singularly and adversely effects the development of the children involved in these dissolved marriages.

Some sociologists and humanists on the other hand take a somewhat different view. They feel divorce is a safety valve that allows the institution of monogamous marriage to continue. They say that were it not for the possibility of divorce, fewer people would marry, and that those individuals who do get divorced, for the most part, remarry. If they get divorced again, they remarry again. The idea, then, is that those people who are inclined toward divorce are those people who are inclined to marry, and this is the only way the monogamous marital state can continue to exist.

As a corollary, the rate of marital infidelity is also rather drastically increasing. Estimates indicate that 60% of all married men and 30 to 35% of all married women have at least one extramarital affair. Here, too, the sociologists and the moralists come into some area of conflict.

The moralist will argue that there is no question that an individual who is betrayed and finds out about it will respond by feeling humiliated, deceived, and filled with a desire for revenge. Thus the act causes at least one partner a tremendous degree of unhappiness. The possibility also exists that the partner who undertakes what initially is interpreted as a casual extramarital affair may become deeply involved emotionally, thus depriving the spouse of emotional support. To be sure, most extramarital affairs in American society are quite casual, in contrast to the more deeply involved European romances. Yet American society is not immune to deep involvement, and the straying partner may eventually find himself or herself in a dilemma.

Some sociologists, on the other hand, look at infidelity, as well as at divorce, as a safety valve. They contend that whereas in the past it was felt the adulterer was notoriously neurotic, unhappily married, and out of sorts in general, this pattern is no longer the case. Many of the unfaithful, perhaps even a majority, are not seriously dissatisfied with their marriages or their mates, and a fair number or more live happily married lives. Only about one-third, and perhaps fewer, appear to seek extramarital sex for neurotic motives; the rest do so for nonpathological reasons.

Many of the unfaithful, perhaps even a majority, do not feel that they, their mates, or their marriages have been harmed. Some even contend that their marriages have been helped and in some cases saved by this activity

THE ROLE PLAYED BY EACH INDIVIDUAL WITHIN THE FAMILY. In the family of the early 1900's, everyone had a succinct place, which, even though it might have been undesirable, did offer some element of security and importance. In today's family, this condition frequently does not exist. Mother has now become a breadwinner. Not only is she now a breadwinner and a mother, but some of her historical maternal duties have been taken over by the father. The father then becomes a breadwinner, a father, and a part-time mother (cf. Chapter 13, Gender Roles).

The children's position in the family is also altered. The child lacks the loyalty for an apartment complex that he had for the farm. He therefore frequently has to go to external areas for recognition. He must attain his rewards and self-satisfaction from academic or other achievements outside the home, for he no longer can be recognized for those things which he does "around the house."

There also seems to be a tendency toward children becoming buddies of their parents. This situation may have healthy emotional repercussions, but at the same time such a situation may confuse children about the roles they and their parents play within the family unit.

CHILD REARING.   The family faces two questions regarding child rearing. First, which parent is responsible, and to what degree, for the physical needs of the child and his general well-being? Second, which parent, and to what degree, is responsible for the emotional growth and the installation of value systems within the child?

Such tasks as feeding and clothing children have been traditionally handled by the mother of the family, whereas the father more often was saddled with providing adequate housing and finance. One notes now, for example, in cases of divorce, that either parent seems quite capable of handling both chores adequately. If a radical change has occurred in the family, it has occurred now only in that children are more involved with decision making, such as making their own meals or choosing their own clothing.

The second question traditionally offered no problem to the family, inasmuch as the authority figure, usually the father, as previously mentioned, set the tone, and a code of strict obedience was adhered to. Following World War II, however, a more permissive, almost laissez-faire attitude began to develop by which the child frequently set the tone as to what he could or could not do. The parents, out of fear of suppressing the child, and frequently out of fear of their own uncertainty, acquiesced to childhood demands. This has lead to the creation of many problems within the family regarding rules and expectations.

More recently, it is refreshing to note, parents are again beginning to set standards of behavior and demanding some adherence to them. However, in contrast to the more traditional patterns, parents are now modifying these standards when necessary or when the standards appear to be unjust or unreasonable. They also are defending them where and when necessary. As in any other social situation, the proof of the pudding is in the eating. It takes a generation raised in a certain environment to answer whether that environment was a wholesome one.

Solving The Problems

How has the family of today attempted to rectify some of these problems and with what success? One method employed has been the avant-garde method of communal living. Here, 3 to possibly 100 individuals join in a single family unit. To date, although this relationship has worked for some, it has generally failed. Problems arising with interpersonal communication, such as jealousies or differences in the willingness to cooperate, have turned people away from this Utopian concept. It is possible that in the future a similar system may evolve which is more satisfactory, but I believe it would require some change in human nature as we know it today.

An even greater number of individuals are engaging in a form of trial marriage. The concept of young people living together as husband and wife without being legally wedded has existed for many years among the poorer elements of the population. Recently, however, the more affluent middle-class young adult has found himself in this situation and has seemingly adjusted quite well to it. Here the motivations are certainly the prime indicator of the success of such an endeavor. If these motivations are basically healthy, and one individual is not really exploiting another, this type of trial marriage may frequently lead to legal marriage. If it does not, both individuals may leave their relationship with each more mature and better prepared for eventual legal marriage elsewhere.

In some instances, a marriage contract has been devised that stipulates precisely the role to be enacted by each of the individuals entering the marriage. This is a product of a more sophisticated and intellectual group, in which the wife frequently will have a career of her own that financially equals, or may even exceed, that of her spouse. By this method careful guidelines are drawn delineating what each partner will contribute and take from the marriage.

Some married couples have attempted to attain a more liberalized attitude toward sexuality. They may take separate vacations. Others are allowing their mates one night a week on the town. Still others have organized sexual groups of two or more couples and exchanged marital partners with the hope of removing the boredom that they claim has surrounded their marital life as well as their sexual experiences. One cannot say that this latter attempt is doomed to failure, but one can comment that this has not been avidly accepted, and many individuals who initially were excited about the concept have abandoned it. Whereas the rules stated the encounter was to be only with one individual and purely sexual, frequently other circumstances arose. Such complications as indiscriminate gossip and blackmail occurred.

As far as child rearing is concerned, studies indicate rather conclusively that a child is better off reared in the environment of a home, however bad it may be, as compared with that of an institution with no parental involvement whatever. In the kibbutzim of Israel, where children were literally taken from their parents and reared as products of the kibbutz, it has been found desirable to increase the amount of time children spend with their parents to allow the former greater identification with the latter and to make the children a part of the family unit, although they are still part of the greater family unit, namely, the kibbutz. Certainly additional experimentation will be tried, which leads to our final topic, the family of the future.

The Family Of The Future

Alvin Toffler, among other authors, in his book *Future Shock* has dared to make some predictions on the future of the family. His views are worth examining.

In his early speculation Toffler quotes other authors. For example, Ferdinand Lundberg states, "The family is dead except for the first year or two of child raising." William Wolfe parallels this by saying, "This will be its only function." Family optimists, on the other hand, feel that the family is in for a golden age. They theorize that as leisure time increases, families will spend more time together and will derive great satisfaction from joint activity. This concept is embodied in the saying, "The family that plays together, stays together." Toffler also quotes Dr. Irvine W. M. Greenberg's view, "People will marry for stable structure." According to Greenberg, the family serves as one's portable roots, "anchoring one against the storm of change." In short, the more transient and novel the environment, the more important the family will become. A similar opinion is espoused by Morton Hunt, who theorizes that marriage is a microcosm and that we are living now in a rather cold macrocosm. Hunt implies that individuals have many neighbors but few lifelong friends. He states, "Our lives are controlled by remote governments, huge companies, and insensate computers. Alone and impotent, one can find intimacy and warmth only in the confines of a family relationship, a loving relationship, and a marriage relationship." I share this viewpoint and personally feel that the family will continue and will serve a much more psychological function than in the past, and possibly a less economic one.

Toffler predicts other events.

1. The end of motherhood. Toffler sees, as we have alluded in Chapter 8, Genetic Engineering, that motherhood will become a thing of the past. Not only from the standpoint of physical motherhood, but from the standpoint of emotional motherhood, the female will no longer feel a bond and responsibility in raising an infant.

2. The streamlined family. As discussed earlier in this chapter, the family of today has been streamlined to a father, a mother, and two or three children, excluding such relatives as aunts,

uncles, and grandparents. Toffler's streamlined family goes a step further and excludes even the children. The family will become a highly mobile couple who can move freely from place to place. He expects people of the future to further streamline the marriage by matching individuals as to career, similar educational and social goals, and similar desires for geographical location (cf. Chapter 13, Gender Roles).

3. Biological parents and professional parents. The chapter on genetic engineering presents the view that it is wholly possible for a couple to have children to order, as it were, with one or neither of the couple being the biological parent. Toffler presents the possibility that additional specialization should be entertained with professional parents rearing the child rather than amateur parents. The moral implications of this thought, however, are at the moment at least beyond the average comprehension.

4. Communes and homosexual daddies. Toffler points to the concept of communes as an alternative to marriage as we know it. He anticipates that with a mobile working force, however, this will become somewhat impractical and suggests that, ". . . communal experiments will first proliferate among those in the society who are free from the industrial discipline —the retired population, the young, the dropouts, the students, as well as among self-employed professional and technical people. Later, when advanced technology and information systems make it possible for much of the work of society to be done at home via computer-telecommunication hookups, communalism will become feasible for larger numbers." He also suggests that homosexual communes will be acceptable, but does not hazard the guess as to whether the adopted children of those communes will be of the same or opposite sex of its adult members.

5. Sequential marriage. For the future Toffler seems to envision the concept of love as we know it today as disappearing. The relationship of a couple will be defined as "parallel development," whereby two people will move side-by-side along similar paths of development and at the same rate of speed to maintain their one-to-one relationship. Toffler believes, however, that the odds are almost impossible for such a relationship to extend through a lifetime. One individual will go a bit

faster, the other slower, and although the two may retain sight of one another for a while, it is highly unlikely they will do so for a lifetime. He therefore propounds that an individual will have a series of marriages. The first will be a trial marriage and have no legal standing. If it is successful, it may develop into a second marriage for childbearing and rearing. There may be another marriage after the children have left home and possibly one or more additional marriages at the time of retirement. The marital lives of people then will be characterized by what Toffler calls "marriage trajectories," a series of marriages, rather than by whether they are married or not married as we think of the union today.

Conclusion

I do not believe one can draw any valid conclusions about the future of the family at this point. I do think the reader is well-advised to realize that the family is in a state of flux and that the family of today is neither the family of yesterday nor the family within which he will find himself in the very near future. I think the reader should adjust his goals and thinking with new knowledge and scientific advances in mind and should seek a marital mate who fits a wide variety of criteria. The person so doing should be able to make adjustments with the mate selected, rather than to simply "fall in love" and let the devil take the hindmost.

References

LANTZ, H. R., AND E. C. SNIDER. 1969. *Marriage*, 2nd ed. New York: Wiley.

TOFFLER, ALVIN. 1970. *Future Shock*. New York: Random House. Also New York: Bantam, 1971.

23

religious attitudes toward sexuality

Through the centuries organized religion and individual sexual practices have been intimately associated. The theologic basis for this marriage is deep-rooted in Judeo-Christian precepts. This basis originated with the concept of original sin and the subsequent fall of man following Adam's indiscretion. It continues through such basic doctrines as the Ten Commandments, of which two succinctly relate to sexuality: (1) Thou Shalt not Commit Adultery; and (2) Thou Shalt not Covet Thy Neighbor's Wife. Christianity, with its focus on the virgin birth and subsequent orders lauding celibacy, has further intermeshed religious and sexual thoughts.

Moreover, in a rather pragmatic way, as the theologians attempted to focus on man's moral conduct, they frequently equated morality with proper sexual behavior. Sexuality offered an undertaking that was common to all believers and that rather clearly demonstrated the lust of man. Somehow this sexuality tied into his animal ancestry. Control of this lust, therefore, raised man to a higher, more God-like plane. This concept was rather easy for the average man to understand and accept.

In a book of the type I am writing, I have focused much attention on the feelings and the emotional aspects of sexuality. It therefore seems quite appropriate to present a brief discussion of religious attitudes toward sexuality, for there is no question but that much adult sexual behavior is dictated by what has been learned in childhood religious experiences. Certainly much of the guilt associated with sexuality in the past has had its basis with theological teaching. Modern religious leaders have amended this problem but still retain a germane influence on sexual teaching.

The expanse and intricacy of religious attitudes offer major difficulties in discussing the relations between sexuality and religion. Each individual has his own religious beliefs, and it is difficult for any one person to evaluate the subject of religion as a whole. Moreover, there are so many religious sects, even within the major religions, that it is difficult to express a single opinion for any one religion. Within Judaism one is confronted with the orthodox, conservative, and reformed viewpoints; in Catholicism with the traditional versus the liberal viewpoints; and in Protestantism with the many denominations, each with its own code of moral behavior. Certainly volumes could be written on the subject.

My purpose in devoting these relatively few pages to sex and religion is really to stimulate thought, rather than to cover any one phase of sex and religion in depth. What I present here, therefore, is a brief summary of those topics of sexuality that are discussed in some way by all religious groups. The reader can then fall back on his own religious experience and the references to analyze the viewpoint of any single religion.

The Stand Of Religion On Five Major Sexual Topics

The five most prominent sexual subjects on which religion has taken a stand are premarital coitus, homosexuality, adultery, contraception, and abortion.

PREMARITAL COITUS. Organized religion suggests that this is

not preferential behavior, but organized religion is also quite aware that this coitus exists and that it may be on the increase. Whereas older religious teachings emphasized the unholiness of the act and the concept that it was a sin, modern religious leaders emphasize that this behavior is emotionally unhealthy for the individual. The trend, then, is toward a psychological reason for keeping coital activity within the framework of a marriage. The average clergyman, when questioned, has certainly seen the messes into which younger members of society have gotten themselves by premarital coitus and suggests that these difficulties could have been avoided through abstinence. The clergy stresses the value of the individual and the fact that by engaging in premarital activity one might be selling himself short by not maintaining proper stature.

HOMOSEXUALITY.   For the most part organized religion does not approve of homosexual activity. It considers the act to be unnatural and in being so runs contrary to the will of God. Moreover, organized religion is also extremely interested in the family and its preservation, and homosexuality runs contrary to the usual concept of family life. However, religious leaders are now involving themselves in the treatment of homosexuality to some degree, counseling on it, and have taken a stand that the punishments for being identified as a homosexual may be overly harsh.

ADULTERY.   Adultery to organized religion is wrong. This activity of man is contrary to the word and spirit of God. Within the Ten Commandments it is stated "Thou Shalt not Commit Adultery." In a more subtle fashion, of course, adultery also deteriorates family relationships, and the churches are concerned that the family is a unit and should be preserved.

CONTRACEPTION.   Most religious organizations believe that contraception is permissible. Orthodox Judaism and traditional Catholicism oppose any form of contraception. The theological grounds for this are that it is an unnatural act, that the Scriptures repeatedly instruct man to be fruitful and multiply, and that any overt behavior contrary to this attitude is unnatural.

ABORTION.   The abortion question is currently in a state of flux from the standpoint of theology. Three general viewpoints are expressed. The first is that there is no justification for abortion on any grounds, that abortion per se is taking a human life, and that this is basically sinful. This is perhaps best typified by traditional Catholicism. The second is that abortion is acceptable to preserve the health of the mother. The majority of religions are in general agreement on this point, and the more liberal beliefs will allow that mental, as well as physical, health should be included.

The third viewpoint concedes that abortion on demand is the ideal rule and that no woman under any circumstances need complete a pregnancy if she does not want to do so. The length of pregnancy, of course, makes a significant difference. Only the most liberal religious groups hold to this point of view.

Conclusion

The foregoing comments, to be sure, offer only a brief review of a very complicated situation, one which is not only replete with philosophical thoughts and writings but which also embodies a great deal of emotion in each of us. My aim in this brief presentation is to show that religion and sexuality are closely associated and play a very significant role in our lives and social structure. To ignore this role is to do a disservice to one's self as well as to the subject matter.

References

ELLIS, ALBERT, AND ALBERT ABARBANEL (eds.). 1961. *Encyclopedia of Sexual Behavior*, Vol. 2. New York: Hawthorn.

GITTELSOHN, ROLAND B. 1965. *Consecrated Unto Me, A Jewish View of Love and Marriage*. New York: Union of American Hebrew Congregations.

THIELICKE, HELMUT. 1964. *The Ethics of Sex*. New York: Harper and Row.

WIER, FRANK E. 1962. *Sex and the Whole Person; A Christian View*. New York: Abingdon.

24

sex and the civil law

There is a legal code specifically written regarding marriage and family. The rationale behind this code seems to fall into two categories. In the first place, the state wishes to fix financial responsibility to insure that the state will not have to bear the burden of supporting dependent women and children. Second, the state is interested in marital unions that produce offspring acceptable to the state. Since the state has in a sense pledged itself to a society based on the family as the prime unit, it also encourages sexual activity within the boundaries of a legal marriage.

Restrictions On Marriage

AGE. There are usually two restrictions regarding age that are placed on individuals who are going to get married. The younger level will allow marriage with parental consent. The older level will allow marriage without parental consent. In many states, should the girl be pregnant, these restrictions are waived.

RELATIONSHIP. All states have some definition of family relationships within which people may not marry. In no state can a parent marry his child, a grandparent his grandchild, a brother his sister, an aunt her nephew, or an uncle his niece. As to how distant the relationship may be before marriage is permitted varies markedly from state to state.

RACE. A number of states prohibit marriage between people of different races. However, these statutes have recently been under heavy attack on constitutional grounds, and it is anticipated that those that remain will be declared invalid in the near future.

MENTAL AND PHYSICAL HEALTH. Most states now have some law requiring individuals to seek medical testing before they are allowed to marry. The most common requirement is a premarital test for venereal diseases. Some states further prohibit the marriage of mental defectives, drug addicts, and alcoholics. Unfortunately, these laws are difficult to enforce.

Laws Regarding The Role Of Sex In Marriage

The implication of marriage laws is twofold. First, some degree of "normal" sexual relations shall be maintained. Second, adultery is not permitted. Breaching either of these principles constitutes grounds for divorce or annulment.

IMPOTENCE. Most laws regarding impotence imply that the impotence was present at the time of marriage. Were it to occur after marriage, the impotence could be considered an illness. In other aspects of the marriage vow, illness is not in and of itself a cause for divorce.

STERILITY. Sterility, as with impotence, is allowable as a cause for divorce if the sterility existed at the time of the marriage and if the individual who was sterile knew but concealed this fact from the other party. An element of fraud is thus involved and as such constitutes grounds for divorce or annulment.

PHYSICAL INCAPACITY. If one spouse refuses for reasons of physical incapacity to enter into a sexual relationship with the other, divorce or annulment is allowed in some states.

ABNORMAL SEXUAL PRACTICES.   As stated before, the law suggests that an individual getting married might expect "normal" sexual
intercourse with his mate. There is no obligation per se to submit to
"abnormal" or "unnatural" sexual acts on either part, and insistence
on this type of sexual involvement by one member of the marriage
may well be grounds for divorce. In many states abnormal sexual
practices connote a criminal act as well.

ADULTERY.   With a fair degree of uniformity the laws of the
various states stipulate that a spouse is entitled to the exclusive right
of intercourse with his mate. Therefore, an adulterous act committed
by one member of the marriage becomes grounds for divorce. Interestingly enough, in some states if one member permits or condones
adultery on the part of the mate, that specific adulterous experience
is invalid as a cause for divorce. Another interesting legal ramification
is the situation of one partner of a marriage bringing suit against a
third person for alienation of affection of the other partner. This
alienation of affection may or may not involve adultery.

25

sex and the criminal law

A *maze of laws relates to sexual offenses. These laws vary markedly from state to state and have been summarized in the accompanying chart (Fig. 25–1). It is interesting that most of these laws are not enforcible. Even when circumstances allow them to be enforced, they are frequently ignored.*

However, whereas other areas of law have been changing dynamically during the last 50 years, little change has been made in the laws regarding sexual offenders.

Legal Requirements Concerning Sexual Intercourse

It is somewhat easier to understand the crimes involved if we first understand the positive aspects of sexual intercourse and what is implied legally by sexual intercourse.

sex and society

STATE PENALTIES FOR

STATE	ADULTERY	COHABITATION	FORNICATION	CRIMES AGAINST NATURE**	GENERAL LEWDNESS
ALABAMA	up to 6 months and/or $100 up	up to 6 months and/or $100 up		2–10 years (a, b, c, d)	up to 12 months and/or up to $500
ALASKA	up to 3 months or up to $200	1 to 2 years and/or up to $500		1–10 years (b)	3–12 months or $50–$500
ARIZONA	up to 3 years	up to 3 years		1–5 years (a) 5–20 years (b, c)	1–5 years
ARKANSAS		$20–$100		1–21 years (a, b, c)	
CALIFORNIA	up to 1 year and/or up to $1000			up to 15 years (a) not less than 1 year (b, c)	up to 6 months and/or up to $500
COLORADO					
CONNECTICUT	up to 12 months and/or up to $1000			up to 12 months and/or to $1000 (c, d)	up to 6 months and/or up to $1000
DELAWARE	up to 1 year and/or up to $500			up to 3 years plus up to $1000 (a, b, c)	sentence at the court's discretion
DISTRICT OF COLUMBIA	up to 1 year and/or up to $500		up to 6 months and/or up to $300		up to 90 days and up to $250
FLORIDA	up to 12 months and/or up to $1000	up to 60 days and/or up to $500	up to 60 days and/or up to $500	up to 1 year (under common law) (a, b, c)	up to 60 days and/or up to $500
GEORGIA	up to 12 months and/or up to $1000		up to 12 months and/or up to $1000	1–20 years (a, b) 1–5 years (c)	up to 12 months and/or up to $1000
HAWAII*	(men) 2–12 months and/or $30–$100 (women) 2–4 months and/or $10–$30		1–3 months or $10–$50	up to 20 years and up to $1000 (a, b, c)	up to 1 year and/or up to $1000
IDAHO	3 months–3 years and/or $100–$1000	6 months and/or $300	6 months and/or $300	not less than 5 years (a, b, c, d)	6 months and/or $300
ILLINOIS	up to 1 year and/or up to $500	up to 6 months and/or up to $200	up to 6 months and/or up to $200		
INDIANA	up to 6 months and/or up to $500	up to 6 months and/or up to $500		$100–$1000 (a, b, c) up to 2 to 14 years	$5–$100 up to 6 months
IOWA	up to 3 years or up to 1 year and up to $300	up to 6 months or up to $200		up to 10 years (a, b, c)	up to 6 months or up to $200
KANSAS	up to 1 month and/or up to $500			up to 6 months and/or up to $1000 (a, b, c)	up to 6 months and/or up to $1000
KENTUCKY	$20–$50		$20–$50	2–5 years (a, b, c)	up to 1 year and/or up to $200
LOUISIANA				up to 5 years and/or up to $2000 (a, b, c)	up to 5 years and/or up to $1000
MAINE	up to 5 years or up to $1000	up to 5 years or up to $300	up to 60 days plus up to $100	1–10 years (a, b, c, d)	up to 6 months and up to $25
MARYLAND	$10			up to 10 years and/or up to $1000 (a, c, d) 1–10 (b)	up to 60 days and/or up to $50
MASSACHUSETTS	up to 3 years or up to $500	up to 3 years or up to $300	up to 3 months or up to $30	up to 5 years or $100–$1000(a) up to 20 years (b, c)	up to 3 years or up to $300
MICHIGAN	up to 4 years and/or up to $2000	up to 1 year or up to $500	up to 5 years or up to $2500	up to 5 years or up to $2500(a, d) up to 15 years (b, c)	up to 1 year or up to $500
MINNESOTA	up to 1 year and/or up to $1000 (doesn't apply if female unmarried)		up to 90 days or up to $100	up to 1 year and/or up to $1000 (a, b,) up to 90 days or up to $100 (c, d)	up to 90 days or up to $100

NOTE: IN MANY STATES, THE VIOLATIONS MUST BE PROVED TO BE "OPEN AND NOTORIOUS."
* Effective January 1, 1973, consensual sex between adults is legal under the revised Penal Code.
**Key: a. Oral intercourse (fellatio, cunnilingus)　b. Anal intercourse　c. Sex with animals　d. Sex with the dead

FIGURE 25-1.

CONSENSUAL SEX OFFENSES

STATE	ADULTERY	COHABITATION	FORNICATION	CRIMES AGAINST NATURE**	GENERAL LEWDNESS
MISSISSIPPI	up to 6 months and up to $500	up to 6 months and up to $500		1–10 years (b,c)	up to 6 months or up to $500
MISSOURI	up to 1 year and/or up to $1000			not less than 2 years (a,b,c)	up to 1 year and/or up to $1000
MONTANA		up to 6 months and/or up to $500		not less than 5 years (a,b,c)	
NEBRASKA	up to 1 year	up to 6 months and up to $100		up to 20 years (a,b,c)	up to 90 days or up to $100
NEVADA				1–6 years (a,b,c)	up to 1 year and/or up to $1000
NEW HAMPSHIRE	up to 1 year		up to 1 year or $50	up to 1 year (a,b,c,d)	up to 1 year and/or up to $200
NEW JERSEY	up to 3 years and/or up to $1000		up to 6 months and/or up to $50	up to 20 years and/or up to $5000 (b,c,)	up to 3 years and/or up to $1000
NEW MEXICO				2–10 years and/or up to $5000 (a,b,c)	up to 6 months and/or up to $100
NEW YORK	up to 3 months and/or up to $500			up to 3 months and/or up to $500 (a,b) up to 1 year and/or up to $1000 (c,d)	
NORTH CAROLINA		up to 6 months and/or up to $500		up to 10 years and/or any fine (a,b,c)	
NORTH DAKOTA	1–3 years or up to 1 year and/or up to $500	30 days–1 year or $100–$500	up to 30 days and/or up to $100	up to 10 years (a,b,c,d)	1–5 years and/or up to $1000
OHIO		up to 3 months plus up to $200		1–20 years (a,b,c)	
OKLAHOMA	up to 5 years and/or up to $500			up to 10 years (a,b,c)	up to 5 years and/or up to $5000
OREGON					
PENNSYLVANIA	up to 1 year and/or up to $500		up to $100	up to 10 years and up to $5000 (a,b,c)	up to 1 year and/or up to $500
RHODE ISLAND	up to 1 year or up to $500		up to $10	7–20 years (a,b,c)	up to 1 year and/or up to $5000
SOUTH CAROLINA	6–12 months and/or $100–$500	6–12 months and/or $100–$500	6–12 months and/or $100–$500	5 years and/or not less than $500 (b,c)	sentence at the court's discretion
SOUTH DAKOTA	up to 5 years and/or up to $500			up to 10 years (a,b,c)	up to 1 year and/or up to $2000
TENNESSEE				5–15 years (a,b,c)	
TEXAS	$100–$1000	$50–$500	$50–$500	2–15 years (a,b,c)	$50–$200 and/or 1–6 months
UTAH	up to 3 years	up to 5 years (polygamous cohabitation only)	up to 6 months or up to $100	up to 6 months and/or up to $299 (a,b) 3–20 years (c)	up to 6 months and/or up to $300
VERMONT	up to 5 years and/or up to $1000			1–5 years	up to 5 years or up to $300
VIRGINIA	$20–$100	$50–$500	$20–$100	1–3 years (a,b,c)	up to 1 year and/or up to $1000
WASHINGTON	up to 2 years or up to $1000	up to 1 year and/or up to $1000		up to 10 years (a,b,c,d)	up to 90 days or up to $250
WEST VIRGINIA	not less than $20	up to 6 months and/ or not less than $50	not less than $20	1–10 years (a,b,c)	up to 30 days and/or not less than $50
WISCONSIN	up to 3 years and/or up to $1000	up to 1 year and/or up, to $500	up to 6 months and/or up to $200	up to 5 years and/or up to $500 (a,b,c)	up to 1 year and/or up to $500
WYOMING	up to 3 months plus up to $100	up to 3 months plus up to $100	up to 3 months and up to $100	up to 10 years (a,b,c)	

First, it implies that the parties are legally married when they engage in the act. Second, it seems that the only type of intercourse that is legally permitted is the insertion of the penis within the vagina. Other forms and variations of sexual gratification are prohibited. Third, the act of intercourse must be voluntary for both participants. If it is involuntary, the subject of rape is introduced. Fourth, sexual intercourse must take place in a relatively private confine. Coitus performed in public or in the company of friends is frequently a crime.

Crimes Involving Sexual Intercourse

FORNICATION.   Fornication by definition is the act of sexual intercourse by an unmarried person. If one member of the copulating pair is unmarried, the act becomes fornication and therefore illegal.

ADULTERY.   Although some aspects of adultery are covered by civil law, in some states adultery is also considered a criminal offense. It is fascinating to note the report by the lawyer, Robert V. Sherwin, that in the state of New York there have been fewer than five convictions for adultery during this century, even though adultery has been the only ground for divorce in that state and thousands of divorces have been granted.

RAPE.   The offense of rape falls into two categories. The first is actual rape in which the act occurs "against the will' or "without lawful consent" of the raped individual. Actual rape implies that the act is either forcibly performed or that consent is given out of fear of the alternative consequences. A variation of this theme is rape of an individual who is in no condition to refuse because of the use of such agents as drugs or alcoholic beverages.

The second type of rape is statutory rape. In this case the major factor is the age of the individual involved, and consent or nonconsent is no longer considered. The only defense for a person who has been indicted for statutory rape is (1) to deny that sexual intercourse occurred, or (2) to prove the individual was of legal age of consent. This age of consent varies from state to state. The major difficulty for an accused male in such cases has been that it is almost impossible to tell a young lady's age any more by her outward appearance because of the use of such items as cosmetics, false eyelashes, and hair dyes. It therefore well behooves the male who is suggesting intercourse to establish the age of his paramour.

The punishments for rape are severe—a great deal more severe than for any of the other acts considered.

ABDUCTION. The major factor of concern here is the purpose for which the individual was abducted. If sexual intercourse is involved, punishment is more severe than otherwise. If a state line is crossed in the course of an abduction for sexual purposes, Federal law is also involved by the Mann Act.

SEDUCTION. The underlying premise of seduction is the promise of marriage that has not been fulfilled. As can well be imagined, seduction is a difficult crime to prove.

PROSTITUTION. The element that sets prostitution apart, legally speaking, from fornication or adultery is that the prostitute permits access to her sexual parts in return for a fee.. The offense here lies with the individual who is doing the prostituting. The whole subject of prostitution is a work unto itself as it now falls into the realm of "big business" and has many individuals involved who are not actively engaged in intercourse itself. For example, the operator of the house and the agent or pimp are also legally at fault.

There have often been attempts made to legalize prostitution. One is uncertain what the future of prostitution will be. It is interesting to note that our motion-picture industry in the shows of the late sixties and early seventies tended to glorify the prostitute. Many award-winning movies had their basis in the exciting life herein portrayed.

In general, however, it has been found that the life of the prostitute is a rather unpleasant one and might even be considered in some ways unwholesome, as her emotional sequelae are rather severe.

INCEST. Incest was briefly considered under civil law. It can also be a criminal offense.

Other Aspects Of Sex And Criminal Law

To this point we have discussed laws regarding sexual intercourse. There are also laws regarding sexuality in which sexual intercourse is not a part.

MASTURBATION. There are no laws directly condemning masturbation, but there are certainly laws in reference to it. For example, an individual who masturbates in public might well be convicted of indecent exposure.

Mutual masturbation, regardless of the sexes involved or whether the participants are single or married, is considered illegal in many states as a crime against nature.

Devices that can be used for purposes of masturbation are labeled under the laws of some states as indecent. Hence, to sell or manufacture such articles becomes an offense.

SODOMY AND CRIMES AGAINST NATURE. This area is difficult to interpret under the law as most sexual authorities now condone these acts as part of a total sexual relationship. However, they still exist in the legal codes of various states as criminal offenses whether within or without the confines of marriage.

HOMOSEXUAL BEHAVIOR. In many states an individual who is caught in a homosexual relationship faces the possibility of criminal action. Also an individual who solicits for homosexual purposes or who represents himself as a prostitute for homosexual purposes is subject to prosecution.

Lesbians, although subject to the same laws, are much less frequently arrested for these offenses than the male homosexuals.

In *Sexual Freedom and the Constitution* Walter Barnett, a lawyer who has been a professor at various schools of law, makes an excellent case against the laws governing sodomy and, in turn, a case for homosexuality, as sodomy is frequently a form of homosexual behavior among males. He asserts that there is need to guarantee individual sexual rights in the pursuit of happiness when no one is harmed. His treatise, a fascinating approach to a difficult problem, marshals constitutional arguments against existing Federal and state laws.

OBSCENE AND LEWD BEHAVIOR. There are multiple laws regarding variations upon obscene and lewd behavior. Some statutes have specific "peeping Tom" laws. Obscene telephone conversations or letters may involve a crime as well. The purveyance of pornographic items and the sale of obscene literature are criminal offenses.

Conclusion

Certain aspects of sexuality, such as artificial insemination and changing one's sex, lack legal direction, and the laws attempting to govern sterilization are in a state of uncertainty. By and large the present situation regarding sex and the law is well stated by the lawyer Robert Veit Sherwin in his contribution to *The Encyclopedia of Sexual Behavior*:

> The majority of authorities in the fields of sex and law recognize the need for change in laws that apply to sex, but thus far little has been done toward this end. Instead of changing the laws, it has been the practice of the courts and law-enforcement bodies simply to ignore them. It goes without saying that ignoring the law is not the same as amending it, or legally nullifying it. Failure to enforce existing laws in effect breaks down public respect both for the observed and for the ignored laws.
>
> Many law enforcement authorities and law-revision committees have taken the position that laws concerning sexual behavior should be confined to three major areas: (1) sexual acts that involve the use of force or the threat of force; (2) sexual acts performed in public; (3) sexual acts that involve minors. According to these authorities, all other laws concerning sexual behavior should be eliminated as being unenforcible, useless, antiquated, inapplicable, and generally not within the province of law enforcement in the first place. Although a number of important studies have been made on the subject, all of them coming to approximately the same conclusions as those just stated, to date they have had little effect on the state legislatures.

References

Barnett, Walter. 1973. *Sexual Freedom and the Constitution*. Albuquerque, N.M.: University of New Mexico Press.

Pilpel, Harriet F., and Theodora S. Zavin. 1967. *Laws on Marriage and Family*, in *The Encyclopedia of Sexual Behavior*, ed. by Albert Ellis and Albert Abarbanel. New York: Hawthorn.

Sherwin, Robert Veit. 1967. *Laws on Sex Crimes*, in *The Encyclopedia of Sexual Behavior*, ed. by Albert Ellis and Albert Abarbanel. New York: Hawthorn.

index

A

Abduction, legal aspects of, 265
Abnormal sexual behavior, legal
    aspects of, 260
Abortion, 101, 103, 213–225
  anesthesia and, 218
  bizarre methods of, 219–220
  Colorado law and, 222
  complications from, 220–221
  dilation of cervix and, 218
  emotional consequences of, 221
  estrogen and, 219
  legal aspects of, 108, 187, 222–224
  methods of, 217–220

Abortion (*cont.*)
  morality of, 224–225
  morning-after pill and, 219
  physiological activity of fetus
    and, 107
  prostaglandins and, 219
  religious views regarding, 214,
    221–222, 256–257
  statistics on deaths from, 220–221
  statistics on incidence of, 214,
    216–217
  those who seek an, 214–216
Adrenal cortex, 76
Adultery:
  legal aspects of, 260–264
  religious view regarding, 256

269

Amniocentesis, 100
Amniotic fluid:
    abortion and, 219
    amniocentesis and, 100
    weight of, 111–112
Ampulla:
    of breast, 61–62
    of vas deferens, 48–50
Anal-genital sex: 140
    gonorrhea and, 235–236
    homosexuality and, 173
    syphilis and, 230, 234
Analgesia during childbirth, 120–121
Anal phase of psychosexual
        development, 129
Anesthesia:
    abortion and, 218
    childbirth and, 120–121
    Queen Victoria and, 38
Anthropological techniques and
        sexuality, 240
*Appetitional Theory of Sexual
        Motivation, An* (Hardy), 142
Areola of breast, 61
Arsphenamine, 229
Atresia, 69
Attitudes, sexual, 5–6, 12–13
Autosomes, 11, 97–99

B

Barnett, Walter, 266
Barr body, 101
Bartholin glands, 74–75
    relation to bulbourethral glands, 75
    sexual activity and, 92
    venereal disease and, 235
Bauman, K. E., 212
Beach, F. A., 240
Belzer, E. G., Jr., 19
Benedict, Ruth, 239
Bergler, Edmund, 58
Bergström, S., 219
Berne, Eric, 18

Bestiality in ancient Rome, 25
Bieber, Irving, 175–176
Biological theory of psychosexual
        development, 127–128
Birth control, 186–187
Blackman, Justice Harry A., 222
Blair, Ralph, 176
Blastocyst, 99
Blowing, 173
Body language, 18
Body Language (Fast), 18
Braxton-Hicks contractions, 113
Breast, 61–64
    artificial, 63
    enlargement of, 63
    female libido and, 63
    hormones and, 64
    pregnancy and, 111
    sexual activity and, 86–87
Breast-feeding:
    bottle-feeding versus, 124
    menstruation and, 116
Broad ligament, 67
Brutality, ancient Roman sexual, 25
Buggery, 173
Bulbocavernosus muscle, 49, 55, 96
Bulbourethral glands: 49–51
    pre-ejaculatory emission and, 54,
        192
    relation to Bartholin glands, 75

C

Cabeza de negro, 199
Calderone, Mary S., 214
Catholicism, Roman:
    abortion and, 221–222
    contraception and, 193
    sexual views of, 255–257
Cervical plugs, 191
Cervix:
    abortion and, 217–218
    anatomy and physiology of, 66–67,
        70–71

Cervix (*cont.*)
  childbirth and, 114, 116
  diaphragms and, 195
  functions of, 71
  incompetent, 71
  labor and, 114
  pregnancy and, 111, 122
Cesarean birth, 121, 209–210
Cesarean operation, 209–210
Chang, Chin-Chuan, 40
Chastity, female gender role and, 161
Chemotaxis, ovum and, 69
Childbirth methods:
  Dick-Read, 121
  La Maze, 121
Child rearing, 248–250
Chorionic gonadotropin, 79
Christianity, early:
  antisexual teachings of, 27
  penitentials and, 28
  sexuality during, 25–27
Chromosomes, 97
  autosomes, 97–99
  sex, 98–99
Circumcision, 22, 52
Climax (*see* Orgasm)
Clitoris, 4, 66, 72, 74
  sexual activity and, 88–91
  uniqueness of, 159
Coition (*see* Sexual intercourse)
Coitus (*see* Sexual intercourse)
Coitus interruptus, 192
Colorado, abortion law in, 222
Communes, family, 252
Condom, 32, 193–194
  ancient Rome and, 191
  venereal disease and, 234, 236
Contraception, 190–212
  appliance methods of, 193–203
  history of, 191
  moral concepts, population and, 187
  nonappliance methods of, 192–193
  poor and, 210–211
  religious views regarding, 211, 256
  supplies and, 210
  underdeveloped nations and, 187

Contraceptives:
  condom, 32, 193–194
  copper T, 197–198
  criteria for the perfect, 191–192
  Dalkon shield, 197
  diaphragm, 194–196
  foam, 202
  intrauterine device (I.U.D.,
    I.U.C.D.), 196–198
  jelly, 202
  Lippes loop, 197–198
  pill:
    combination, 199
    sequential, 199
  vaginal douche, 202–203
Copper T, 197–198
Copula carnalis, 27
Copula fornicatoris, 27
Copulation, 33 (*see also* Sexual
    intercourse)
Corona of penis during coitus, 93
Corpus albicans, 68–69, 78
Corpus cavernosum (*pl.* corpora
    cavernosa), 46, 51–53
Corpus luteum, 67–68, 76, 78
Cortisol, 64
Counseling about sexual intercourse,
    152–157
Couple, The (Mr. and Mrs. "K"), 140
Cowper's glands (*see* Bulbourethral
    glands)
Creatinine, 101
Cremasteric muscle, 46–48
Crimes against nature, 266
Cryptorchism, 47
Cunt, 18

D

Dalkon shield, 197
D&C (*see* Dilation and curettage)
Darkfield test for syphilis, 233
Dark Ages, sexuality during 27–29
Dartos muscle, 46, 48

Decter, Midge, 161
Demerol, 120
Diaphragm, contraceptive, 194–196
Dickinson, R. L., 82, 86
Dick-Read, Grantley, 121
Dilation and curettage (D&C), 217
Dilation, cervical, 71, 114, 116
Dilaudid, 120
Dildo, 173
Divorce, 246–247
Don Juan complex, 156
Donovania granulomatis, 227
Double standard among Jews, 21–22
Douche:
    vaginal, 202–203
    venereal disease and, 234
Dualism, 23, 25–26
Ductless glands, 33 (*see also*
        Endocrine glands)
Ductus deferens (*see* Vas deferens)
Dyspareunia, 149

E

EDC (Estimated Date of
        Confinement), 107
EEG (*see* Electroencephalogram)
Ehrlich, Paul (German bacteriologist
        and pathologist), 229
Ehrlich, Paul R. (American biologist),
        185, 187
Eighteenth century, sexuality during,
        35–36
Ejaculate, 54–55
Ejaculation:
    physiological aspects, 54–55, 95
    premature, 148
    psychological aspects, 96
    sociological aspects, 96
Ejaculatory duct, 49–51
Electroencephalogram and detection
        of life, 108
Embryo, 105–106
Encylcopedia of Sexual Behavior
        (Ellis and Abarbanel), 11, 267

Endocrine glands (Ductless glands),
        63
    adrenal, 76
    ovaries, 64, 66–69, 76, 200, 206
    pituitary, 64–65, 74, 200
    placenta, 64, 76, 79, 119
    testes, 46–50, 56
Endocrines (*see* Hormones)
Endometrium, 67, 70, 76–78
Enlightenment, The, 35–36
Enovid, 199
Ephron, Nora, 161
Epididymis (*pl.* epididymides), 48–50
Episiotomy, 116, 120
Equal Rights Amendment, 160
Erection:
    coitus and, 93
    foreplay and, 93
    paraplegic men and, 53
    parasympathetic nervous system,
        and, 53
    physiology of, 52–54
    sexual intercourse and, 93
    sympathetic nervous system and,
        53
Erythroblastosis fetalis, 113
Escutcheon, 73
Essay on Population (Malthus), 36
Estrogens:
    breast and, 63–64
    contraceptive pill and, 199–201
    corpus luteum and, 69
    labor onset and, 114
    menopause and, 80
    morning-after pill and, 219
    ovarian follicles and, 68–76
    placenta and, 64, 119
    production and activity of, 76–80
Estrous cycle, 77–79
    estrogen (proliferation) phase of, 77
    menstrual phase of, 78
    pregnant phase of, 78
    progesterone (secretory) phase of, 77
Eunuchoidism, 99
*Everything You Always Wanted to
        Know about Sex
        but Were Afraid to Ask*
        (Reuben), 11

Extramarital coitus:
   not condoned, 245
   number having, 247
   in Sparta, 23

F

Fallopian tube (*see* Uterine tube)
Family:
   change in structure of, 188
   future, 251–253
   sex and, 244–253
   today's, 246–249
   traditional American, 245–246
Fast, Julius, 18
Father, role of the modern, 248
Fellatio in ancient Rome, 25
Fellator, 180
Female gender role, 160–163, 188
Fertilization, 78, 97–99
Fetal membranes, 106
Fetal triangle,100
Fetology, 105–110
Fetus:
   abortion and, 218–219
   definition of, 105
   determination of life in, 108
   growth of, 107–109
   parasitic nature of, 112, 119
   physiological activity of, 107, 109–110
   weight of, 105-106
Flagellation, 31, 35, 38
Fluorescent treponemal antibody test (FTA) for syphilis, 233
Foams, contraceptive, 202
Follicles:
   atretic, 68–69
   in elderly women, 77
   ovarian, 68
   ruptured, 68
Follicle stimulating hormone (FSH), 56, 76–78, 175
Ford, C. S., 240
Foreskin:
   female, 91
   male, 52

Fornication:
   legal aspects of, 264
   penance and, 28
Fornix, 66, 71
Fourchette, 72, 74
Frei test, 227
Frenulum clitoris, 74
Freud, Sigmund, 10
Freud, work of:
   historical import of, 39–40, 82–83
   homosexuality and, 175
   psychoanalytical theory of, 128–133
   vaginal versus clitoral orgasm in, 162
Frigidity, 147
Frottage, 173
FSH (*see* Follicle stimulating hormone)
FTA test for syphilis, 233
Fuck, 17–18
Fucking, 15
Future Shock (Toffler), 189, 251

G

Gagnon, John, 134–135
Gebhard, Paul H., 40
Gender roles, 158–164
   female, 160–163
   male, 163–164
Generation gap, sexuality and, 19–20
Genetic engineering, 97–104
Georg, I. E., 193
German measles, 106
Gestation time, 107
Glands:
   adrenal, 76
   Bartholin's, 74–75
   bulbourethral, 49–51, 54, 75, 192
   Cowper's (*see* Bulbourethral glands)
   ductless, 63
   endocrine (*see* Endocrine glands)
   of endometrium, 70, 77
   mammary, 60–64
   milk, 61–62
   ovaries, 63–64, 66–69, 76–78, 200, 206

Glands (*cont.*)
    pituitary, 55–56, 64–65, 76–78, 200
    placenta, 64, 76, 79, 119
    prostate, 75, 49–51, 55
    seminal vesicles, 48–50, 54
    Skene's, 75
    testes, 46–48, 56
    urethral, 51
Glans:
    of clitoris, 74
        during coitus, 91
    of penis, 46, 49–50, 52
        during coitus, 93
Gonadotropin, chorionic, 78
Gonorrhea, 234-236
    clinical manifestations of, 235
    diagnosis of 235–236
    epididymis and, 48
    history of, 234–235
    preventive measures against,
        236–238
    serologic test for, 238
    treatment of, 236
Graafenberg, E., 196–198
Granuloma inguinale, 227
Greece, ancient:
    homosexuality in, 24
    Lesbianism in, 24
    masturbation in, 24
    sexuality in, 23–27
Greenberg, Irving W. M., 251

H

Hackett, Thomas D., 57
Hardy, Kenneth R., 142
Harlow, Harry, 4
Heat flash, 80
Hemophilia, 101
Hemophilus ducreyi, 227
Hetaera, 24, 30
Heterosexuality, mammalian, 241
History, sexuality and, 19–40
Hoffman, Martin, 176

Home, sexuality in, 5
Homo sapiens, 240
Homosexual Community Counseling
        Center (HCCC), 176
Homosexual daddies, 252
Homosexuality, 170–181
    ancient Greeks and, 24
    ancient Jews and, 22
    ancient Romans and, 24
    cause of, 174–177
    definition of, 172
    disease hypothesis of, 178
    eighteenth century England and, 35
    facets of, 179–180
    hormones and, 174–175
    idolatry associated with, 26
    legal aspects of, 266
    mammalian, 177, 241–242
    matter of choice and judgment,
        163–164
    primate, 177
    religious views regarding, 256
    situational, 172
    theories of origin of, 174–177
    twelfth century and, 31
    Victorian era and, 38
Homosexuals:
    compulsiveness of, 180
    instability of, 180
    masturbation by, 180
    numbers of, 173
    sexual activities of, 173
    types of, 171
    venereal diseases and, 238
Hooker, Evelyn, 178
Hormonal physiology:
    female sexuality and, 79
    immature female and, 75–77
    male sexuality and, 55–56
    mammary glands and, 63–65
    mature nonpregnant female and,
        77–78
    mature pregnant female and, 78–79
    menopause and, 80
Hormones, 4, 63, 76, 79
    chorionic gonadotropin, 78–79
    cortisol, 64

Hormones (*cont.*)
  estrogens, 63–64, 68, 76–80, 114,
    119, 199–201, 219
  follicle stimulating (FSH), 56,
    76–78, 175
  gonadotrophic, 55
  homosexuality and, 174–175
  insulin, 64
  interstitial-cell-stimulating
    (ICSH), 56
  luteinizing (LH), 56, 76–78, 175
  male, 46–47
  oxytocin, 64–65
  placental lactogen, 79
  progesterone, 63–64, 68, 76–79,
    111, 114, 119, 199–201
  prolactin, 64–65
  prostaglandins, 219
  testosterone, 56–57, 174
  thyroxin, 64
Hot flash (*see* Heat flash)
Human Sexual Inadequacy (Masters
    and Johnson), 83, 146
Human Sexual Response (Masters
    and Johnson), 83
Hunt, Morgan, 251
Hymen, 36, 74–75
Hypothalamus, 56
  milk flow and, 64–65
Hysterectomy, 70
Hysteria, 24

I

ICSH (*see* Interstitial-cell-stimulating
    hormone)
Implantation of embryo, 78, 97, 99,
    106
  artificial, 104
Impotence, 54, 147–148
  legal aspects of, 259
Incest:
  human versus subhuman, 242
  legal aspects of, 265
Incubi, 31

Infanticide in ancient Greece, 191
Infertility, 149 (*see also* Sterility)
  epididymis and, 48
Infidelity, 247–248
Inquisition, 32–33
Insemination, 99
Institute for Sex Research, 40
Insulin, 64
Intercourse (*see* Sexual intercourse)
Interstitial cells, 47, 56
Interstitial-cell-stimulating hormone,
    56
Intrauterine contraceptive device,
    196–198
  cervical plug as, 191
Ischiocavernosus muscle, 55
I.U.C.D. (*see* Intrauterine
    contraceptive device)
I.U.D. (*see* Intrauterine contraceptive
    device)

J

Jellies, contraceptive, 202
Jesus Christ, sexual views of, 25–26
Jews:
  abortion and, 221
  contraception among ancient, 191
  contraception among modern, 256
  double standard among, 21–22
  sexuality among ancient, 20–22
  sexuality among modern, 22,
    255–257
Johnson, Virginia E., 82
Jones, Ernest, 128
Joy of Sex, The (Comfort), 140
Judaism, sexual views of, 255–257

K

Kibbutz of Israel, 250
Kinsey, Alfred, 40

Kinsey, work of Alfred:
  historical aspect of, 82–83
  homosexuality and, 174
  marital infidelity and, 145
  masturbation and, 9, 166–167
Kirkendall, L. A., 13
Klinefelter's syndrome, 98–99, 101
Kolodny, R. C., 174

L

Labium majus (*pl.* Labia majora), 66
  72–73
  during sexual activity, 88–91
Labium minus (*pl.* Labia minora), 66,
  72-74
  during sexual activity, 88–91
Labor, 113–118
  anesthetics and, 116
  causes of, 113
  false, 114
  forceps, use of, during, 116
  stages of, 114–116
  true, 114
Lactiferous duct, 61–63
Lactogen, placental, 78
La Maze method of childbirth, 121
Laminaria tents, 218
Lantz, H. R., 246
Laparoscope, 102, 206–207
Laparoscopy, 206-207
Law, civil:
  marriage and, 258–259
  sex and, 258–260
Law, criminal:
  sex and, 261–267
Learning sexuality, 3–8
Lesbianism, 171–172
  ancient Greece and, 24
  ancient Rome and, 24
  incidence of, 174
  legal aspects of, 266
  women's liberation and, 161
Let-down of milk (*see* Milk flow)
Levirate marriage, 21

Lewd behavior, legal aspects of, 266
Leydig, cells of, 47
LH (*see* Luteinizing hormone)
Libido, 132
  contraceptive pill and, 201
  sterilization and, 206
Life:
  determination of, 108
  inception of, 107
Ligament:
  broad, 67
  ovarian, 67
  round, 67
Lippes loop, 197
Logic, sexuality and, 10
Loop (*see* Intrauterine contraceptive
  device)
Lorenz, Konrad, 127
Love:
  no justification for marriage, 29
  parameters of, 138
  true versus false, 30
Love Doctors, The (McGrady), 11
Love Story (Segal), 138
Lundberg, Ferdinand, 251
Luteinizing hormone (L.H.), 56,
  76–78, 175
Lymphogranuloma venereum, 227

M

Male chauvinist pig, 161
Male gender role, 163–164
Male rebellion, 57–58
Male sex characteristics:
  primary, 56
  secondary, 56
Malthus, Thomas, 36
Mammalian sexual behavior, 240–242
Mammary glands, 60–64
Mann Act, 265–266
Marital infidelity, 145–146
Marker, Russell, 199
Marmor, Judd, 177
Marriage (Lantz and Snider), 246

Marriage:
  inability to achieve harmony in, 149–150
  legal aspects of, 250
  legal sex role in, 259–260
  monogamous, 247
  restrictions on, 258–259
  sequential, 252–253
  trajectories, 253
  trial, 249–250
Martin, Clyde E., 40
Maslow, A. H., 13
Masters, William H., 82
Masters and Johnson, work of, 12, 83-96
  experimental participants, 83
  female sexual response:
    Bartholin glands, 75, 92
    breast, 86–87
    clitoris, 91
    general, 84–86
    labia majora, 91
    labia minora, 91
    ovary, 92
    sex flush, 87
    uterine tubes, 92
    uterus, 92
    vagina, 72, 87–90
  historical background, 40–82
  male sexual response:
    general, 92–93
    penis, 93–95
    scrotum, 95
    testes, 95
  methodology, 83
  orgasm:
    clitoral versus vaginal, 162
    female, 92
    inability to achieve, 146
    male, 95–96
  sexual problems:
    couples versus individuals, 145
    inability to achieve orgasm, 146
    premature ejaculation, 148
Masturbation, 165–169
  ancient Greece and, 24
  erroneous concepts regarding, 9

Masturbation (*cont.*)
  female, 167
  frequency of, 166–167
  history of, 165–166
  homosexuals and, 173
  legal aspects of, 265
  mammals and, 241
  Masters and Johnson's work on, 84
  mechanism of, 167
  motivations for, 167–169
  mutual, 173
  number performing, 166
  Onan and, 28
  Victorian view of, 37
McGrady, Patrick M., Jr., 11, 14
MCP (*see* Male chauvinist pig)
Medieval Ages, sexuality during, 27–29
Menarche, 76
Menopause:
  female, 80
  male, 57–58
Menses and sexual desire, 79
Menstruation:
  anovulatory, 75–77
  early, 77
  ovulatory, 77
Micronor, 200
Milk ejection, 64
Milk flow, 64–65
  psychological aspects of, 65
Milk gland, 61–62
Mithraism, 27
Mongolism, 101
Monkeys, Harlow's research on, 4
Mons pubis, 66, 72–73
Mons veneris (*see* Mons pubis)
Morphine, 120
Mother:
  change in role, 188
  role of modern, 248
Motherhood, end of, 251
Motivation:
  fewer children and, 187
  masturbation and, 167–169
  sexual intercourse and, 140–144
Myometrium, 67, 70
Myotonia, 84

N

Neisseria gonorrhoeae, 227
Neo-Freudian psychoanalytical
    theory, 130–131
Neurohypophysis, 65
New York, abortion law in, 222
Nineteenth century, sexuality during,
    36–39
Nipple of the breast, 61–63
    during sexual activity, 86–87
Nobile, Philip, 147–148
Nocturnal emission, penance and, 28
Norinyl, 199
Novocaine, 120
Nulliparous female, 69

O

Obscenity, legal aspects of, 266
Oedipus complex, 130
    homosexuality and, 175
Onan and masturbation, 28
Oracon, 200
Oral-genital sex, 140
    complications associated with
        pregnancy, 124
    gonorrheal pharyngitis and, 236
    homosexuals and, 173, 180
    mammals and, 242
    syphilis and, 230
Oral phase of psychosexual
    development, 129
Orgasm:
    clitoral versus vaginal, 162
    female, 92
    frequency during pregnancy, 123
    inability to achieve, 146
    male, 93, 95
    number of females reaching, 146
Original sin, 27–28
Ortho-novum, 200

Ovarian ligament, 67
Ovary, 63–64, 66–69, 76–78
    contraceptive pill and, 200
    germ cells and, 99
    sexual activity and, 92
    sterilization and, 206
Overpopulation, 185–189
Ovulation, 99, 193
Ovulen, 199
Ovum, 68
    chromosomes within, 99
    entrance into uterine tube, 69
    securing, 102
Oxytocin, 64–65

P

Papanicolau smear, 71
Paraplegic men, erection and, 53
Parasympathetic nervous system,
    erection and, 53
Parents:
    biological, 252
    professional, 252
Parturition, 113–118
Patterns of Culture (Benedict), 239
Patterns of Sexual Behavior (Ford and
    Beach), 240
Pederasty:
    ancient Rome and, 25
    homosexuality and, 173
Peer group and sexuality, 6
Penicillin, 229, 236
Penis, 46, 49–54
    erection and, 52–54, 93
    sexual activity and, 93–95
Penitentials, sexual behavior and, 28
Perimetrium, 67, 70
Physiological changes during
    pregnancy, 111–113
Physiology, female sex (*see* Sexual
    intercourse, female)
Physiology, male sex (*see* Sexual
    intercourse, male)

Physiology, sexual, 81–96 (*see* also
    Masters and Johnson, work of)
  importance of knowing, 81
Pill, contraceptive, 199–202
  blood clots and, 201
  combination, 199
  morning-after, 219
  ovary and, 200
  pituitary gland and, 200
  sequential, 199
  side effects of, 201
Pincus, Gregory, 40, 191, 199
Pituitary gland, 55–56
  contraceptive pill and, 200
  estrous cycle and, 76–78
  growth and, 76
  milk flow and, 64–65
Placenta:
  formation of, 78–79, 100
  functions and growth, 119
  milk production and, 64
  nourishment of, 111
  progesterone and, 76
  transfers through, 106, 119
Placental lactogen, 79
Planned Parenthood, 211–212
  contraceptives and, 198
Pomeroy, Wardell B., 40
Population Bomb, The (Ehrlich), 185
Population Council, 220
Population, doubling time for,
    185–186
Postpartum period, 116
Predestination, Calvin's doctrine of, 35
Pregnancy, 105–125
  complaints during, 123
  metabolic changes during, 111–112
  physiological changes during,
    111–113
  psychological preparation for, 124
  sexual intercourse after, 117
  sexual intercourse during, 117
  tests for, 110
  weight gain during, 111–112, 122
Premarital coitus, religious views
    regarding, 255–256

Premature infants, 107
Prenatal care, 121–122
Prepuce:
  circumcision and, 22
  of clitoris, 74, 91
  of penis, 52
Priapism, 53
Prick, 18
Primates, 5
Progesterone:
  breast and, 63–64
  contraceptive pill and, 199-201
  estrous cycle and, 76–79
  labor onset and, 114
  ovary and, 68–69
  placenta and, 119
  plant source of, 199
  pregnancy and, 111
Prolactin, 64–65
Prostaglandins, 219
Prostate fluid, 49–50
Prostate gland, 49–51, 55, 75
  ejaculation and, 55
  relation to Skene's glands, 75
  removal, 51
Prostatitis, 51, 54
Prostitution, female:
  ancient Greeks and, 24, 30
  ancient Jews and, 22
  Crusades and, 32
  eighteenth century England and, 36
  legal aspects of, 265
  Renaissance Rome and, 32
  Victorian England and, 38
Prostitution, male:
  ancient Greece and, 24
Protestantism:
  abortion and, 221
  sexual views of, 255–257
Protestant Reformation, sexual
    reasons for, 34
Psychoanalytical theory of
    psychosexual development,
    128–133
  adolescent period, 132–133
  adult period, 133, 137–151

Psychoanalytical theory (*cont.*)
  infantile period, 129–130
  latency period, 131–132
  Oedipal period, 130–131
  prepuberty period, 132
Psychological preparation for
    pregnancy, 124
Psychosexual development, 126–136
  anal phase of, 129
  biological theory of, 127–128
  oral phase of, 129
  psychoanalytical theory of, 128–133
  sociological theory of, 134–135

R

Rape:
  legal aspects of, 264–265
  seminal fluid and, 48
Reiss, I. L., 13
Religion:
  abortion and, 221–222, 256–257
  adultery and, 256
  contraception and, 193, 256
  homosexuality and, 256
  premarital coitus and, 255–256
  sex and, 254–257
Renaissance, sexuality during 31–35
Reproductive Biology Research
    Foundation, 174
Reuben, David, 10
Revolt of the Middle-Aged Man, The
    (Bergler), 58
Rh factor, 112–113, 119, 122, 210
Rhogam, 113
Rhythm method of contraception,
    192–193
Right to Life advocates, 214, 224
Rock, John, 40, 191, 199
Romantic era, sexuality during, 29–31
Rome, ancient:
  bestiality in, 25
  fellatio in, 25
  homosexuality in, 24
  pederasty in, 25

Rome Ancient (*cont.*)
  sexual brutality in, 25
  sexuality in, 23–27
Round ligament, 66
Rousseau, Jean Jacques, 35

S

Saint Paul, sexual views of, 26
Salvarsan, 229
Satyriasis of Henry VIII, 34
School of sexuality, 7
Scientific method, 10
Screw, 18
Scrotum, 47
  during sexual activity, 93–95
  sterilization and, 204
Seduction, legal aspects of, 265
Semantics, sexual, 15
Seminal fluid, 48–49, 219
Seminal vesicle, 48–50, 54
Sensuous Man, The ("M"), 140
Sensuous Woman, The ("J"), 140
Sex and the College Student
    (Committee on the College
    Student), 133
Sex determination, 99, 101, 103
Sex drive, male versus female, 160
Sex flush, 87
Sex Information and Education
    Council of the United States
    (*see* SIECUS)
Sex in Human Loving (Berne), 18
*Sexual Behavior in the Human
    Female* (Kinsey), 82
Sexual Behavior in the Human Male
    (Kinsey), 82
Sexual customs, ebb and flow of, 39
Sexual desire, female, estrous cycle
    and, 79
Sexual Freedom and the Constitution
    (Barnett), 266
Sexual intercourse, 137–150
  biological aspects of, 137–138
  effect of repeated casual, 155

index 281

Sexual Intercourse (*cont.*)
  evaluation of early, 155
  frequency of, 139–140
  illegal, 28
  imprint on experience and
      personality of, 154
  legal aspects of, 261, 264
  love and, 138
  marital, 27
  motivations for, 140–144
  nonmarital, 27
  pregnancy and, 123–124
  primate, 159
  problems regarding, 144–150
  pros and cons of adolescent, 153
  religious views regarding
      premarital, 255–256
  technique of, 140
  truisms about, 154
  unacceptable behavior and, 148–149
  universality of, 154–155
  Victorian view of, 38
Sexual intercourse, female:
  organ response during:
    Bartholin glands, 92
    breast, 86
    clitoris, 91
    labia majora, 91
    labia minora, 91
    ovaries, 92
    uterine tubes, 92
    vagina, 87–88
  phase of:
    excitement, 89
    orgasmic, 90
    plateau, 89
    resolution, 90
  response cycle during 84
  total response during, 84–86
Sexual intercourse, male:
  organ response during:
    corona, 93
    glans, 93
    penis, 93
    scrotum, 95
    testes, 95
  phase of:
    excitement, 93

Sexual Intercourse male (*cont.*)
    orgasmic, 94
    plateau, 94
    resolution, 95
  response cycle during, 92–93
  total response during, 92–93
Sexuality:
  ancient Greece and, 23
  ancient Rome and, 23–25
  anthropological aspects of,
      239–243
  authoritarian statements and, 11
  changing attitudes regarding, 19–20
  current thinking regarding, 20
  early Christianity and, 25–27
  generation gap and, 19–20
  history of, 19–40
  learning, 3–8
  Medieval Ages and, 27
  psychological aspects of, 66
  reason for studying, 3
  Scandinavian countries and, 7
  statistical surveys and, 11
  teaching, 5–8
  truth and, 9–13
  Victorianism and, 36–39, 82
  where taught, 5–6
Sexual milieu, 7
Sherfy, Mary Jane, 159
SIECUS (Sex Information and
      Education Council of the
      United States), 7
Silicone, 63
Simon, William, 134–135
606 compound, 229
Skene's ducts, 72, 74
Skene's glands, 72, 75
  relation to prostate, 75
SL ratio (*see* Sphingomyelin-
      lecithin ratio)
Smegma, 52
Smoking and pregnancy, 123
Snider, E. C., 246
Sodom and Gomorrah, 20
Sodomy:
  homosexuality and, 173
  legal aspects of, 266
Solomon, Joan, 176

Sparta, extramarital coitus in, 23
Sperm, 99
    viability of, 193
Spermatic cord, 46–48
Sphingomyelin-lecithin (SL) ratio, 102
S-Q contraceptive pill, 200
Sterility, legal aspects of, 259
Sterilization:
    female, 206–209
    indications for, 209–210
    male, 204–206
    motivational aspects of, 210–212
Stillborn, 108
Succubi, 31
Suckling, 64, 79
Suction technique for abortion, 217
Superovulation, 102
Sympathetic nervous system:
    ejaculation and, 54
    erection and, 53
Syndrome:
    Gaugin, 57
    Klinefelter's, 98–99, 101
    sacred amulet, 58
    scapegoat wife, 57
    tired housewife, 145
Syphilis, 227–234
    clinical manifestations of, 229–233
    Henry VIII and, 34
    history of, 32, 227–228
    preventive measures, 233–234,
        236–237
    tests for, 233
    treatment of, 233

T

Taboos:
    homosexuality and, 22
    menstruation and, 224
    research and, 83
    word, 16
Teaching sexuality, 5–8
Ten Commandments, sex and the,
    254, 256

Terminology of sex:
    general, 16
    scientific, 16
    scrambled words and, 18
    vernacular, 17
Testicle (*see* Testis)
Testis (*pl.* testes), 46–50
    germ cells and, 99
    interstitial cells of, 56
    sexual activity and, 93–95
Testosterone, 47, 56–57, 174
Tests:
    fetal normalcy, 101–102
    fetal sex determination, 101–102
    for gonorrhea, 238
    pregnancy, 110
    routine prenatal, 121–122
    for syphilis, 233
Test tube baby, 103
Thalidomide, 106
Thyroxin, 64
Tietze, Christopher, 220–221
Toffler, Alvin, 251–253
Toilet training, 129–130
TPI test for syphilis, 233
Travel and pregnancy, 123
Treponema pallidum, 227, 233
    immobilization test (TPI), 233
Truth About Rhythm, The (Georg),
    193
Truths, sexual, 10–13
Tubal ligation, 206–208
    vaginal, 208
Tuberculosis, genital, 48
Twentieth century, sexuality during,
    39–40
Twilight sleep, 120

U

Umbilical cord, 118
United States, sexual criminal laws,
    262–263
United States Supreme Court,
    abortion and, 222–224

Urethra, 49–52, 55, 66, 72
Urethral glands, 51, 54
Uterine tube, 66, 69
  during sexual activity, 92
  sterilization and, 206–208
Uterus, 66, 69–70
  abortion and, 217
  contraction after labor, 116
  labor and, 114–118
  pregnancy and, 107–108, 111
  rupture of, during abortion, 220
  sexual activity and, 88–92

V

Vagina, 66–67, 70–72, 171
  functions of, 71–72
  lubrication of, 87
  pregnancy and, 111
  sexual activity and, 87–90
Vaginal environment and sex
      determination, 99
Validity, sexual, 9–10, 13
Vas deferens (*pl.* vasa deferentia),
      48–50
  vasectomy and, 204–206
Vasectomy, 48, 204–206
Vasocongestion, 84
VD (*see* Venereal diseases)
VD Day, 238
Venereal diseases, 226–238
Vestibular glands (*see* Bartholin
      glands)
Vestibule, 74

Victorian era, sexuality during, 36–39
Virgo intactus, 24

W

Wasserman test for syphilis, 23
Wife:
  role in today's family, 248
  triple function of, 30
Witches, 32–34
Wolfe, William, 251
Women's Liberation Movement,
      160–162

X

X chromosome, 11, 98–99
X rays, effects on fetus, 106
Xylocaine, 120

Y

Y body, 101
Y chromosome, 11, 98–99

Z

Zygote, 99, 106